Funding the Future

Funding the Future

Financial Sustainability and Infrastructure Finance in Australian Local Government

Brian E Dollery

*Centre for Local Government,
University of New England*

Michael A Kortt

*Southern Cross Business School,
Southern Cross University*

Bligh James Grant

*UNE Business School,
University of New England*

CELEBRATING 25 YEARS
1988 2013
THE FEDERATION PRESS
2013

Published in Sydney by
The Federation Press
PO Box 45, Annandale, NSW, 2038.
71 John St, Leichhardt, NSW, 2040.
Ph (02) 9552 2200. Fax (02) 9552 1681
E-mail: info@federationpress.com.au
Website: http://www.federationpress.com.au

National Library of Australia Cataloguing-in-Publication entry

Dollery, Brian.
Funding the future : financial sustainability and infrastructure finance in Australian local government / Brian E Dollery, Michael A Kortt and Bligh James Grant.

Includes index.
ISBN 9781862878983 (pbk).

Local government - Australia - Finance.
Public administration - Australia.

352.140994

Typeset by The Federation Press, Leichhardt, NSW.
Printed by Ligare Pty Ltd, Riverwood, NSW.

Table of Contents

Preface

The existence of a financial crisis in Australian local government cannot be gainsaid. Over the past decade, a host of state and national inquiries have established that not only do a large number of local councils suffer straitened financial circumstances, but an immense local infrastructure backlog has also developed. Moreover, the infrastructure shortfall is intensifying as local authorities divert funds away from desperately needed infrastructure investment and maintenance in an effort to maintain current service provision. As a result, the funding required for local infrastructure now exceeds the financial capacity of most local councils using 'own-source' revenue.

Despite almost universal agreement on the causes and consequences of the fiscal crisis, no corresponding consensus holds on the most suitable public policy measures for remedying the problem. Numerous solutions have been advanced, from 'internal' reform aimed to improve asset management, through to 'external' funding derived from Commonwealth and state transfers. While debate on optimal public policy has been vigorous in the popular press, substantive contributions have been scattered in copious and often obscure official documents issued by public agencies, departments and inquiries, as well as articles in far-flung academic journals. This has led to a curious fragmentation of the debate and a dearth of serious engagement between protagonists of different public policies.

This most unsatisfactory state of affairs has provided the impetus for this book. Founded on academic research conducted by scholars working through the Centre for Local Government at the University of New England, this book seeks to build on the labours of these scholars in an effort to gather under a single cover the complex and often disparate strands of argument over financial sustainability and the local infrastructure backlog in Australian local government. It follows the publication of a book on shared services in Australian local government by the same authors, entitled *Councils in Cooperation: Shared Services and Australian Local Government* (Dollery, Grant and Kortt, 2012), also published by Federation Press.

The Centre for Local Government represents one of the very few organisations in Australia which is focused on rigorous research into Australian local government. Members of the Centre are drawn from universities across Australia and abroad, as well as comprising numerous current and retired experts who have worked in the local government sector. They bring together a remarkable variety of skills, mostly from the disciplines of accounting, economics, finance, political science and public administration, as well as vast experience derived from decades as senior executives and elected representatives in Australian local government. Since its establishment in 1994, members of the Centre for Local Government have produced a wealth of research into Australian local government.

Literally hundreds of academic papers on various dimensions of local government have been published in scholarly journals. Australian outlets include: *Accounting, Accountability and Performance; Agenda; Australian Geographer; Australian Journal of Political Science; Australian Journal of Public Administration; Australian Journal of Social Issues; Australian Planner; Australasian Journal of Regional Studies; Canberra Bulletin of Public Administration; Economic Analysis and Policy; Economic Papers; Economic Record; Public Administration Today; Transactions of Multi-Disciplinary Engineering; Public Administration Today; Regional Policy and Practice; Sustaining Regions; Urban Futures;* and *Urban Policy and Research.* Papers have also appeared in international journals, such as: *Applied Economics; International Review of Public Administration; Economia; Engineering Economist; Journal of Public Budgeting, Accounting and Financial Management; Local Government Studies; Public Administration; Public Administration Quarterly; Public Choice; Public Productivity and Management Review; Publius; Review of Policy Research; Studies in Economics and Econometrics;* and *the Yokohama Journal of the Social Sciences.*

The Centre for Local Government has also done a great deal of commissioned work for various government departments, official inquiries, local government bodies, individual local authorities and the like. Significant published monographs derived from this work include: 'Regional Capacity Building: How Effective is REROC?' (Dollery, Marshall, Johnson and Witherby, 2004); 'Australian Local Government: An Annotated Bibliography, 1988-1998' (Kimber, Dollery, Marshall and Witherby, 1999); and 'Local Government: One Industry, Many Perspectives' (Witherby, Dollery, Marshall and Auster, 1999).

Over the years, members of the Centre have actively published their research in books as well. This corpus of work includes: *Australian Local Government: Reform and Renewal* (Dollery and Marshall, 1997), *The Political Economy of Local Government* (Dollery and Wallis, 2001); *Reshaping Australian Local Government: Finance, Governance and Reform* (Dollery, Marshall and Worthington, 2003); *Australian Local Government Economics* (Dollery, Crase and Johnson, 2006); *Reform and Leadership in the Public Sector: A Political Economy Approach* (Wallis, Dollery and McLoughlin, 2007) and *Councils in Cooperation: Shared Services and Australian Local Government* (Dollery, Grant and Kortt, 2012). Both *Australian Local Government: Reform and Renewal* and *Reshaping Australian Local Government: Finance, Governance and Reform* have been translated into Mandarin.

The present book joins this body of work as yet another successful research project completed by members of the Centre. In many respects it represents the culmination of more than a decade of pure and applied research into financial sustainability and the local infrastructure backlog in Australian local government. The book thus builds on the research foundations laid by numerous scholars connected with the Centre.

We are grateful to several individuals and organisations for the kind assistance they have rendered. In particular, express our gratitude to the Commonwealth Department of Infrastructure, Transport and Regional Development for providing invaluable financial support necessary to ensure the publication of this book. We also thank Emeritus Mayor Dr Ian Tiley, Kylie Flack from the UNE Business School, Alison Basden from Academic and Scientific Editing and Linda Nix from Golden Orb Creative, and the Staff at Federation Press in Sydney, especially Christopher Holt, Ann Cunningham and Josephine Romeo for their helpful assistance in bringing this book to fruition. We place on record our sincere gratitude to the countless people in Australian local government who have freely given us the benefits of their insights into local government.

Brian Dollery is Professor of Economics and Director of the Centre for Local Government at the University of New England. He has previously held academic positions at the University of South Africa, Rhodes University and the University of Cape Town in the Republic of South Africa, East Carolina State University and Creighton University in the United States, and Yokohama National University in Japan. Brian has published extensively on the theoretical aspects of local government economics, finance and structure, as well as Australian local government. Brian thanks his wife Therese Burton for her patience, love and support during the preparation of this book. Brian also records his profound indebtedness to his mother Joan Livingstone Dollery – an indomitable spirit, lifelong anti-apartheid crusader, social worker to the poorest of the poor in Port Elizabeth and scholar extraordinaire – for engendering in him a 'life of the mind'.

Michael Kortt is a Senior Lecturer in Applied Economics and Director of Research Training for the Southern Cross Business School at Southern Cross University (SCU). He holds a PhD in economics from the University of New England, a masters degree in pharmaceutical sciences from the University of Arizona and an honours degree in economics from La Trobe University. Prior to joining SCU in 2011, Michael spent 10 years working in the government sector as a senior research manager for the Department of Veterans' Affairs, the Department of Families, Housing, Community Services and Indigenous Affairs, and the Department of Health and Ageing. His principal research interest is in the field of local government economics, with a particular emphasis on empirical analysis. Michael thanks his wife Samantha and his son Harrison for their patience, understanding, love and support in the writing of this book.

Bligh Grant is Lecturer in the UNE Business School at the University of New England. Before this he was Research Lecturer in Local Government Studies and Deputy Director of the Centre for Local Government at the University of New England (UNE), a position he held from 2008. Alongside pursuing research interests in local government studies, he works in the areas of Australian politics, public administration, business ethics and the Australian wine industry. Bligh would like to thank his students in local government studies in the MBA Program at UNE for their hard work and enthusiasm for the topic, and the many individuals working in local and state government who have generously contributed their time to furthering research and understanding.

Chapter 1
Introduction

1.1 Introduction

Australian local government, in common with many other local government systems across the world, has undergone sweeping changes in the past few decades (Denters and Rose, 2005; Dollery, Garcea and LeSage, 2008). Not only has the role of local government steadily expanded away from its traditional focus on 'roads, rates and rubbish' to encompass a much wider range of responsibilities, but many of these newfound tasks have been forced upon its unwilling shoulders by higher tiers of government (Dollery, Byrnes and Allan, 2007). Moreover, scores of these additional and unsolicited functions have come with limited financial assistance or even no funding at all (Dollery, Crase and Johnson, 2006). One consequence of the transformation of the functions of Australian local government, without any compensating change in its capacity to fund its activities, has been a steady deterioration in the financial sustainability of the local government sector and the emergence of a massive local infrastructure backlog. From a public policy perspective, these allied problems represent not only by far the most pressing difficulties facing Australian local government, but also the most intractable.

In the Australian local government sector, three main engines of reform have been deployed. In the first place, in line with New Public Management (NPM) doctrine (Dollery and Wallis 2001), state and territory governments have attempted to improve the efficiency of local authorities by modernising their Local Government Acts, in expectation that greater legislative latitude would give local councils the flexibility to adapt more easily to changing circumstances. Second, in paradoxical contrast to this increased local autonomy, higher tiers of government have simultaneously sought to control the manner in which local authorities discharge their responsibilities through prescriptive legislation, hypothecated intergovernmental grants and other 'top-down' measures (Hawker Report, 2003). Finally, state governments have episodically imposed programs of involuntary structural reform involving compulsory amalgamation, especially on regional, rural and remote local government entities. Over the past two decades South Australia, Victoria, Tasmania, New South Wales, Queensland and the Northern Territory have all experienced bouts of forced mergers, with Western Australia the only jurisdiction to have thus far escaped the dogma that 'bigger is better' in local governance.

Several lessons have flowed from these episodes of structural reform. First, as a general rule, the pecuniary benefits of compulsory council consolidation promised by the architects of structural reform have not eventuated. As a result, large numbers of local authorities in all jurisdictions remain fiscally distressed. It is especially noteworthy that no discernible difference in the degree of financial sustainability is evident between Western Australian councils - which have escaped forced amalgamation - and their consolidated counterparts in the other states. Second, in the light of the unsatisfactory economic, political and social consequences of council mergers, the local government sector is increasingly sceptical of the extravagant claims made by advocates of amalgamation. As a result, local councils across Australia have explored models of local government collaboration which present alternative modes of securing the advantages of scale and scope in suitable local services without the need for enforced amalgamation. These models are usually based on sharing resources or services, or other voluntary arrangements, and have often displayed high levels of ingenuity.

Our book *Councils in Cooperation* (Dollery, Grant and Kortt, 2012) considered shared services in Australian local government in great detail. One of the conclusions we drew from this analysis was that while various forms of inter-council collaboration have reaped numerous benefits, the financial dividend in terms of cost savings have been modest. Thus, although carefully selected and well implemented shared service arrangements proved worthwhile, they nonetheless fell far short of representing a solution to the Damoclean fiscal problems facing Australian local government.

The existence of acute financial distress in Australian local government cannot be disputed. Indeed, both ubiquitous financial unsustainability and a concomitant local infrastructure backlog have been exhaustively documented in a series of state inquiries in South Australia, New South Wales, Queensland, Western Australia and Tasmania, as well as in several national inquiries, including the PriceWaterhouseCoopers report, *National Financial Sustainability Study of Local Government* (PWC Report, 2006). These inquiries have found that the major symptom of financial distress in Australian local government has been a systemic neglect of local infrastructure investment and maintenance. The result has been the emergence of a massive infrastructure renewal backlog, far in excess of the fiscal capacity of most local authorities to address from 'own-source' revenue alone. Put differently, the sheer scale of the problem radically surpasses the current financial capacity of many municipalities.

This poses especially thorny problems for public policy-makers. These difficulties are compounded by two crucial characteristics of contemporary Australian fiscal federalism. In the first place, like many other federal systems, Australian federalism is plagued by vertical fiscal imbalance between its three tiers of government. In terms of the Australian Constitution and its later refinement by the High Court, revenue-raising powers are concentrated largely in the federal government. By contrast, a disproportionate level of public expenditure is undertaken by state and local government. The net effect has been the evolution of a more acute degree of vertical imbalance than in comparable federal systems, such as Canada, Germany and the United States (see, for example, Groenewegen, 1990; Mathews, 1994).

Four generic methods of dealing with vertical fiscal imbalance in federal systems of government have been identified in the literature (Bahl and Linn, 1994). In the institutional context of the Australian federation, these methods have been summarised as follows by Dollery, Fletcher and Rao (1998, 485): 'taxation powers could be shifted to the two lower tiers of government from the Commonwealth Government'; 'expenditure powers could be transferred from state and local governments to the

Commonwealth'; 'revenue-sharing arrangements could be instituted', which has subsequently occurred with the Goods and Services Tax (GST) collected by the federal government and transferred to state and territory governments; and 'a system of intergovernmental grants could be employed', already a highly developed and long-standing practice in Australian fiscal federalism. Indeed, in Australia grants have historically been the major policy instrument used to tackle both vertical and horizontal fiscal imbalance. Prior to the introduction of the GST in 2000, Financial Assistance Grants (FAGs), in the form of General Purpose Payments (GPPs) and Special Purpose Payments (SPPs) through the Commonwealth Grants Commission, represented the predominant mechanism used to deal with fiscal imbalance in Australia (Worthington and Dollery, 1998). In the period since 2000, grants have been augmented by tax sharing through the GST as the main methods of addressing vertical fiscal imbalance. While we are concerned in this book primarily with funding of local government, it is obvious that the financial crisis in Australian local government has its roots in the structure of Australian fiscal federalism and, more specifically, the assignment of expenditure functions relative to revenue-raising powers between the three tiers of government. For this reason, Part A of this book is devoted to an analysis of Australian fiscal federalism and local government revenue in the context of this federalist structure.

The local government grants system in Australia has four distinctive characteristics. First, Australian local government raises almost 90% of its total revenue (with the remainder coming from grants and subsidies), compared with around 65% for its US counterpart. Second, although in historical terms the Commonwealth in Australia has provided the necessary finance, the specific allocation and distribution of grants to local governments has been done by state-based Local Government Grants Commissions (LGGCs). Notwithstanding the fact that each Australian state has its own LGGC, each LGGC applies allocative principles drawn from a common legislative core. The most important of these universal principles are that monies are allocated on a full horizontal equalisation basis; the functional requirement of any given local authority is determined at a standard not lower than the average standard of other local councils in the state; revenue and expenditure needs and disabilities are assessed; and 'effort neutrality' in raising revenue is prescribed between different local government areas in a given state. Third, general financial assistance grants represent by far the largest source of grants made to Australian local governments, in stark contrast to local government grants in the United States, which are chiefly hypothecated. Finally, the ability of individual local authorities to influence the grants process through their revenue-raising or expenditure decisions is extremely limited. Indeed, it has been argued that even if specific councils are given information on the assessment of their revenue and expenditure needs and the disability factors applied to them, they cannot determine their relative funding outcomes (see, for instance, Australian Urban and Regional Developing Review, 1994a, 1994b).

In addition to these transfers, in recognition of the deteriorating condition of local government infrastructure, especially the network of local roads in non-metropolitan areas, in November 2000 the Commonwealth Government announced that it would be providing direct funding of $1.2 billion to local government – under the banner of the *Roads to Recovery* (R2R) Program – to assist in the construction and maintenance of the local road network (DOTARS, 2003; Auditor-General, 2006). While the R2R Program was originally intended to run from January 2001 to June 2005, it has subsequently been extended five times. The most recent extension of the R2R Program was announced in the 2012/13 Commonwealth Budget through which the Australian Government will provide a further $350 million per annum from 2014/15 to 2018/19. Although it has undoubtedly made a valuable contribution to remediating local government infrastructure, and especially the network of local roads, its operational efficiency has been questioned (Lopez, Dollery and Byrnes, 2008, 2009), and its constitutional validity is uncertain (Pape, 2005; Grant and Dollery, 2010).

While the nature of Australian fiscal federalism, derived partly from the Australian Constitution, certainly creates a harsh financial environment for the local government sector, especially in terms of its ability to raise 'own-source' revenue, it is by no means the only contributing factor to the fiscal distress in Australian local government. As we have seen, a host of national and state inquiries into the financial circumstances of local government have spawned a wealth of information. One interesting lesson to emerge has been the difficulties involved in satisfactorily defining financial sustainability in local government. This echoes international experience. For instance, after reviewing the voluminous literature, Honadle, Costa and Cigler (2004, 18) have drily observed that there is not even consensus about 'the terminology surrounding fiscal health'. While Australian work typically employs the term 'financial sustainability', US scholars use numerous expressions, including 'fiscal health' (Berry, 1994), 'financial condition' (Lin and Raman, 1998), 'fiscal stress' (Pagano and Moore, 1985) and 'fiscal capacity' (Johnson and Roswick, 1991). Dollery and Grant (2011, 42) have argued that the Australian research embodied in most public inquiries into financial sustainability has fallaciously 'conflated fiscal sustainability with fiscal viability', which are not equivalent concepts. Furthermore, it has relied too heavily on an 'accounting-based KPI methodology', which is misplaced given its 'poor predictive record' and 'inherent bias' against rural shires.

The absence of agreement on the meaning of financial sustainability should hardly be surprising in the democratic non-profit local public service environment in which local authorities operate. After all, Aulich (2005) and other scholars have long underlined the inevitable tensions between local democracy and economic efficiency in the municipal milieu. However, several other factors complicate the quest for financial sustainability in local government. For instance, Kloha, Weissert and Kleine (2005) have stressed the difficulties involved in constructing comparative financial indicator indexes as an 'objective' measurement tool in a highly charged political environment. Similarly, in the Australian context, Worthington and Dollery (2000b) have stressed the significance of 'nondiscretionary variables' in performance indicators, which cannot be changed by council performance. Furthermore, the immense diversity between metropolitan, regional, rural and remote councils in Australia precludes the use of 'one-size-fits-all' methods of assessing local authorities (Dollery, Wallis and Akimov, 2010). These and other complications mean that additional techniques are required to augment traditional accounting measures and financial KPIs. Part B of the book is devoted to the problem of financial sustainability in Australian local government.

Despite the difficulties in determining the financial sustainability of local government, there can be no gainsaying the existence of a financial crisis in Australian local government. This becomes plain if we consider, for example, the findings of the PriceWaterhouseCoopers report *National Financial Sustainability Study of Local Government* (PWC Report, 2006) commissioned by the Australian Local Government Association (ALGA), which took a national perspective on financial reform and financial sustainability. The PWC Report (2006, 111) found that 20–40% of all Australian councils 'could be unsustainable', a further 10–30% of all councils faced 'sizeable sustainability challenges', New South Wales had the most acute 'financial viability issues', the average annual 'underspend' on 'existing infrastructure renewals' was $1.3–$1.7 million per council, and that, in order to remove the annual infrastructure shortfall plus the accumulated infrastructure backlog, the 'average' council would need to spend an additional $2.6–$3.3 million per year.

The sheer size of the local infrastructure maintenance and renewal backlog is alarming. While considerable uncertainty surrounds the exact magnitudes involved (Dollery and Mounter, 2010), PWC (2006) estimated a national infrastructure backlog of between $12.0 billion and $15.3 billion across all seven Australian local government jurisdictions. In addition, the annual shortfall in expenditure on existing local infrastructure renewal occurs in the range $0.9–$1.2 billion. Based on these projections, PWC (2006) established that funding in the vicinity of $1.8–$2.3 billion per annum is required to address the deficit in maintenance spending on existing infrastructure and eliminate the current local infrastructure backlog. This is the rough equivalent to an additional $2.6–$3.3 million per council per annum or $87–$109 per capita per annum. Part C of this book concentrates on methods of ameliorating the infrastructure shortfall.

Local government has taken numerous steps to address the problem. Apart from the various state-based inquiries, which were all instituted by state local government associations, and which made many useful recommendations, largely ignored by state and territory governments, it is possible to identify various other remedial measures. For instance, in its report *Strong Foundations for Sustainable Local Infrastructure: Connecting Communities, Projects, Finance and Funds*, released on 18 June 2012, Ernst and Young (2012, 10) observed that there had been a 'concerted and creditable effort on behalf of councils themselves to improve their financial management, asset management and prioritisation processes'. Furthermore, whereas 'serious capacity shortages continue to exist in some areas, especially the more geographically remote councils, there are a growing number of examples of best practice implementation and innovative procurement'. However, *Strong Foundations for Sustainable Local Infrastructure* cautioned that 'the reality of today's fiscal environment means that it would not be prudent for local government simply to assume an ever-increasing level of funding from other tiers of government in the future'. It followed that 'the main challenge faced by the local government sector today is how to meet its infrastructure obligations without the ability to rely upon increased funding from states, territories and the Commonwealth'.

Various solutions to the Australian local infrastructure crisis have been proposed in the literature. For example, Byrnes, Dollery, Crase and Simmons (2008) have suggested the establishment of an Australian municipal bond market. In an analogous vein, Dollery, Byrnes and Crase (2007) have presented the case for a federal infrastructure fund for local government infrastructure funding. Similarly, Dollery, Kortt and Grant (2011) have advocated the establishment of a national bond bank to pool individual council risk in aggregated infrastructure bonds issues guaranteed by the Australian Government. However, despite the extension of the *Roads to Recovery* (R2R) program, the creation of Infrastructure Australia and some minor policy initiatives by the Commonwealth Government, as yet no decisive remedial policy action has been taken to tackle the local infrastructure problem.

1.2 Outline of book

Against the background of a deteriorating financial viability in Australian local government and a mushrooming local infrastructure shortfall, this book focuses on the Australian fiscal federalism and the place of local government in this structure, provides a critical assessment of methodologies and findings of the various national and state public inquiries into financial sustainability in local government, explores 'holistic sustainability' as distinct from the narrower 'financial sustainability' in local government, and sets out a detailed assessment of different approaches to funding, including an Australian municipal bond market, a Commonwealth local infrastructure fund, municipal banking and an Australian municipal bond bank. While the emphasis falls squarely on Australian local government, we draw extensively on the international literature, both conceptual and empirical.

The book is divided into three main parts. Part A considers the nature of Australian fiscal federalism and the position of local government in these fiscal federalist arrangements. Part B provides a detailed account of methodologies and findings of the national and state-based inquiries into local government financial sustainability, as well as 'holistic sustainability' in local government. Part C presents a comprehensive analysis of the most promising methods of ameliorating the local government infrastructure backlog, which includes case studies of different bond banks.

Part A comprises two chapters. Chapter 2 provides a synoptic account of Australian fiscal federalism and its characteristics, and is divided into five main sections. Section 2.2 presents a brief overview of the federal system of government in the Commonwealth of Australia and its fiscal federalist structures. Section 2.3 sets out in detail Commonwealth, state and local government public finances. Section 2.4 examines the thorny relationship between Commonwealth, state and local governments which flows from the high degree of vertical fiscal imbalance in the Australian federation. Section 2.5 focuses on horizontal fiscal imbalance and fiscal equalisation. Chapter 2 ends with some brief concluding remarks in section 2.6.

Chapter 3 is divided into four main sections. Section 3.2 provides an overview of local government expenditure with particular reference to local government expenditure on new non-financial assets (ie infrastructure). Section 3.3 contains a broad synopsis of local government revenue, including taxation, grants, the sales of goods and services, and interest from council investments. Section 3.4 investigates in more depth the nature of financial assistance grants, the role that local government grants commissions play in the allocation and distribution of funds to local government, and the efficiency consequences of grant distribution. Chapter 3 ends with some brief concluding remarks in section 3.5.

Part B comprises two chapters. The first, Chapter 4, is divided into three main sections. Section 4.2 deals with financial sustainability and financial reform in local government, which was by far the major concern of the bulk of the 12 inquiries under consideration. Section 4.3 tackles the findings of the inquiries, determining the common issues raised, patterns of policy recommendations and recurring unresolved matters, and it then draws some general conclusions on the policy and practice implications for local government.

Chapter 5 attacks the term 'financial sustainability' and presents the case for a broader concept of 'holistic sustainability' in local government. Chapter 5 is divided into three main sections. Section 5.2 describes the genesis of the term 'sustainability' in policy analysis by way of background. Section 5.3 investigates the inherent tensions in Australian local government which render difficult the problem of determining sustainability in local government. Section 5.4 considers the academic literature on the problem of 'sustainability' in Australian local government. Section 5.5 outlines the taxonomic 'government failure' approach to sustainability. Section 5.6 assesses the main elements of 'holistic sustainability' in Australian local government. Chapter 5 ends in section 5.7 with some brief concluding comments.

Part C comprises four chapters. Chapter 6 sets the historical scene for a detailed evaluation of different policy instruments which could be used to tackle the local government infrastructure backlog. Chapter 6 is divided into two main sections. Section 6.2 describes financial relationships between the Commonwealth and local government during the immediate Second World War and post-war Labor administrations of John Curtin, Ben Chifley and Robert Menzies, through to the Whitlam, Frazer, and Hawke and Keating Governments. It is argued that the Australian local government sector has been treated to acts of munificence - especially under the Whitlam administrations of the 1970s, for example - as well as comparative neglect - notably under the Hawke and Keating Governments. Chapter 6 ends with some brief concluding remarks in section 6.3.

Chapter 7 is divided into five main sections. Section 7.2 provides a synoptic description of the *Roads to Recovery* (R2R) program launched by the Howard Government and the Nation Building Program instituted by the Rudd/Gillard Governments as recent examples of Commonwealth funding of local government infrastructure. Section 7.3 outlines the case for a Commonwealth local government infrastructure fund, drawing largely on Dollery, Byrnes and Crase (2007). Section 7.4 then juxtaposes this approach with the *modus operandi* of Infrastructure Australia - a statutory body established by the Commonwealth in 2008 - and argues that Infrastructure Australia is functionally distinct from a local government infrastructure fund since it mostly occupies an advisory role on infrastructure designated as 'nationally significant' (Infrastructure Australia, 2008, 12). Section 7.5 provides an assessment of the case for a federally financed local government infrastructure fund. Chapter 7 ends in section 7.6 with some brief concluding remarks.

Chapter 8 is divided into five main sections. Section 8.2 outlines the infrastructure renewal problem currently facing local government in New South Wales, concentrating on the water and wastewater sector as an example of how municipal revenue bonds could operate. Section 8.3 provides a brief account of municipal bond finance in the United States which could be adopted in Australian local government. Section 8.4 describes the main principles embodied in the Byrnes, Dollery, Crase and Simmons (2008) approach relating to the cost of capital and the structure of asset-backed securities. Section 8.5 considers the long-term debt which could be raised by local authorities through asset-backed securities. Chapter 8 ends in section 8.6 with some brief concluding remarks.

Chapter 9 is divided into four main parts. Section 9.2 considers municipal banking as a possible solution to the Australian local government infrastructure shortfall. Section 9.3 sets out the case for a national bond bank. Section 9.4 considers three 'case studies' of existing municipal bond banks: the Local Government Finance Authority of South Australia (LGFA), the New Zealand Local Government Funding Agency (NZLGFA), and the Municipal Finance Authority of British Columbia (MFABC). Chapter 9 ends with some brief concluding remarks in section 9.5.

PART A

Australian Fiscal Federalism and Australian Local Government

Chapter 2
Australian Fiscal Federalism

2.1 Introduction

The Australian federal system consists of three different tiers of government: the Commonwealth Government, state government and local government. Two major features dominate Australian fiscal federalism (Dollery, 2002). First, the assignment of expenditure functions and revenue-raising capacities has resulted in significant vertical fiscal imbalance (VFI) because the Commonwealth Government raises more revenue than it needs to meet its existing expenditure obligations, while the converse is true for state and local governments. In other words, state and local governments have expenditure requirements that are not matched by a corresponding capacity to raise revenue (Dollery, Crase and Johnson, 2006). In principle, the problem of VFI can be addressed through four main avenues: expenditure responsibilities can be shifted between the different tiers of government, taxation powers reallocated, intergovernmental transfers used to redistribute funds, and tax-sharing arrangements instituted (Dollery, 2002, 27). Since the birth of Australian federation in 1901 all of these methods have been employed in an effort to rectify VFI.

Second, the incidence of horizontal fiscal imbalance (HFI) is manifest at both state and local government levels since these lower tiers of government differ substantially in terms of revenue-raising capacity and the cost of service delivery (Dollery, 2002). In the context of Australian fiscal federalism, the problem of HFI 'was initially addressed by special grants to financially distressed state and local governments and from 1933 onwards through equalisation procedures administered by the Commonwealth

Grants Commission' (Dollery, 2002, 27), a process that is commonly referred to as horizontal fiscal equalisation (HFE).

Against this background, the purpose of this chapter is to provide a broad overview of Australian fiscal federalism, with a particular emphasis on the federal system of government, intergovernmental financial relations, VFI and HFE. While the subject of local government financing is introduced here, its details are covered in Chapter 3.

This chapter is divided into five main sections. Section 2.2 provides a brief overview of the federal system of government, fiscal federalism and competitive federalism. Section 2.3 provides a synoptic description of Commonwealth, state and local government public finances. Section 2.4 examines the problematic relationship between Commonwealth, state and local governments which stems from the high degree of VFI. Section 2.5 explores the principle of HFE, how fiscal equalisation operates in practice (including the role of the Commonwealth Grants Commission) and theoretical motivations for fiscal equalisation. The chapter ends with some brief concluding remarks in section 2.6.

2.2 The Australian federal system of government

2.2.1 Federal system of government

In a federal system of government, the allocation of powers between the different levels of government is fundamentally important. In practice, the allocation of powers is chiefly determined by historical conditions and constitutional considerations. Despite the significance of these factors, a range of alternative paradigms have been advanced by social scientists in an effort to determine why these existing arrangements have endured. These paradigms can also be helpful in assessing the relative efficiency of governmental structures by providing a 'benchmark model of institutional optimality' (Dollery, Crase and Johnson, 2006, 43). In the current context, the following conceptual approaches are particularly relevant: (i) the principle of subsidiarity and the notion of decentralisation, (ii) the theory of fiscal federalism and (iii) the concept of competitive federalism.

One way to establish the most efficient allocation of function within a federal system of government is to call upon the principle of subsidiarity, which holds that 'all social functions should be performed by the smallest organisational unit possible' (Dollery, Crase and Johnson, 2006, 43). Subsidiarity involves determining the most suitable tier of government at which decision-making should be undertaken (ie, local, state or national). Adherence to this principle involves the optimum allocation of functions between the various levels of government, the most effective coordination of decisions between these levels, and the most suitable forms of accountability and consultation in the decision-making process. While the principle itself does not tell policy makers how to realise these objectives it does, however, suggest that some degree of decentralisation in the decision-making process is warranted.

In considering the concept of decentralisation, Bailey (1999, 18–19) has identified three different types of decentralisation: (i) *economic decentralisation,* which focuses on the locality of economic decision-making and functions, (ii) *political decentralisation,* which signifies the 'devolution of political decision-making to local and regional governments', and (iii) *administrative decentralisation,* which refers to the establishment of regional offices for national or state government agencies 'with or without decision-making powers independent of sanction with the centre'.

The question of whether a specific function should be decentralised or centralised can be approached from at least four main viewpoints: (i) constitutional, (ii) economic, (iii) managerial and (iv) social. A constitutional approach would take into account a range of factors such as constitutional powers and the rule of law. In comparison, an economic perspective would consider matters related to economic efficiency and equity, especially in terms of VFI and HFI. A managerial approach would focus on questions related to managerial practice, including roles, responsibility, reporting lines and accountability. Finally, a social approach would be concerned primarily with matters such as societal well-being, social participation and social cohesion.

Since we are principally concerned with the economic foundations of the allocation of functions – especially in the context of Australian fiscal federalism – we adopt an economic perspective.

However, it needs to be borne in mind that the application of constitutional, economic, managerial and social approaches to the question of whether or not a function should be centralised or decentralised in no way leads to a consensus view. This is because 'value judgements lie at the core of most of these perspectives' (Dollery, Crase and Johnson, 2006, 44). Supporters of centralisation will generally put forth a case that it guarantees uniform standards, reduces inequalities and circumvents the duplication of services. On the other hand, exponents of decentralisation tend to champion the enhancement of local autonomy, greater customisation and innovation.

By way of example, government functions that require universal knowledge of a system (such as the national economy) should be managed by national government agencies. In contrast, government functions that rely on non-transferable local knowledge (as in the case of local community festivals) should be handled by local government agencies. Finally, intermediate government functions which require sub-national knowledge (as in the case of region-specific nature reserves) would be best served by state governments.

2.2.2 The theory of fiscal federalism

In his *Fiscal Federalism*, Wallace Oates (1972) established a theoretical framework for the assignment of functions between different tiers of government. Oates (1972, vi) described fiscal federalism as 'the division of fiscal functions among levels of government [and] the extent to which such a theoretical structure can explain the organization and workings of the public sectors of different countries'.

Within this context, Dollery, Crase and Johnson (2006) recognised that the main challenge facing the theory of fiscal federalism rests on the question of which government functions are best handled at the national, state or local government levels. In keeping with the conceptual taxonomy advanced by Richard Musgrave (1959), who distinguished between the allocation, distribution and stabilisation functions of government, most of the literature in the 'optimal federalism' tradition focuses on 'the assignment of function to different levels of government and the appropriate fiscal instruments for carrying out these functions' (Oates, 1999, 1121). Thus, from a policy perspective, the principal aim of this literature is not simply to determine the optimal assignment of governmental functions *per se*, but also to reorganise the public sector in order to enhance its performance.

According to King (1992), the theory of fiscal federalism offers policy makers a framework with which to address four significant questions: (i) What functions should be assigned to state and local governments as opposed to national governments? (ii) What is the optimal size of sub-national governments? (iii) How should the activities of state and local government be funded? (iv) To what extent should the activities of state and local government be controlled by the national government?

The *correspondence principle* is central to the theory of fiscal federalism. In essence, the correspondence principle states that the 'jurisdiction that determines the level of provision of the public good includes precisely the set of individuals who consume the good [so as to] internalize the benefits from the provision of each good' (Oates, 1972, 34). This means that each function of government should be provided by the smallest unit (ie, the lowest tier) of government such that there are no spatial spillovers into neighbouring administrative jurisdictions (Dollery, Crase and Johnson, 2006).

Moreover, the concept of a *benefit region* is important for the assignment of governmental functions in a federal system, especially since nearly all public goods and services confer benefits on constituents within limited geographical boundaries. For example, while some public sector functions, such as national defence, have a nationwide benefit, other functions, such as street lighting, are spatially confined. If the geographical boundary is restricted, then the benefits of that specific public good or service are limited to those residents in that particular area. Furthermore, if the costs associated with providing the 'public service are met by these residents (and if these costs would be the same for any level of government), then economic efficiency will be achieved if the service provision is provided by the lowest level of government possible' (Dollery, Crase and Johnson, 2006, 47). This represents the heart of Oates's (1972, 54) decentralisation theorem, which states that:

> In the absence of cost-savings from the centralized provision of a good and of inter-jurisdictional external effects, the level of welfare will always be at least as high (and typically higher) if Pareto-efficient levels of consumption of the good are provided in each jurisdiction than if any single, uniform level of consumption is maintained across all jurisdictions.

Thus, by tailoring the outputs of those local public services to 'the particular preferences and circumstances of their constituencies, decentralized provision increases economic welfare above that which results from the more uniform levels of such services that are likely under national provision' (Oates, 1999, 1121–2). The fundamental point is that the efficient level of output 'is likely to vary across jurisdictions as a result of both differences in preferences and cost differentials' and, in order to maximise 'overall social welfare', it is required that 'local outputs vary accordingly' (Oates, 1999, 1122).

The theory of fiscal federalism can also shed light on the optimal size of government (Dollery, Crase and Johnson, 2006). For instance, if we bring into play the plausible assumption that the benefits of public goods are not precisely contained within specific geographic regions, the fundamental nature of the problem can be articulated as follows:

> [T]he determination of the optimal-sized group to consume jointly the public good involves a trade-off between the increased cost-savings from joint consumption in larger groups versus the greater welfare from more response levels of consumption in smaller groups (Oates, 1972, 41–2).

Thus, the optimal size of a jurisdiction will occur when the benefits accumulating from decreasing per capita costs of providing a particular public service exactly equal the rising costs associated with having more individuals move into an area. In other words, the efficient size of government is determined when the marginal social benefit of consumption is equal to the marginal social cost associated with congestion (Dollery, Crase and Johnson, 2006).

At a more general level, the normative framework presented by fiscal federalism seeks to prescribe the level of government most appropriate to address the problems of allocation, distribution and stabilisation (Musgrave, 1959). The theory of fiscal federalism contends that 'the central government should have the basic responsibility for the macroeconomic stabilization function and for income redistribution in the form of assistance to the poor' (Oates, 1999, 1121). For example, a central government can exercise both monetary and fiscal policy, in contrast to lower tiers of government that have fiscal discretion only. Thus, it would appear that a central government would enjoy a comparative advantage in addressing the macroeconomic problem of stabilisation (Dollery, Crase and Johnson, 2006). Similarly, as noted by Oates (1999, 1121), the 'mobility of economic units can seriously constrain attempts to redistribute income'. For instance, a locally administered program to support low income households may generate an 'influx of the poor and encourage an exodus of those with higher income who must bear the tax burden'. Put differently, if the mitigation of poverty is viewed as a national public good, then it is best addressed at the national level. Following this line of reasoning, King (1984, 6) has argued that:

> [T]he general consensus seems to be that sub-national authorities will have little or no part to play in the distribution function, and that they will have no part at all to play in the stabilisation function.

However, the allocation function of government provides a much stronger case for a multi-tiered federal system of government (Dollery, Crase and Johnson, 2006). According to Oates (1972, 13), a decentralised government has three 'economically desirable characteristics'. First, multiple jurisdictions are more likely to be responsive to spatial variation in the demand for public goods and services. Second, the competition stimulated between different jurisdictions and the potential mobility of constituents along the lines predicted by Tiebout (1956) should enhance economic efficiency. Finally, a decentralised system of government may advance 'better public decision-making by compelling a more explicit recognition of the cost of public programs' (Oates, 1972, 13).

An interesting line of inquiry pursued in the literature has indicated that local authorities are more likely than their national government counterparts to meet the wishes of their constituents (Dollery, Crase and Johnson, 2006). For example, Peacock (1977) has remarked that local government politicians are better informed about local preferences because they tend to live in the local area and contest elections on local issues. Along similar lines, some authors also maintain that in a multi-level federal system of government constituents are able to exercise a greater level of control over the machinery of government because 'decentralisation with a number of tiers of government can simultaneously increase the ratio of representatives to officials and reduce the number of fields in which each representative has to operate' (King, 1984, 23).

Another field of inquiry in the literature emphasises the efficiency-enhancing features of multi-level government (Dollery, Crase and Johnson, 2006). For example, one of Oates's (1972) original insights was that a decentralised system of government is more likely to generate greater innovation in the provision of local public goods and services. More recently, Oates (1999, 1132) has also remarked that:

> In a setting of imperfect information with learning-by-doing, there are potential gains from experimentation with a variety of policies for addressing social and economic problems. And a federal system may offer some real opportunities for encouraging such experimentation and thereby promoting "technical progress" in public policy.

King (1984) has outlined several reasons why local authorities are inclined to be somewhat more adventurous than their national counterpart, 'not least because innovation in one municipal jurisdiction might compel other local governments to follow course' (Dollery, Crase and Johnson, 2006, 50). With respect to government administration, Helm and Smith (1987, ix) have argued that the decentralisation of functions to local government enhances economic efficiency due to 'informational economies' and that local government enjoys a comparative advantage in the possession 'of more and better information'.

Economists have also developed convincing arguments against the decentralised provision of local public goods and services. For example, several authors have advanced a Tiebout-style reasoning focusing on competitive federalism arguments. More specifically, it has been asserted that decentralisation results in 'shifting some of the burden of local taxes onto non-residents' (Dollery, Crase and Johnson, 2006, 50). Where intergovernmental grants are designed to supplement the revenues of local governments, the problem of tax shifting will be further compounded since a municipality's total revenue will be artificially overstated. In a similar vein, 'beggar-thy neighbour' policies, such as tax rebates employed to attract firms to specific local government areas, can lower total revenue and result in the sub-optimal provision of services (Breton, 1995).

As noted by Dollery, Crase and Johnson (2006), there are a number of public choice arguments against decentralisation. In the first place, it is held that 'fiscal illusion' among local voters may result in excessive local government expenditure. In this respect, King (1984, 25) has noted that:

> [T]here is the possibility that overprovision would occur if taxes levied by sub-central authorities were not perceptible to citizens, because they might underestimate the cost of service provision.

An argument derived from the 'median voter model' emphasises the risk of excessive local government expenditure. For example, some scholars maintain that efforts devoted toward enticing median voters can result in excess local government expenditure, since these constituents only bear a relatively small proportion of the cost associated with public expenditures. As Dollery, Crase and Johnson (2006, 51) have observed, this is a particularly 'telling point in the context of rural Australian councils who are heavily dependent on grants from the state and Commonwealth governments'. Moreover, local government authorities with highly mobile populations may also 'resort to the overprovision of services, since current voters know they will bear relatively few future costs' (Dollery, Crase and Johnson, 2006, 51).

A range of other arguments has been mounted against the decentralised provision of local public goods and services. For example, Peacock (1977) has contended that local government service delivery may be inefficient (especially for new services) due to inexperience. King (1984) has also argued that local councils may ignore positive externalities to non-residents, which will subsequently result in an under-provision of local public goods and services.

Finally, a number of practical arguments have been directed against the decentralisation of governmental functions. For example, Dillinger and Fay (1999, 20) have contended that 'as a practical matter, it is often difficult to define the scope and benefits of a specific service and to determine which specific jurisdiction will reap these benefits'. Even if benefit regions could be identified and established for particular public services, each service may, in fact, have a different benefit region, indicating that a three-level federal system of government could not suitably accommodate all of them (King, 1984). Expressed differently:

> [G]iven that there are many public goods at all sorts of levels, and given we cannot have an infinite number of layers of government, how do we decide at what level to set up government functions (Helm and Smith, 1987, iv).

The arguments presented above against decentralisation naturally point towards a need for local public goods and services to be provided by a more centralised system of government.

2.2.3 Competitive federalism

A federal system of government established in accordance with the theory of fiscal federalism will be characterised by a single national government, several state or provincial governments and a variety of local government systems, each consisting of a considerable number of community authorities. While the national government will benefit from some degree of monopoly power as a result of having various revenue-raising and expenditure powers, the position of state and local government is not immediately obvious. In his *Competitive Governments*, Albert Breton (1995) argued that, under a federal constitution, state and local government could either 'act in collusion in their expenditure and taxation behaviour' or 'compete with each other in terms of levels of taxation and patterns of expenditure and service delivery' (Dollery, Crase and Johnson, 2006, 52). In other words, competitive federalism accepts the premise that several lower levels of government in a federal system will compete with each other by using both their revenue-raising and expenditure powers.

The notion of competition between local government authorities can be traced backed to a seminal paper by Charles Tiebout (1956). According to Tiebout (1956), if there were a sufficiently large number of municipalities, and if each municipality offered a different array of public goods and services, 'then each individual could be thought to select that local community to live in which provides a level of public good output corresponding to his preference' (Brown and Jackson, 1990, 258). Thus, citizens will relocate to municipalities that offer the best combination of services and taxes that accord with their individual preferences (Dollery, Crase and Johnson, 2006). By 'voting with their feet' constituents concurrently reveal their preferences and promote the efficient allocation of local public goods among the community. Individuals are free to exit those municipalities that do not provide services that meet their needs and relocate into competing municipalities that provide a better mix of local public goods and services.

The model developed by Tiebout (1956) has a number of interesting implications for local government. To begin with, the larger the number of competing local government authorities, the greater will be the economic welfare accumulating to constituents, since they can more readily locate to a combination of local public goods and services that align with their preferences (Dollery, Crase and Johnson, 2006). Second, as the number of competing local government authorities in a given area increases, competition will increase as each local government authority attempts to realise its optimum size. Third, the more municipalities that are in a particular metropolitan area, the more demographically homogeneous each council will become, because 'people will migrate to areas that suit their preferences in accordance with self-selecting ethnic and socioeconomic characteristics' (Dollery, Crase and Johnson, 2006, 53). Finally, the differing levels of taxation and provision of local public goods in a local government area will be reflected in the property values. The enhanced provision of local public goods in a particular municipality will thus stimulate inward migration, which in turn will place upward pressure on property values.

A sizeable but inconclusive empirical literature exists on the Tiebout (1956) model, set primarily in the context of the US institutional environment. Abelson (2003) has contended that the Tiebout (1956) model is broadly applicable to US local government, where there are a 'large number of municipalities containing homogenous population, highly mobile households, vigorous municipal tax competition, limited spatial income redistribution through equalising intergovernmental grants, and individual local government bodies producing a wide range of key local goods and services, including health, policing and public schools' (Dollery, Crase and Johnson, 2006, 53–4). However, Abelson (2003) has also argued that the Tiebout (1956) model is not readily transferable to Australian local government. For example, many important services, such as education, health, and law and order, are provided in Australia by state governments and, since these services represent significant reasons for US mobility between local areas, there is correspondingly little, if any, incentive to relocate from one local government area to another within an Australian state (Dollery, Crase and Johnson, 2006).

However, it can be argued that the Tiebout (1956) model may still be applicable to public sector behaviour in Australia if we invoke Breton's (1995) model of competitive federalism and widen the scope of intergovernmental competition from competition between local government authorities to competition between *all* levels of government in a federal system (Dollery, Crase and Johnson, 2006). Against this background, Dollery, Crase and Johnson (2006, 54) have remarked that 'in recent years Australian state governments have withdrawn or reduced many of their services to remote and rural areas, and local councils have in many cases been obliged to replicate these services for their residents'. This unfortunately is a negative aspect of contemporary 'competitive federalism' in Australia whereby cost-shifting occurs and local government bears the greatest burden.

2.2.4 A brief history of Australian federalism

After the United States (1789), Switzerland (1848) and Canada (1867), the Commonwealth of Australia is one of 'the oldest continuing federal systems in the world' (Dollery, 2002, 26). On 1 January 1901, the Constitution of the Commonwealth of Australia came into being after a decade of concerted effort and brought the six self-governing British colonies into a federation. In essence, the forefathers of Australian federation partly followed the US model of federalism by specifying a relatively limited number of federal exclusionary powers, in addition to a significant number of concurrent powers, while leaving a range of unspecified residual powers to the state governments (Dollery, 2002). The most important federal powers are derived from section 51 of the Constitution and bestow on the Commonwealth Government the sole responsibility for activities such as defence, trade and immigration, while the states maintain responsibility for important public services such as education, health, and law and order (Dollery, 2002).

Taking into account the comparative longevity and stability of the Australian federation, it is instructive to consider its inherent strengths and weaknesses. In support of federalism, Maddox (2000) has contended that such a system enables the appropriate level of government to remain 'close to the people', in addition to reinforcing the notion of decentralised democracy. Moreover, it is also argued that a federal system of government and its associated political and legal institutions provide a greater opportunity for individual participation, which may create an environment that fosters innovation and new ideas. In other words, the system of federalism can offer a 'competitive laboratory' in which different bureaucracies across the states and territories can produce ingenious solutions to complex policy problems along the lines pictured by Breton (1995) and other advocates of competitive federalism (Burgess, 2006).

The principal weakness of the federal system of government in Australia is the duplication of political activities and institutions (Maddox, 2000). Along similar lines, Mathews (1983) has argued that the duplication within a federal system of government stems from a lack of policy coordination between the Commonwealth and state governments on a variety of issues ranging from the environment to transport. Contrary to Breton (1995), it has also been suggested that competition between the states and territories could lead to decision making that is not in the best interests of citizens. To illustrate this problem, Maddox (2000) has provided an example whereby a state or territory government which attempts to attract a mining company to a region – in an effort to stimulate economic development – may offer 'cheap electrical power, concession tax rates and infrastructure assistance' and may not assign appropriate weight to environmental concerns (Maddox, 2000, 154–5).

Another weakness identified by Maddox (2000, 156) is that 'policy vacuums' may arise when the federal system of government allows for 'indecision, inaction and buck-passing' to occur between the national and state and territory governments. This problem has both political and structural dimensions and, from time to time, there will be a range of policies in which national and state governments may not be prepared to act or may disagree on the appropriate policy response. This circumstance is able to exist within the Australian context because the notion of 'divided responsibility' forms part of the federal system of government. In relation to this issue, Parker (1980, 17) has also remarked that 'the mere division of powers between the federal and state parliament ... diffuse responsibility between sets of ministers at different levels ... and frustrates attempts in any one parliament to hold its ministers accountable'.

2.3 Public finance

In section 2.2 we considered the federal system of government in Australia with particular reference to the theory of fiscal federalism and competitive federalism. In this section we provide a synoptic overview of Commonwealth, state and local government public finances, which, for ease of exposition, have been grouped into the following categories: (i) economic transactions, (ii) expenditure by purpose, and (iii) source of taxation revenue.

2.3.1 Commonwealth finance

The Commonwealth Government Operating Statement in Table 2.1 records the economic transactions for the Commonwealth Government covering the period 2007/08 to 2010/11. Over 90% of Commonwealth revenue is sourced from taxation and the major expenditure categories include gross operating expenses, current transfers and capital transfers. The operating statement itself comprises two balancing items. The first is the 'Net Operating Balance', which is simply derived by subtracting total expenses from total revenues. In this context, total revenue and total expenses are defined as 'inflows and outflows of economic value arising from operational transactions, and usually result in a change to net worth' (ABS, 2005, 27). The second balancing item in Table 2.1 is 'Net Lending(+)/Borrowing(-)', which is 'derived as the net operating balance less net acquisition of non-financial assets' and is used to measure 'the public sector's financing requirement' and ascertain how the 'financing requirement was financed' (ABS, 2005, 27).

Table 2.1. Commonwealth Government Operating Statement 2007/08 to 2010/11

	2007/08 $m	2008/09 $m	2009/10 $m	2010/11 $m
Revenue				
Taxation revenue	285,672	278,002	267,171	288,075
Current grants and subsidies	0	0	0	0
Sales of goods and services	5,814	6,911	8,301	8,436
Interest from public non-financial corporations	0	81	0	0
Interest from public financial corporations	2,108	1,063	727	568
Interest from other	3,215	3,594	3,222	4,141
Dividend income	2,848	3,475	7,658	2,359
Other	3,634	5,157	4,933	5,354
(1) Total Revenue	**303,291**	**298,282**	**292,013**	**308,933**
Expenses				
Gross operating expenses				
Depreciation	4,218	4,926	4,914	5,218
Employee expenses	21,379	23,064	25,357	27,425
Other operating expenses	52,867	57,466	61,887	66,171
Nominal superannuation interest expenses	6,011	6,715	6,687	6,997
Other interest expenses	4,136	4,711	6,920	9,894
Other property expenses	0	0	0	0
Current transfers				
Grant expenses to state governments	69,483	73,088	75,682	79,978
Grant expenses to the private sector	11,819	13,019	16,561	14,521
Grant expenses to universities	7,349	6,692	8,808	8,250
Grant expenses to local governments	89	46	12	14
Other Grant expenses	0	0	0	0
Subsidy expenses to public corporations	220	188	198	195
Subsidy expenses to other	7,299	8,058	8,215	8,495
Other current transfers	86,398	111,548	98,490	105,559

	2007/08 $m	2008/09 $m	2009/10 $m	2010/11 $m
Capital transfers				
Grant expenses to public non-financial corporations	426	9	81	0
Grant expenses to public financial corporations	0	0	0	0
Grant expenses to other levels of government	5,012	10,978	21,608	18,609
Other Grant expenses	1,624	1,892	2,293	2,943
Other capital transfers	0	15	0	0
(2) Total Expenses	**278,330**	**322,416**	**337,714**	**354,269**
(3) Net Operating Balance: (1) – (2)	**24,961**	**-24,133**	**-45,701**	**-45,336**
(4) Net acquisition of non-financial assets				
Gross fixed capital formation	7,040	8,956	10,080	9,210
less Depreciation	4,218	4,926	4,914	5,218
plus Change in inventories	762	600	661	764
plus Other transactions in non-financial assets	46	209	1,340	1,198
(5) Total Net acquisition of non-financial assets	**3,631**	**4,839**	**7,166**	**5,954**
(6) Net Lending(+)/Borrowing(–): (3) – (5)	**21,330**	**-28,972**	**-52,867**	**-51,290**

Source: Australian Bureau of Statistics, *Government Finance Statistics* (Cat. No. 5512.0) (ABS, 2012b).

Table 2.1 reflects that the period of fiscal restraint ended in 2007/08. With the emergence of the global financial crisis in 2007, there was a pressing need for the Commonwealth Government to undertake countervailing stimulatory policy measures. As a result, the Commonwealth's 'Net Lending(+)/Borrowing(–)' position shifted from $21,330 million in 2007/08 to –$51,290 in 2010/11.

Over this period, total Commonwealth Government outlays increased from $278,330 million in 2007/08 to $354,269 million in 2010/11, as illustrated in Table 2.2, while total Commonwealth Government taxation remained relatively stable, as shown in Table 2.3.

Table 2.2 also indicates that most of the growth in expenditure occurred in education (81%), housing and community amenities (88%), health (27%), social security and welfare (20%) and defence (19%). However, a noticeable decrease was observed for expenditure in the agriculture, forestry and fishing (–33%) category.

Table 2.2. Commonwealth Government Expenses by Purpose 2007/08 to 2010/11

	2007/08 $m	2008/09 $m	2009/10 $m	2010/11 $m
General public services	15,049	15,159	15,433	18,348
Defence	16,570	18,341	19,350	19,666
Public order and safety	3,503	3,557	3,844	3,828
Education	18,694	21,905	35,709	33,794
Health	44,235	49,145	51,525	56,023
Social security and welfare	97,843	124,905	109,133	116,951
Housing and community amenities	2,955	5,146	9,090	5,543
Recreation and culture	3,221	3,105	3,371	3,234
Fuel and energy	5,368	5,791	8,537	5,929
Agriculture, forestry and fishing	3,819	2,714	2,905	2,546
Mining, manufacturing and construction	1,410	1,911	1,630	1,456
Transport and communications	4,273	7,183	6,754	4,731
Other economic affairs	5,893	6,493	9,062	9,042
Nominal interest on superannuation	6,011	6,715	6,687	6,997
Public debt transactions	4,136	4,711	6,921	9,894
Other	45,351	45,636	47,763	56,287
Total	**278,330**	**322,416**	**337,714**	**354,269**

Source: Australian Bureau of Statistics, *Government Finance Statistics* (Cat. No. 5512.0) (ABS, 2012b).

Table 2.3. Commonwealth Government Taxation Revenue 2007/08 to 2010/11

	2007/08 $m	2008/09 $m	2009/10 $m	2010/11 $m
Personal income tax	124,075	123,946	121,264	135,075
Fringe benefits tax	3,796	3,581	3,523	3,348
Company income tax	66,661	62,784	54,490	58,118
Income tax paid by superannuation funds	11,916	9,201	6,164	6,683
Income levied on non-residents	2,132	1,857	1,574	1,707
Employers' payroll taxes	381	377	507	505
Taxes on property	15	16	12	13
General taxes (sales taxes)	1,105	1,090	1,247	1,236
Goods and services tax (GST)	44,381	42,626	46,553	48,093

	2007/08 $m	2008/09 $m	2009/10 $m	2010/11 $m
Excises and levies	24,297	25,137	25,303	26,619
Taxes on international trade	6,081	6,289	5,762	5,839
Other	834	1,098	771	838
Total	**285,672**	**278,002**	**267,171**	**288,075**

Source: Australian Bureau of Statistics, *Taxation Revenue Australia* (Cat. No. 5506.0) (ABS, 2012c).

Table 2.3 also shows the dominating influence of personal income tax and company tax, which in 2010/11 accounted for two-thirds (67%) of total Commonwealth Government taxation revenue. It is also worth noting that personal income tax in and of itself accounted for nearly half (47%) of all taxation revenue in 2010/11.

2.3.2 State finance

State finances for the years 2007/08 to 2010/11 are summarised in Table 2.4 (economics transactions), Table 2.5 (expense by purpose) and Table 2.6 (taxation revenue). As noted by Mathews and Grewal (1997), a relatively high proportion of state government outlays is characterised by fixed capital expenditure and states thus need to rely heavily on borrowings in order to fund infrastructure projects. For instance, the total state borrowing requirements increased from –$4,318 million in 2007/08 to –$15,337 million in 2010/11.

In reviewing the state government operating statement in Table 2.4, it is important to consider the role of Commonwealth–state financial relations. Over this period, state governments received around 45% of their total revenue from the Commonwealth Government in the form of grants and subsidies, despite a steadily increasing revenue stream from state-based taxes and the sale of goods and services.

With respect to state government expenses by purpose, shown in Table 2.5, the largest increases in expenditure between 2007/08 and 2010/11 were for social security and welfare (34%), housing and community amenities (28%), education (26%), health (25%), public order and safety (23%), and recreation and culture (23%). In terms of total outlays, education and health represent

25% and 26%, respectively, of all state expenditure between 2007/08 and 2010/11.

Table 2.4. State Government Operating Statement 2007/08 to 2010/11

	2007/08 $m	2008/09 $m	2009/10 $m	2010/11 $m
Revenue				
Taxation revenue	53,134	50,631	54,536	58,121
Current grants and subsidies	72,289	78,148	85,771	85,991
Sales of goods and services	15,342	16,680	17,981	19,333
Interest income	840	2,978	3,452	4,041
Other	19,558	25,438	32,811	32,808
(1) Total Revenue	**161,163**	**173,875**	**194,551**	**200,294**
Gross operating expenses				
Depreciation	7,565	8,611	9,272	9,628
Employee expenses	69,586	75,734	80,586	85,739
Other operating expenses	39,384	43,047	46,446	49,854
Nominal superannuation interest expenses	2,743	3,417	4,488	4,345
Other interest expenses	2,658	3,265	3,916	4,791
Other property expenses	0	2	2	2
Current transfers				
Grant expenses	19,080	21,718	24,208	25,357
Subsidy expenses	8,479	9,385	8,554	8,914
Other current transfers	1,475	1,780	1,984	1,902
Capital transfers				
Grants to local governments	872	969	1,224	1,597
Other capital transfers	5,342	5,734	10,530	6,072
(2) Total Expenses	**157,184**	**173,663**	**191,210**	**198,199**
(3) Net Operating Balance: (1)–(2)	**3,979**	**212**	**3,342**	**2,094**
(4) Net acquisition of non-financial assets				
Gross fixed capital formation	15,069	18,425	25,658	25,929
less Depreciation	7,565	8,611	9,272	9,628
plus Change in inventories	48	181	44	52
plus Other transactions in non-financial assets	746	941	1,275	1,078
(5) Total net acquisition of non-financial assets	**8,297**	**10,936**	**17,706**	**17,431**
(6) Net Lending(+)/Borrowing(-): (3)–(5)	**–4,318**	**–10,724**	**–14,364**	**–15,337**

Source: Australian Bureau of Statistics, *Government Finance Statistics* (Cat. No. 5512.0) (ABS, 2012b).

Table 2.5. State Government Expenses by Purpose 2007/08 to 2010/11

	2007/08 $m	2008/09 $m	2009/10 $m	2010/11 $m
General public services	4,611	4,850	5,710	6,004
Defence	0	0	0	0
Public order and safety	15,952	17,370	18,277	19,643
Education	39,522	43,215	48,987	49,824
Health	41,243	44,784	48,273	51,654
Social security and welfare	10,762	12,084	13,073	14,389
Housing and community amenities	8,301	10,519	12,617	10,617
Recreation and culture	3,791	4,070	4,294	4,662
Fuel and energy	1,653	1,619	912	1,136
Agriculture, forestry and fishing	3,478	3,218	3,165	2,789
Mining, manufacturing and construction	703	656	703	730
Transport and communications	15,753	18,175	19,618	19,874
Other economic affairs	3,135	3,278	3,774	4,088
Nominal interest on superannuation	2,743	3,417	4,488	4,345
Public debt transactions	2,676	3,268	3,934	4,814
Other	2,861	3,139	3,385	3,631
Total	**157,184**	**173,663**	**191,210**	**198,199**

Source: Australian Bureau of Statistics, *Government Finance Statistics* (Cat. No. 5512.0) (ABS, 2012b).

Table 2.6. State Government Taxation Revenue 2007/08 to 2010/11

	2007/08 $m	2008/09 $m	2009/10 $m	2010/11 $m
Payroll taxes	16,026	16,926	16,796	18,086
Land taxes and rates	5,467	6,761	7,049	7,428
Government borrowing guarantee levies	253	386	677	830
Stamp duties on conveyances	14,289	9,526	12,292	12,330
Other stamp duties	957	313	231	317
Taxes on the provision of goods and services	61	69	69	69
Taxes on gambling	4,850	5,028	5,054	5,147
Taxes on insurance	4,250	4,505	4,597	5,035
Motor vehicle taxes	6,386	6,458	6,992	7,461
Franchise taxes	3	4	4	1
Other	591	655	775	1,416
Total	**53,134**	**50,631**	**54,536**	**58,121**

Source: Australian Bureau of Statistics, *Taxation Revenue Australia* (Cat. No. 5506.0) (ABS, 2012c).

Table 2.6 shows the principal sources of state government taxation revenue over the period 2007/08 to 2010/11. During this period, state government taxation, on average, increased by 9.4% between 2007/08 and 2010/11. Increases were also observed for land tax (36%), insurance tax (18%), motor vehicle tax (17%), payroll tax (13%) and gambling tax (6%). However, a decrease in taxation revenue was observed for stamp duties on conveyance (–14%).

2.3.3 Local government finance

Local government finances for the years 2007/08 to 2010/11 are summarised in Table 2.7 (economic transactions) and Table 2.8 (expense by purpose). In reviewing the local government operating statement, shown in Table 2.7, the following points are worth noting. First, around 10% of local government revenue in 2010/11 was derived from grants and subsidies from higher tiers of government, both Commonwealth and state. The remaining source of local government expenditure was derived from property taxes (37%), the sale of goods and services (25%), interest income (4%) and other (24%).

Second, a relatively high proportion of local government expenditure is also devoted to capital expenditure, which relies heavily on borrowing in order to fund infrastructure projects. For example, in 2010/11, the net operating balance for the local government sector was $4,180 million. However, the corresponding net acquisition of non-financial assets in 2010/11 was $4,548 million, which subsequently resulted in a net borrowing position of –$369 million. It is also worth noting that the depreciation on capital formation plays a significant role in local government financing. For instance, of the $10,204 million spent on gross capital formation in 2010/11, depreciation accounted for $5,794 million or 59%.

Table 2.8 shows local government expenditure by purpose for the years 2007/08 to 2010/11. Over this period, the main increases in local government expenditure were for public order and safety (44%), education (44%), transport and communications (28%), recreation and culture (26%), and social security and welfare (19%). In terms of taxation, local municipal rates (ie, property taxes) were the preponderate source of taxation revenue for local government.

Table 2.7. Local Government Operating Statement 2007/08 to 2010/11

	2007/08 $m	2008/09 $m	2009/10 $m	2010/11 $m
Revenue				
Taxation revenue	10,139	10,896	11,607	12,408
Current grants and subsidies	2,306	3,370	2,895	3,376
Sales of goods and services	8,092	8,634	9,245	8,466
Interest income	819	760	669	1,192
Other	6,438	7,047	7,602	8,060
(1) Total Revenue	**27,794**	**30,706**	**32,019**	**33,503**
Expenses				
Gross operating expenses				
Depreciation	4,847	5,355	5,588	5,794
Employee expenses	8,855	9,464	10,127	10,891
Other operating expenses	9,558	10,528	10,660	11,447
Other interest expenses	428	375	453	578
Current transfers				
Grant expenses	148	116	126	193
Subsidy expenses	0	4	1	2
Other current transfers	135	188	152	197
Capital transfers				
Grant expenses	13	21	64	20
Other capital transfers	21	26	339	201
(2) Total Expenditure	**24,005**	**26,077**	**27,509**	**29,323**
(3) Net Operating Balance: (1)–(2)	**3,790**	**4,629**	**4,509**	**4,180**
(4) Net acquisition of non-financial assets				
Gross fixed capital formation	8,349	10,176	11,091	10,204
less Depreciation	4,847	5,355	5,588	5,794
plus Change in inventories	17	49	−173	−159
plus Other transactions in non-financial assets	154	230	385	297
(5) Total Net acquisition of non-financial assets	**3,674**	**5,100**	**5,716**	**4,548**
(6) Net Lending(+)/Borrowing(–): (3)–(5)	**116**	**-471**	**–1,206**	**-369**

Source: Australian Bureau of Statistics, *Government Finance Statistics* (Cat. No. 5512.0) (ABS, 2012b).

Table 2.8. Local Government Expenses by Purpose 2007/08 to 2010/11

	2007/08 $m	2008/09 $m	2009/10 $m	2010/11 $m
General public services	4,573	4,849	5,118	5,611
Public order and safety	535	592	662	769
Education	100	134	155	144
Health	295	308	300	332
Social security and welfare	1,411	1,504	1,599	1,684
Housing and community amenities	5,780	6,493	6,892	6,451
Recreation and culture	3,462	3,880	4,107	4,359
Fuel and energy	34	15	12	15
Agriculture, forestry and fishing	40	38	30	29
Mining, manufacturing and construction	300	307	301	356
Transport and communications	5,169	5,632	5,827	6,640
Other economic affairs	914	940	976	1,016
Public debt transactions	428	375	453	578
Other	964	1,013	1,078	1,336
Total	**24,005**	**26,077**	**27,509**	**29,323**

Source: Australian Bureau of Statistics, *Government Finance Statistics* (Cat. No. 5512.0) (ABS, 2012b).

2.4 Vertical fiscal imbalance

In section 2.3 we provided a synoptic sketch of Commonwealth, state and local government finances. In this section we examine the problematic relationship between Commonwealth, state and local governments that stems from the high degree of VFI. In reviewing the state government operating statement in Table 2.4, it is important to consider the role of Commonwealth-state financial relations. Over this period, state governments received around 45% of their total revenue from the Commonwealth Government in the form of grants and subsidies, despite a steadily increasing revenue stream from state-based taxes and the sale of goods and services. In other words, the fiscal relationship between the Commonwealth and the states is characterised by VFI: a situation where the state's own revenue sources are inadequate to fund their expenditure responsibilities, while the Commonwealth Government's revenue sources are greater than is required for its responsibilities.

In principle, VFI can be addressed in four ways: (i) responsibilities for expenditure can be transferred between different levels of government; (ii) taxation powers can be reallocated; (ii) funding between different tiers of government can be redistributed via the introduction of intergovernmental grants; and (iv) revenue-sharing arrangements can be developed and implemented (Dollery, 2002). However, it has been argued that intergovernmental grants may not be efficient because these grants 'have zero opportunity cost from the perspective of the states and local government' and furthermore there is 'little incentive to expend these funds judiciously' (Dollery, Stewart and Worthington, 2000, 18).

In recent times, two main types of federal grants have been employed to overcome vertical fiscal imbalance: General Purpose Payments (GPPs) and Specific Purpose Payments (SPPs). GPPs are provided to state and local governments and can be used for any purpose. In other words, the funding associated with this type of grant is *untied*. On the other hand, SPPs are funds that are provided for a purpose as specified by the Commonwealth Government. Thus, the funding associated with this type of grant is *tied* to a specific purpose. Between 1969/70 and 1994/95, SPPs rose relative to GPPs and 'state and local governments have experienced a relative decline in Commonwealth Government grant income and have raised increasing proportions of their income from own source income' (Dollery, Stewart and Worthington, 2000, 18). In essence, this has two main repercussions for state and local governments: (i) reduced autonomy in spending Commonwealth grants; and (ii) an increased reliance on own-source taxation. Moreover, as SPPs are allocated in accordance with the procedures and recommendations of the Commonwealth Grants Commission (CGC), it is possible that the allocation of these grants may be 'much more amenable to party political calculation, and thus can be employed to maximise electorate support' (Dollery and Worthington, 1996, 81).

Thus, in the context of public choice theory, it could be argued that the Commonwealth Government's increasing reliance on SPPs may be motivated by political self-interest, although Dollery and Worthington (1996, 84) have argued that 'the increment in political support is directed to recipient government politicians, rather than those of the donor government'. It is also interesting to note that referring to VFI as a criticism of the federal system of governance may be misplaced. For instance, Dollery (2002, 29) has argued that many examples of both federal and unitary systems of government have decentralised fiscal responsibilities and therefore VFI should be viewed as a problem 'generic to all forms of democratic government that embody a division of powers'.

The changing nature of VFI is illustrated in Table 2.9, which shows the proportion of revenue collected under Commonwealth and state legislation over the last century. In 1901/02, the proportion of revenue collected under Commonwealth legislation was 41%. The corresponding proportion of revenue collected under state legislation was 59%. The proportion of all state revenue from Commonwealth transfers was 36.7%. In 1946/47, following the Second World War (WW2), the proportion of revenue collected under Commonwealth legislation was 84.9%, compared with 15.1% of revenue collected under state legislation. The corresponding proportion of all state revenue from Commonwealth transfers was 46.1%. In 2009/10, the proportion of revenue collected under Commonwealth legislation was 75%, compared with 25% of revenue sourced under state legislation. The proportion of all state revenue attributable to Commonwealth transfers was 49.8%.

Table 2.9. Proportion of Revenue Collected under Commonwealth and State Legislation

	Proportion collected under Commonwealth legislation	Proportion collected under State legislation	Proportion of all State revenue from Commonwealth transfers
	%	%	%
1901/02	41.0	59.0	36.7
1938/39	46.6	53.4	13.9
1946/47	84.9	15.1	46.1
1980/81	78.3	21.7	62.0
2009/10	75.0	25.0	49.8

Source: Commonwealth Grants Commission, *Report on GST Revenue Sharing Relativities – 2011 Update* (CGC, 2012).

Dollery, Crase and Johnson (2006) provide an excellent historical account of Commonwealth-State financial relations, which is summarised in Table 2.10.

Table 2.10. Historical Perceptive of Commonwealth–State Financial Relations

Time Period	Standing of Commonwealth–State Financial Relations
1901–1909	The Constitution required states to surrender their main source of revenue (ie, customs duties) although the federal government was required to return 75% of these funds to the states and any 'surplus' revenue.
1910–1918/19	Payment of 'surplus' funds to the states was abolished and a system of equal per capita payments commenced. The federal government introduced personal income tax in 1915 creating concurrent taxing powers with states.
1919/20–1932/33	Special Commonwealth grants to states commenced. Per capita payments ceased and an annual payment to the states was introduced. During this period, the Australian Loan Council was established to coordinate Commonwealth and state borrowings. The states remained largely self-financing although evidence was emerging of vertical fiscal imbalance.
1933/34–1941/42	The Commonwealth Grants Commission (CGC) was established to oversee the payment of funds to the states. The essential doctrine established by the CGC was 'the obligation of the Commonwealth to make it financially possible for any state to give its people a standard of service approximately equal to that of other states, without being forced to tax more severely than the average of other states' (Giblin, 1949, 3).
1942/43–1946/47	In 1942 the Commonwealth assumed the sole power to apply personal income tax. It was initially understood that this arrangement would continue for the period of WW2 plus one additional year. In 1946, the Commonwealth legislated to retain these taxation powers.
1947/48–1958/59	The vertical fiscal imbalance established by the Commonwealth's assumption of taxation powers was reinforced by the Commonwealth's control of the Australian Loan Council, which imposed strict controls on state borrowing.
1959/60–1971/72	During the 1950s Financial Assistant Grants, special grants and Specific Purpose Grants were employed to address vertical fiscal imbalance between the Commonwealth and states. Greater emphasis on the latter led Groenewegen (1979, 53) to remark that 'the states are more and more becoming administrative spending agencies of federal government'.
1972/73–1975/76	The election of the Whitlam Government escorted in major reforms to the financial relations between Commonwealth, state and local government. The general growth in public sector outlays was accompanied by a commensurate increase in intergovernmental transfers to the states. In the context of local government, General Purpose Assistance Payments were introduced.

Time Period	Standing of Commonwealth–State Financial Relations
1976/77–1982/83	The Fraser government put in place revenue sharing arrangements with the states. The previous reliance on Specific Purpose Payments was reduced with an intention of providing the states with a greater degree of autonomy.
1983/84–1995/96	Under the Hawke and Keating Governments, tax-sharing arrangements were abolished and Specific Purpose Payments were again increased to substitute for General Purpose Payments. The Hawke and Keating Governments (like the Fraser Government) continued to decrease payments to the states.
1996/97–2007/08	Under the Howard Government, significant attention was devoted to the reduction of government debt. The Howard Government also sought to expand the competition reforms introduced under the Hawke and Keating years. In terms of Commonwealth–State relations, the introduction of the goods and services tax (GST) from 2000/01 and the associated Intergovernmental Agreement on the Reform of Commonwealth–State Financial Relations in 1999 represents the most important development during this period. Under the conditions of this agreement, state governments' share of GST and receipt of other Commonwealth revenues was conditional upon the delivery of state taxation reform.

Source: Adapted from Dollery, Crase and Johnson (2006).

Table 2.11. Taxation by Level of Government 2007/08 to 2010/11

	2007/08 $m	2008/09 $m	2009/10 $m	2010/11 $m
Commonwealth Government	285,672	278,002	267,171	288,075
Less intergovernmental taxes	14	3	9	8
Tax revenue net of intergovernmental taxes	285,658	277,999	267,161	288,066
State Government	53,134	50,631	54,536	58,121
Less intergovernmental taxes [AQ 5]	575	610	644	665
Tax revenue net of intergovernmental taxes	52,560	50,021	53,893	57,456
Local Government	10,139	10,896	11,607	12,408
Total	**348,347**	**338,905**	**332,649**	**357,917**

Source: Australian Bureau of Statistics, *Taxation Revenue Australia* (Cat. No. 5506.0) (ABS, 2012c).

In more recent times, VFI in the Australian milieu has remained relatively stable. For example, Table 2.11 shows the level of taxation by tier of government for the period 2007/08 to 2010/11. During this time, the Commonwealth Government collected just over 80% of all taxation. Own-source revenues as a percentage of own-purpose outlays (a measure of VFI) are around 144% for the

Commonwealth and 55% for the states. Commonwealth grants to the states represent around 45% of total state revenue.

Within the context of contemporary Australian fiscal federalism, the principal method of addressing VFI is by means of intergovernmental financial transfers from the Commonwealth Government to the states. Grants are made annually and often in conjunction with other actions. For instance, since 2000/01, the revenue from the GST has been transferred to the states (Table 2.10). When intergovernmental transfers are made, governments need to consider: (i) the total amount of grants to be transferred each year, (ii) the type of transfer (ie, whether the grant is unconditional, tied or mixed) and (ii) how the transfers will be allocated among the different states and territories in the Commonwealth (CGC, 2012).

Under the present Rudd–Gillard Labor Government, which came to power in 2007, the architecture of Australia's fiscal federal relations has been governed by the 2008 Council of Australian Governments (COAG) *Intergovernmental Agreement on Federal Financial Relations* (IGA). This agreement came into force on 1 January 2009 and was intended to provide 'a strong foundation for COAG to pursue economic and social reforms to underpin growth' in addition to clearly specifying the 'roles and responsibilities of each level of government so that the appropriate government is accountable to the community' (Commonwealth of Australia, 2012a, 123). The main features of the current IGA consist of:

- GST distributed to the states and territories on the basis of recommendations made by the Commonwealth Grants Commission (CGC);
- Specific Purpose Payments (SPPs) grouped into five areas (healthcare, schools, skills and workforce development, disability services and affordable housing); and
- the introduction of National Partnership Payments (NPPs) that were designed to: (i) fund the states for specific projects, (ii) offer financial incentives to states to facilitate reforms and (iii) reward those states that actually delivered reforms (Australian Government, 2012a).

The financial characteristics of the current IGA agreement over the period 2010/11 to 2014/15 are summarised in Table 2.12. In 2010/11, Commonwealth payments to the states totalled $93,880 million. Of this total, $45,450 million was received by the states in the form of GST entitlements, which can be used by the states for any purpose as they see fit. The remaining payments to the states comprised SPPs ($26,264 million), NPPs ($21,092 million) and 'other revenue assistance' ($1,074 million).

Table 2.12. Total Commonwealth Payments to States 2010/11 to 2014/15

	National SPPs	National Health Reform funding	NPPs[a]	GST entitlement	Other revenue assistance	Total
	$m	$m	$m	$m	$m	$m
2010/11	26,264	--	21,092	45,450	1,074	93,880
2011/12	28,010	--	17,505	48,350	1,109	94974
2012/13	16,152	13,676	16,782	51,750	1,103	99,464
2013/14	17,199	14,598	17,702	54,700	1,112	105,311
2014/15	18,360	16,154	9,843	57,400	1,098	102,855

Source: Australian Government, 2012b.
Note: (a) Includes Financial Assistance Grants for local government and payments direct to local government.

In considering the current specific purpose arrangements in Table 2.12, it is worth noting that prior to 2009 the states received payments from more than 90 different SPPs. As previously noted, SPPs have now been 'broad banded' into five national SPPs and the agreements between the Commonwealth and the states for each new payment contain 'objectives, outcomes, outputs and performance indicators' (Commonwealth of Australia, 2012a, 27). With respect to the NPPs shown in Table 2.12, it is important to note that these payments include Financial Assistant Grants (FAGs) for local government, in addition to payments made by the Commonwealth Government directly to local government authorities. The subject of Australian local government finance is considered in detail in Chapter 3.

2.5 Horizontal fiscal equalisation

In section 2.4 we examined the subject of VFI within the context of Australian fiscal federalism, a situation whereby the state's own revenue sources are inadequate to fund their expenditure responsibilities, while the Commonwealth's revenue sources are greater than is required for its own responsibilities. In an effort to address VFI, the 'surplus' Commonwealth Government revenue is then distributed to the states in a combination of conditional grants (such as SPPs and NPPs) and 'unconditional general revenue payments' (Petchey, 2011, 207). This latter payment, more commonly referred to as the GST, is collected by the Commonwealth and distributed amongst the states using a methodology developed and employed by the Commonwealth Grants Commission (CGC). In this section, we consider the principle of HFE, how fiscal equalisation operates in practice, including the role of Commonwealth Grants Commission (CGC), and the theoretical motivation for fiscal equalisation.

2.5.1 Horizontal fiscal equalisation

Economic and social differences between different regions within a country may lead to differing revenue-raising capacities and associated expenditure requirements. This situation is known as horizontal fiscal imbalance (HFI). In a unitary state, these differences may be addressed directly, since the government can decide how to apply the revenue-raising and expenditure policies across the entire country. In a federal system of government, however, direct regional transfers to different sub-national jurisdictions do not automatically take place. The problem of HFI is addressed by a process of horizontal fiscal equalisation (HFE). In Australia, the CGC employs the principle of HFE to derive 'relativities' that are applied to the GST revenue pool to decide state shares (Petchey, 2011). These relativities are calculated so:

> State governments should receive funding from the pool of goods and services tax revenue such that, after allowing for material factors affecting revenues and expenditures, each would have the fiscal capacity to provide services and the associated infrastructure at the same standard, if each made

> the same effort to raise revenue from its own sources and operated at the same level of efficiency (CGC, 2012, 31).

In other words, the aim of HFE is to provide all states with the same fiscal capacity to deliver the same standard of services, 'without imposing differential burdens on their populations' (Petchey, 2011, 207). However, it is important to note that the principle of HFE *does not* 'provide the capacity for equal services in all regions' of the various states and territories. Rather, the principle of HFE 'reflects the policies' of all states to afford 'different services to people living in different regions' (CGC, 2012, 32). Moreover, the principle of HFE 'provides the capacity for equal service in comparable regions but for different levels of service between those regions' (CGC, 2012, 32). It also needs to be borne in mind that the principle of HFE focuses on equalising each state's *capacity* to provide services – the *actual* level of service provision is a matter for each state (Warren, 2008).

2.5.2 Operation of horizontal fiscal equalisation

The primary role of the CGC is to provide advice on how the GST revenue should be distributed among the states in order to equalise their fiscal capacities (CGC, 2012). To fulfil its advisory role, the CGC employs an HFE model that is comparatively complex and 'not generally well understood by people outside a small group of state and federal policy-makers' (Petchey, 2011, 207).

In essence, the HFE model is used to estimate *relativity factors* for each state. The relativity factor itself 'is an index number calculated over a three-year period' that is 'applied to the GST pool in any particular year to derive the general revenue payment' for a particular state in a given year (Petchey, 2011, 208) and the 'population-weighted average of the relativities necessarily sums to one' (Williams, 2005a, 112). Therefore, an equal per-capita payment would mean a relativity factor of 1, but this is adjusted by revenue and expenditure requirements which are determined on a state-by-state basis. Thus, in terms of state-specific revenue and expenditure needs:

> Relatively high-cost states are assessed to have positive expenditure needs and low-cost states are assigned negative expenditure needs. Similarly states with a relatively strong

tax base are assessed to have negative revenue needs and those with weak tax bases a positive revenue need (Petchey, 2011, 208).

The revenue and expenditure needs for each state will ultimately determine whether a state's relativity factor will lie above or below 1. Relativity factors below 1 denote that a state will receive less than an 'equal per capita share of total GST revenue allocated' and relativity factors above 1 denote that a state will receive 'assistance above that which it would be entitled to if GST funds were allocated on a per capita basis' (Williams, 2005a, 112). Thus, horizontal fiscal equalisation is designed to provide each state with a grant payment equal to its 'per capita share of the GST pool, adjusted by needs that account for difference in service provision expenses and the strength of tax bases' (Petchey, 2011, 208). The relativity factors derived from the application of the horizontal fiscal equalisation formula are shown in Table 2.13 for each state spanning the years 2010/11 to 2014/15 (projection).

Table 2.13. GST Relativities

	NSW	VIC	QLD	WA	SA	TAS	ACT	NT
2010/11	0.95205	0.93995	0.91322	0.68298	1.28497	1.62091	1.15295	5.07383
2011/12	0.95776	0.90476	0.92861	0.71729	1.27070	1.59942	1.11647	5.35708
2012/13[a]	0.97137	0.90508	0.93389	0.67510	1.25339	1.59147	1.10956	5.38098
2013/14[a]	0.98251	0.89344	0.97890	0.63254	1.24010	1.53220	1.05197	5.21688
2014/15[a]	0.98395	0.89556	0.97839	0.64497	1.23411	1.51872	1.05077	5.08175

Source: Australian Government, 2012a.
Note: (a) Treasury projection.

For instance, New South Wales (NSW), Victoria (VIC), Queensland (QLD) and Western Australia (WA) have relativity factors below 1, signifying that they receive less than their equal per capita share of the GST pool of funds. In general, this is because these states benefit from a comparatively stronger revenue base, particularly in the case of WA, in which the CGC remarked that:

> Western Australia's relative revenue raising capacity has steadily increased over the period 2006-07 to 2009-10, mainly due to the continued strength of its mining sector and the flow-on effects to other parts of its economy. In 2009-10 it was

> the only State to have a revenue capacity significantly above average (CGC, 2012, 77).

On the other hand, the relativity factors for South Australia (SA), Tasmania (TAS), the Australian Capital Territory (ACT) and the Northern Territory (NT) lie above 1, denoting that these states receive more than their equal per capita share of GST funds. Apart from the ACT, these states have a comparatively weaker revenue base in addition to relatively higher service delivery costs, especially in the case of the NT, which led the CGC to comment:

> The Northern Territory has the lowest assessed fiscal capacity due to its above average assessed expenses, infrastructure and net lending requirements and below average revenue raising capacity. Its high expense requirements are due to above average shares of government school pupils, Indigenous people, young males and people in remote areas, and above average population growth. It also has below average non-State provision of health services, above average wage levels and diseconomies of scale in administration (CGC, 2012, 23).

One way to assess the influence of HFE is to compare each state's 'share of GST payment using the GST relativities, with a notional distribution on an equal per capita basis' (Commonwealth of Australia, 2012a, 125). For example, of the $48,350 million in the 2011/12 GST pool, a total of $3,880.4 million (or 8% of the all GST payments) will be re-distributed across the states by application of the appropriate relativity factors. The influence of HFE is shown in Table 2.14, where one can observe the extent to which the relativity factors re-allocate GST revenue payments across the states.

In reviewing Table 2.14, the per capita redistribution estimates put into perspective the impact of 'inter-state redistribution' from HFE (Petchey, 2011, 208). In 2011/12, for example, WA effectively 'lost' $597 per capita from HFE while the NT 'gained' $9,242 per person. The remaining states that 'lost out' to HFE include VIC ($200 per capita), QLD ($149 per capita) and NSW ($87 per capita), while TAS ($1,274 per capita), SA ($576 per capita) and the ACT ($249 per capita) all 'gained' from HFE. It needs to be borne in mind that the influence of HFE reflects 'the different structures of state economies' and takes into account the 'emergence of the multi-speed national economy' in which states endowed with natural resources – most notably WA – have become high growth areas (Petchey, 2011, 209). Overall, the results presented in Table 2.14 reflect the 'revenue and expenditure disabilities' of disadvantaged states and territories (Groenewegen, 1990, 256).

Table 2.14. The Influence of Horizontal Fiscal Equalisation 2011/12

	GST distribution using adjusted population	Equal per capita distribution of GST	Redistribution[a]	Projected population	Per capita redistribution
	$m	$m	$m	'000	$
NSW	14,949.8	15,592.3	–642.5	7,360.3	–87.3
VIC	10,888.5	12,021.7	–1,133.2	5,674.8	–199.7
QLD	9,138.9	9,830.8	–691.9	4,640.6	–149.1
WA	3,598.5	5,011.3	–1,412.9	2,365.6	–597.3
SA	4,492.6	3,531.7	960.9	1,667.2	576.4
TAS	1,743.0	1,088.6	654.4	513.9	1,273.5
ACT	866.5	775.3	91.2	366.0	249.3
NT	2,672.1	498.3	2,173.9	235.2	9,242.4
Total	**48,350.0**	**48,350.0**	**3,880.4**	**22,823.7**	

Source: Australian Government, 2012.
Note: (a) The total GST redistribution of $3,880.4 million is the sum of the positive items.

2.5.3 Theoretical motivations for horizontal fiscal equalisation

As emphasised by Warren (2008), the principle of HFE focuses on equalising each state's *capacity* to provide services – the *actual* level of service provision is an issue for the states. Thus, without some type of HFE, different states will deliver different levels of government services relative to their tax base, which has led Williams (2005b, 354) to ask 'Does this matter?'

The main economic argument for HFE is one of equity (Williams 2005a; Williams 2005b; Petchey, 2011), where all citizens in a federal system of governance 'should have access to similar government services' (Williams, 2005a, 114). Thus, without HFE, more prosperous states will be able to deliver services at a lower tax rate than less prosperous states or, in other words, 'for a given set of tax rates the government in the poorer region will be compounding the disadvantages of its citizens by offering lower standards in the provision of services' (Williams, 2005b, 354). Accordingly, in the absence of intergovernmental transfers, more affluent states with lower tax rates are more likely to attract mobile workers, which will in turn drive up property values and 'further increase the social stratification of the nation' (Williams, 2005b, 354).

The economic efficiency argument for intergovernmental transfers can be traced back to the pioneering work of economist James Buchanan (1950, 1952), which Petchey (2011, 211) refers to as the 'efficiency of migration':

> The idea is that state budgets and location-specific economic rents from natural resources create externalities that distort the location choices of mobile capital and labour. The literature argues that there is an efficient inter-state transfer that, if implemented by a central authority, can compensate for these externalities to establish an optimal distribution of capital and labour.

The theoretical rationale is also summarised by Hancock and Smith (2001) in *Financing the Federation*. The authors provide a number of examples where, in the absence of HFE, the variation in net fiscal benefits – defined as the 'difference between the cost of unrequited benefits provided to the individual by government and the unrequited contributions extracted from the individual' (Hancock and Smith, 2001, 79) – may result in individuals migrating from one state to another due to 'differences in demographic structure under redistributive policies' or 'differences in state government claims on natural resources and endowments' (Hancock and Smith, 2001, 82). While several researchers have attempted to assess the efficiency of HFE in the Australian milieu, these 'scholarly critiques have not yet drawn firm conclusions about how Australian equalisation measures up to the efficiency of migration case for inter-state transfers, although insights have been obtained' (Petchey, 2011, 212).

2.6 Concluding remarks

This chapter has provided a broad overview of Australian fiscal federalism, with a particular emphasis on the federal system of government, intergovernmental financial relations, VFI and HFE. Within the context of contemporary Australian fiscal federalism, we noted that state governments receive around 45% of their total revenue from the Commonwealth Government in the form of grants and subsidies, despite a steadily increasing revenue stream from state-based taxes and the sale of goods and services. In other words, the fiscal relationship between the Commonwealth and the states is characterised by a significant degree of VFI. We also explored the principle of HFE, how fiscal equalisation operates in practice, and theoretical motivations for fiscal equalisation. While the intergovernmental fiscal framework surrounding local government was introduced in this chapter, a detailed analysis of local government finance is conducted in Chapter 3.

Chapter 3
Australian Local Government Finance

3.1 Introduction

In Chapter 2 we provided a broad overview of Australian fiscal federalism, with particular reference to the federal system of government, intergovernmental financial relations, vertical fiscal imbalance and horizontal fiscal equalisation. While the subject of Australian local government financing was briefly considered in Chapter 2, this chapter undertakes a detailed analysis of local government finance in Australia.

This chapter is divided into four main sections. Section 3.2 provides an overview of local government expenditure with particular reference to local government expenditure on new non-financial assets (ie, local public sector infrastructure). Section 3.3 discusses local government revenue including taxation, grants, the sales of goods and services, and interest received from council investments. Section 3.4 investigates the nature of Financial Assistance Grants, the role that local government grants commissions play in the allocation and distribution of funds to local government, and the efficiency consequences of these grants. The chapter ends with some brief concluding remarks in section 3.5.

3.2 Local government expenditure

3.2.1 Australian local government functions in perspective

Compared with most other industrialised countries, Australian local government is responsible for considerably fewer functions.

For instance, local government authorities in the United Kingdom provide a range of major social services such as education, housing and some public transport (Worthington and Dollery, 2000a). In Australia, these functions are performed by state and territory governments. However, even when compared with a similar federal system of government, like that of the United States, Australian local government authorities still provide a relatively narrow range of 'services to property' including roads, drainage, water supply, sewage and waste management (McNeil, 1997). For example, US local councils are generally responsible for a far broader array of social services such as hospitals, social security, primary and secondary schools, and policing.

These differences are reflected in the composition of total public sector outlays to own-purpose outlays for each tier of government. In the Australian local government milieu, 'local authority outlays comprised 5 per cent of total public sector outlays' while the states 'accounted for 53 per cent and the Commonwealth contributed the remaining 42 per cent' (McNeil, 1997, 27). Moreover, McNeil (1997, 27) noted that local government has 'held this relative position steady for a number of years'. Latest Australian Bureau of Statistics (ABS) estimates from 2010/11 – which support McNeil's (1997) initial observation – indicate that local government expenditure still accounts for around 5% of total public sector outlays in recent years. In the United States, however, it is estimated that the share of local government expenditure amounts to 26% of total expenditure, with 'state governments accounting for 20 per cent and the federal government accounting for 54 per cent' (McNeil, 1997, 27).

3.2.2 Local government expenditures by purpose

Although comprising a relatively small proportion of total public sector expenditure, Australian local government is comparatively more important in certain areas than others. Table 3.1 shows the shares of current outlays by tier of government for 2010/11. While local government was relatively insignificant in terms of public order and safety (3.2%), education (0.2%) and health (0.3%), especially when compared with state and territory governments, its contribution to housing and community amenities and recreation and culture was considerably more important. For example, in 2010/11 local government's spending on housing and community amenities amounted to $6,451 million or 28.5% of total current outlays by all three tiers of government. Local government also contributed $4,359 million or 35.6% of total current outlays for recreation and culture, and significant proportions of total current outlays for mining, manufacturing and construction (14%), and transport and communications (21.3%).

Table 3.1. Current Outlays by Major Function by Level of Government 2010/11

	Commonwealth		***State***		***Local***		***Total***
	$m	%	$m	%	$m	%	$m
General public services	18,348	61.2	6,004	20.0	5,611	18.7	29,963
Defence	19,666	100.0	0	0.0	0	0.0	19,666
Public order and safety	3,828	15.8	19,643	81.0	769	3.2	24,240
Education	33,794	40.3	49,824	59.5	144	0.2	83,762
Health	56,023	51.9	51,654	47.8	332	0.3	108,009
Social security and welfare	116,951	87.9	14,389	10.8	1,684	1.3	133,024
Housing and community amenities	5,543	24.5	10,617	47.0	6,451	28.5	22,611
Recreation and culture	3,234	26.4	4,662	38.0	4,359	35.6	12,255
Fuel and energy	5,929	83.7	1,136	16.0	15	0.2	7,080
Agriculture, forestry and fishing	2,546	47.5	2,789	52.0	29	0.5	5,364
Mining, manufacturing, construction	1,456	57.3	730	28.7	356	14.0	2,542
Transport and communications	4,731	15.1	19,874	63.6	6,640	21.3	31,245
Other economic affairs	9,042	63.9	4,088	28.9	1,016	7.2	14,146
Nominal interest on superannuation	6,997	61.7	4,345	38.3	0	0.0	11,342
Public debt transactions	9,894	64.7	4,814	31.5	578	3.8	15,286
Other	56,287	91.9	3,631	5.9	1,336	2.2	61,254
Total	**354,269**	**60.9**	**198,199**	**34.1**	**29,323**	**5.0**	**581,791**

Source: Australian Bureau of Statistics, *Government Finance Statistics* (Cat. No. 5512.0) (ABS, 2012b).
Note: The figures in Table 3.1 may not sum to the totals due to rounding.

Figure 3.1. Share of Local Government Expenditure by Function 2001/02 and 2010/11

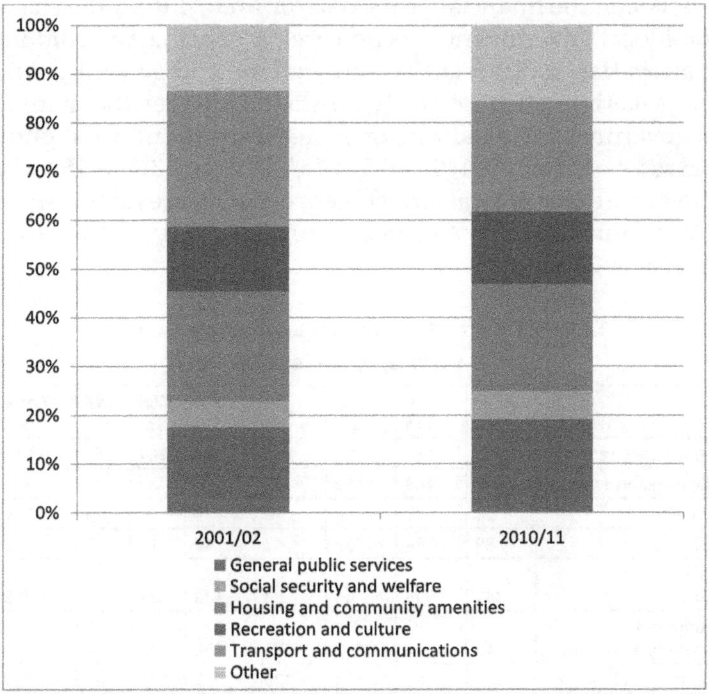

Source: Australian Bureau of Statistics, *Government Finance Statistics* (Cat. No. 5512.0) (ABS, 2012b).

The major share of local government expenditure by function for the financial years 2001/02 and 2010/11 is presented in Figure 3.1. The four largest shares in 2010/11 were in the areas of:

- *transport and communication* ($6,640 million or 23%), which includes road construction and maintenance;
- *housing and community amenities* ($6,451 million or 22%), which incorporates housing and community development, sewerage and street lighting;
- *general public services* ($5,611 million or 19%), which embraces local government administrative functions; and

- *recreation and culture* ($4,359 million or 15%), which includes swimming pools, parks, museums and art galleries.

Between the financial years 2001/02 and 2010/11, the share of total local government expenditure on housing and community amenities, social security and welfare, and general public services has remained relatively constant. However, the share of local government expenditure on recreation and culture slightly increased between 2001/02 and 2010/12, from 13% to 15%. By contrast, the share of local government expenditure for transport and communications between 2001/02 and 2010/11 decreased from 28% to 23%.

Table 3.2. Local Government Expenditure, by Type of Service, by State, 2010/11

	NSW $m	*VIC* $m	*QLD* $m	*SA* $m	*WA* $m	*TAS* $m	*NT* $m	*Total* $m
General public services	1,663	861	2,194	253	374	101	166	5,612
Public order and safety	308	143	162	32	103	6	17	771
Education	54	78	6	0	3	0	3	144
Health	89	84	52	43	49	12	3	332
Social security and welfare	343	998	64	94	138	24	24	1,685
Housing and community amenities	2,349	1,412	1,590	379	508	126	86	6,450
Recreation and culture	1,179	1,165	881	326	659	100	49	4,359
Fuel and energy	0	0	6	8	0	0	1	15
Agriculture, forestry and fishing	1	5	14	9	0	0	0	29
Mining, manufacturing, construction	196	0	101	29	29	0	0	355
Transport and communications	1,734	1,202	2,400	341	741	178	45	6,641
Other economic affairs	291	336	166	67	88	31	38	1,017
Public debt transactions	213	48	249	35	28	4	1	578
Other	666	214	112	138	169	21	16	1,336
Total	**9,088**	**6,544**	**7,997**	**1,753**	**2,890**	**603**	**449**	**29,324**

Source: Australian Bureau of Statistics, *Government Finance Statistics* (Cat. No. 5512.0) (ABS, 2012b).
Note: The figures in Table 3.2 may not sum to the totals due to rounding.

Figure 3.2. Share of Local Government Expenditure by State, 2001/02 and 2010/11

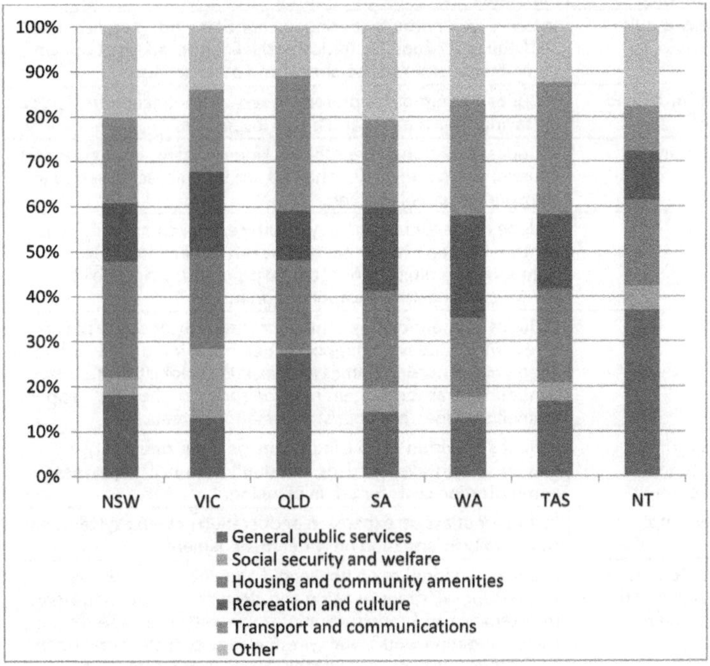

Source: Australian Bureau of Statistics, *Government Finance Statistics* (Cat. No. 5512.0) (ABS, 2012b).

An examination of local government expenditure in Table 3.2 highlights the different emphasis on service provision by local government in Australia. These expenditure figures seem to reflect historical differences in the priorities and allocation of responsibilities for different roles among local and state and territory governments (Worthington and Dollery, 2002a). For example, in 2010/11, local authorities in the Northern Territory, Western Australia and New South Wales outlaid relatively more on public order and safety (3.8%, 3.6% and 3.4%, respectively) than in the other states. On the other hand, Victorian local government directed 15.3% of its outlays to social security and welfare, whereas the corresponding contribution for other states was between 4% and 5%.

Table 3.3. Examples of Local Government Functions Performed under ABS Classifications

ABS category	*Functions*
General public services	Includes expenditures relating to council members and council staff, the cost of administration of the financial affairs of government, management of personnel and other services.
Public order and safety	Includes support of fire protection services, animal protection, surf lifesaving, beach patrol and beach inspection.
Education	Includes operation of pre-schools, kindergartens, adult education courses, support of student hostels, provision of scholarships and transport of school children.
Health	Includes expenditure on baby health centres, community health centres, women's health centres, health inspection services, immunisation clinics, school dental programs, school health services, and health education programs.
Welfare	Includes support for play centres, crèches, day and occasional care centres, outlays in support of neighbourhood services for the aged such as nursing homes and hostels, senior citizens centres, community transport, sheltered workshops for the handicapped, women's refuges, and tourist information bureaus.
Housing and community development	Includes provision of housing for the general community and those with special needs, housing for council employees, administration costs for urban planning.
Water supply	Includes outlays on expansion or operation of water systems and community information on water management.
Sanitation and protection of the environment	Includes expenditure on household garbage and industrial waste disposal, street cleaning and cleaning of recreation areas, maintenance and construction of storm water drainage systems, flood mitigation works, outlays on sewage collection, treatment and disposal systems, septic tank cleaning and inspection, outlays on air quality and noise level monitoring, and outlays on environmental protection research.
Other community amenities	Includes outlays on design, installation, upgrading and maintenance of street lighting, public conveniences, bus shelters, cemeteries, cremation facilities.
Recreational facilities and services	Includes outlays on public recreation halls, civic centres, indoor sporting complexes, swimming pools, football and cricket grounds, tennis courts, golf links, recreational parks and gardens, playgrounds, barbeque areas, walking and cycling paths.
Cultural facilities	Includes costs of library services, museums, art galleries, cultural festivals.
Fuel and energy	Includes outlays on electricity and gas supply.
Transport and communications	Includes outlays relating to road and bridge construction and maintenance, street parking, parking attendants and inspectors.

Source: Australian Bureau of Statistics, *Classifications Manual for Government Finance Statistics, Australia* (Cat. No. 1217.0) (ABS, nd).

In a similar vein, in 2010/11, Western Australian local governments allocated 22.8% of total outlays on recreation and culture, whereas the corresponding contribution in the Northern Territory was 10.9%. Finally, Western Australian and Tasmanian local governments allocated around 25% of total expenditure to transport and communications, Queensland 30% and the Northern Territory a mere 10%. This latter figure reflects the fact that most roads in the Northern Territory are funded directly by the Territory Government, which implies a lower level of council expenditure in this area.

The major shares of local government expenditure by jurisdiction are shown in Figure 3.2 and, as noted earlier, considerable variation exists between states, reflecting a range of contemporary and historical factors (PC, 2008):

- Some Queensland and some New South Wales local government authorities provide water supply and sewerage services.
- A relatively large proportion of Victoria local governments provide some health and community services on behalf of the Victorian and Commonwealth governments.
- Local authorities in Western Australia and Queensland are required to maintain a relatively larger network of local road.
- The Brisbane City Council is responsible for the provision of the urban public transport services in its jurisdiction.

Table 3.3 provides a more detailed account of local government functions. Apart from general local public services, local government in Australia provides a range of different services compared with those delivered by either Commonwealth or state governments. In those specific areas where local government is disproportionally represented in terms of outlays – most notably in housing and community services and in recreation and culture – a wide range of activities are performed. More specifically, housing and community services include: the provision of housing for the general community and those with special requirements; sanitation, water supply and waste management; environmental protection; and services related to street lighting, public conveniences and cemeteries. Recreation and culture services include the provision of libraries and art galleries, community halls, indoor sporting complexes, swimming pools, recreational parks, playgrounds, and walking and cycling paths.

However, even where local governments' contribution to public sector outlays is relatively small, there are ways in which local authorities in Australia can influence local economic development. For instance, local governments' contribution to transport and communication outlays is largely centred in the areas of local roads and bridges, with only highways and major road networks accounted for by state jurisdictions. In a similar vein, local governments' control over zoning, planning and development allows local government in Australia to wield considerable control over matters of regional economic development.

3.2.3 Local government purchases of public sector assets

While the role of local government in current public sector outlays is relatively small, it is far more important in terms of its investment in new non-financial assets (ie, public sector assets). Table 3.4 shows that local government is responsible for approximately $9,198 million or 26% of new non-financial asset expenditure in the state and local government sector.

Table 3.4. Expenditure on New Non-Financial Assets, State and Local Governments 2010/11

	State		*Local*		*Total*	
	$m	%	$m	%	$m	%
NSW	6,489	70.9	2,659	29.1	9,148	100.0
VIC	4,897	75.4	1,602	25.6	6,499	100.0
QLD	8,463	74.0	2,971	26.0	11,434	100.0
SA	1,886	76.2	590	23.8	2,476	100.0
WA	2,870	72.5	1,090	27.5	3,960	100.0
TAS	720	75.9	229	24.1	949	100.0
NT	1,030	94.8	57	5.2	1,087	100.0
Total	**26,355**	**74.1**	**9,198**	**25.9**	**35,553**	**100.0**

Source: Australian Bureau of Statistics, *Government Finance Statistics* (Cat. No. 5512.0) (2012b).

The contribution of local government expenditure on new non-financial assets differs from state to state, and generally corresponds with the differences in the involvement of local

Figure 3.3. Share of Local Government Expenditure on New Non-Financial Assets by State

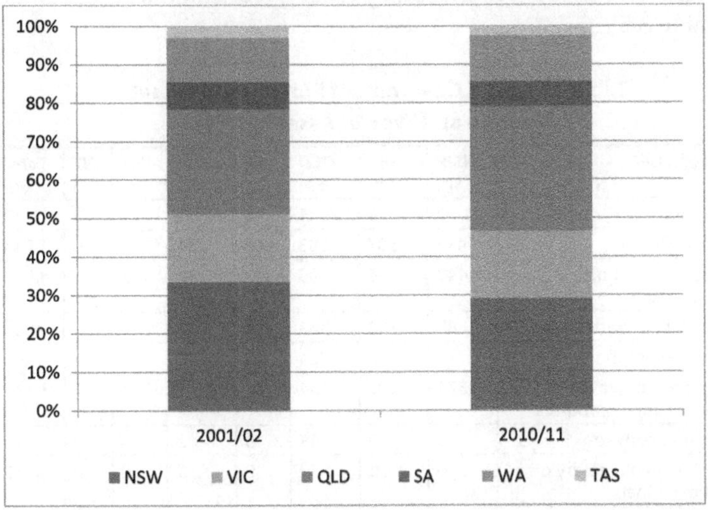

Source: Australian Bureau of Statistics, *Government Finance Statistics* (Cat. No. 5512.0) (ABS, 2012b).

government authorities in the provision of public utilities. For instance, in New South Wales and Queensland, some local authorities are responsible for the provision of water supply and sewerage (Worthington and Dollery, 2000a).

In an effort to gain further insight into local government expenditure on public sector assets, the share of local government expenditure on new non-financial assets by states and territories for 2001/02 and 2010/11 is presented in Figure 3.3. Between 2001/02 and 2010/11, the share of total local government expenditure on new non-financial assets remained fairly constant for local government authorities in Victoria, South Australia, Western Australia and the Northern Territory. However, the share of New South Wales local government expenditure on public sector assets declined between 2001/02 and 2010/11 from 33% to 29%. On the other hand, the share of local government expenditure on non-financial assets in Queensland noticeably increased between 2001/02 and 2010/11 from 27% to 32%.

In 2010/11, local government purchases of public sector assets totalled $9,198 million. Further information on the type of public sector assets purchased by local governments is contained in Table 3.5.

Table 3.5. Local Government Purchases of Assets by State and Type of Asset 2010/11

Type of asset	*NSW* $m	*VIC* $m	*QLD* $m	*SA* $m	*WA* $m	*TAS* $m	*NT* $m	*Total* $m
Dwellings	2	0	11	0	35	1	0	49
Other buildings	412	507	383	106	295	45	0	1,748
Other construction/ infrastructure	1,440	716	1,705	393	496	145	5	4,900
Transport equipment	88	112	350	4	116	10	1	681
Computer equipment	12	0	24	0	15	2	48	101
Equipment other than transport and computers	574	207	194	78	77	11	3	1,144
Computer software	3	0	49	0	3	3	0	58
Entertainment, literary or artistic originals	6	0	2	0	1	0	0	9
Other intangible produced assets	9	0	26	0	26	4	0	65
Land	113	60	227	9	26	8	0	443
Total	**2,659**	**1,602**	**2,971**	**590**	**1,090**	**229**	**57**	**9,198**

Source: Australian Bureau of Statistics, *Government Finance Statistics* (Cat. No. 5512.0) (ABS, 2012b).

The four largest categories of assets purchases by local government in 2010/11 were:

- *Other construction/infrastructure* ($4,900 million or 53%), which 'consists of structures other than buildings, and site clearance and preparation not associated with the cost of buildings'. It also includes 'shafts, tunnels and other structures associated with mining subsoil assets; roads; railways; airfield; airfield runways; bridges; tunnels and subways; waterways and harbours; long distance pipelines, communication and power lines; local pipelines and cables; and mining, manufacturing, sporting and recreational constructions'. Moreover, it includes 'historical monuments which cannot be identified as buildings' and excludes 'major improvements to land such as dams and dykes for flood control' (ABS, 2005, 246).

- *Other buildings* ($1,748 million or 19%), which consists of 'non-residential buildings and all fixtures, facilities and equipment which are integral parts of these buildings' and the 'costs of site clearance and preparation. Includes warehouses, factories, banks, theatres, hotels, restaurants, medical centres and schools' in addition to 'historic monuments identified as primarily non-residential buildings and uncompleted buildings where the ultimate user is deemed to have taken ownership' (ABS, 2005, 246).
- *Equipment other than transport and computer equipment* ($1,144 million or 12%), which includes 'furniture; office equipment; radio, television and communications equipment; medical instruments and appliances; fuel elements for nuclear reactors; musical instruments and sporting goods' but excludes 'equipment acquired by households for final consumption, machinery which is integral to buildings and defence weapons platforms' (ABS, 2005, 246).
- *Transport equipment* ($681 million or 7%), which consists of 'equipment for moving people and objects' and includes 'motor vehicles and trailers; ships; railway and tramway locomotives and rolling stock; and aircraft and spacecraft' (ABS, 2005, 246).

The major shares of local government purchases of assets by state and type of asset for 2010/11 are illustrated in Figure 3.4. The major categories are comprised of (i) 'Other buildings', (ii) 'Other construction/infrastructure', (iii) 'Equipment other than transport and computer equipment' and (iv) 'Other'.

While the purchase of new non-financial assets varies from state to state, it is possible to draw a number of broad inferences. Apart from local governments in the Northern Territory, the greatest share of local government expenditure on new public sector assets was devoted to 'Other construction/infrastructure'. For example, local governments in South Australia, Tasmania and Queensland outlaid relatively more on 'Other construction/infrastructure' (67%, 63% and 57%, respectively) than in Western Australia (46%) and Victoria (45%). Once again, apart from local governments in the Northern Territory, the second largest share of local government expenditure on new public sector assets was

Figure 3.4. Share of Local Government Purchases of Assets by Type and State 2010/11

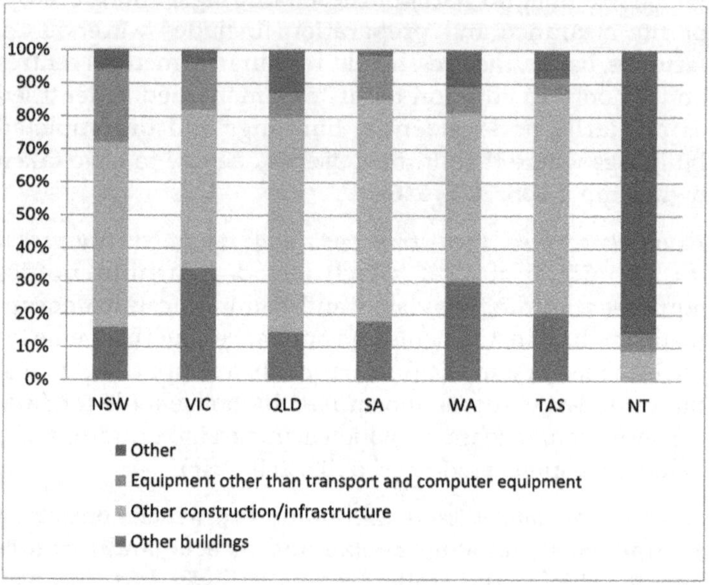

Source: Australian Bureau of Statistics, *Government Finance Statistics* (Cat. No. 5512.0) (2012b).

devoted to 'Other buildings'. Local governments in Victoria and Western Australia outlaid relatively more on 'Other buildings' than in Tasmania (20%), South Australia (18%), New South Wales (15%) and Queensland (13%). Finally, excluding local governments in the Northern Territory, the third-largest share of local government expenditure on new public sector assets was devoted to 'Equipment other than transport and computer equipment'. Local governments in New South Wales outlaid relatively more on the purchase of this type of asset (22%) than did the local government authorities in the other states. The share of local government purchases of assets in the Northern Territory warrants special consideration. Of the $57 million directed towards the purchase of public sector assets in 2010/11, $48 million (or 84%) was used to purchase 'Computer equipment'.

3.3 Local government revenue

Table 3.6 shows that in 2010/11 local government taxation revenue accounted for 3.5% of all taxation revenue raised across all tiers of government in Australia. Commonwealth Government taxation revenue increased by 8% from $20,904 million in 2009/10 to $267,171 million. In 2010/11, Commonwealth Government taxation revenue accounted for 80% of all taxation revenue for all tiers of government. The main sources of taxation revenue for the Commonwealth Government are taxes on income and taxes on the provision of goods and services. In comparison, state government taxation revenue increased by 7% from $54,536 million in 2009/10 to $58,121 million in 2010/11. The main sources of state government taxation revenue are taxes on (i) property, (ii) payroll, (iii) the provision of goods and services, and (iv) the use of goods and performance of activities. Finally, local government taxation revenue increased by 7% from $11,607 million in 2009/10 to $12,408 million in 2010/11. Taxation of property in the form of municipal rates is the only direct source of taxation revenue for Australian local government.

Table 3.6. Share of Taxation Revenue by Tier of Government and Source of Revenue 2010/11

	Commonwealth	*State*	*Local*
Revenue Source	%	%	%
Taxes on income	57.3%	–	–
Employers' payroll taxes	0.1%	5.1%	–
Taxes on property	0.0%	5.8%	3.5%
Taxes on provision of goods and services	23.0%	2.9%	–
Taxes on use of goods and performance of activities	0.2%	2.5%	–
Total	**80.5%**	**16.2%**	**3.5%**

Source: Australian Bureau of Statistics, *Taxation Revenue Australia* (Cat. No. 5506.0) (ABS, 2012c).

Local government financed its activities from a range of different sources including: (i) taxation on property, (ii) grants and subsidies, (iii) the sales of goods and services, and (iv) interest received. Table 3.7 shows that in 2010/11 local government raised approximately 90% of its own revenue, with grants and subsidies accounting for the remaining 10%. However, it needs to be emphasised that individual local authorities have different revenue-raising capabilities, which are not evident from national or state averages. Indeed, the 'difference between urban, rural and remote councils, their population size, rating base and ability to levy user charges, all affect their ability to raise revenue' (DITRDLG, 2012, 8).

Table 3.7. Local Government Revenue Sources by State 2010/11

	NSW $m	*VIC* $m	*QLD* $m	*SA* $m	*WA* $m	*TAS* $m	*NT* $m	*Total* $m
Taxation revenue	3,317	3,410	2,792	1,086	1,420	298	86	12,409
Current grants and subsidies	1,129	801	615	226	385	106	115	3,377
Sales of goods and services	3,229	1,363	2,585	296	773	122	98	8,466
Interest income	350	129	520	29	130	23	11	1,192
Other	2,000	2,285	2,710	255	648	47	115	8,060
Total	**10,025**	**7,988**	**9,221**	**1,891**	**3,356**	**596**	**425**	**33,502**

Source: Australian Bureau of Statistics, *Government Finance Statistics* (Cat. No. 5512.0) (ABS, 2012b).
Note: The figures in Table 3.7 may not sum to the totals due to rounding.

3.3.1 Local government revenue from municipal rates

Municipal rates accounted for $12,409 million or 37% of total Australian local government revenue in 2010/11. Rates are taxes collected from property owners using various methods of valuation, which may include 'a minimum charge or fixed charge, above which an *ad valorem* component may be applied' (PC, 2008, 22). However, as Table 3.7 demonstrates, the proportion of local government revenue attributable to municipal rates varied considerably between jurisdictions in 2010/11, from a high of 57% for South Australia to a low of 20% for the Northern Territory. The difference in per capita revenue for 2010/11 across jurisdictions for all revenues sources is reported in Table 3.8.

Table 3.8. Local Government Revenue Source by State, $ per capita, 2010/11

	NSW	*VIC*	*QLD*	*SA*	*WA*	*TAS*	*NT*	*Weighted Average*
Taxation revenue	$458	$612	$619	$660	$595	$582	$370	$561
Current grants & subsidies	$156	$144	$136	$137	$161	$207	$495	$153
Sales of goods & services	$446	$245	$573	$180	$324	$238	$422	$383
Interest income	$48	$23	$115	$18	$54	$45	$47	$54
Other	$276	$410	$600	$155	$271	$92	$495	$365
Total	**$1,384**	**$1,434**	**$2,043**	**$1,150**	**$1,405**	**$1,164**	**$1,829**	**$1,515**

Source: Australian Bureau of Statistics, *Australian Demographic Statistics* (Cat. No. 3101.0) (ABS, 2012a) and *Government Finance Statistics* (Cat. No. 5512.0) (ABS, 2012b).
Note: The figures in Table 3.8 may not sum to the totals due to rounding.

While South Australian local authorities impose the highest council rates per capita ($660), it needs to be borne in mind that they raise the lowest revenue per capita from the sale of goods and services ($180) and from interest income ($18). Consequently, South Australian local government collects the lowest total per capita revenue, at $1,150 per annum. At the other end of the spectrum, Northern Territory local governments levy the lowest council rates per capita at $370, while they receive the highest per capita revenue from current grants and subsidies at $495. As a result, Northern Territory local governments collect the highest per capita revenue, at $1,829.

Municipal rates in each jurisdiction are based on the valuation of the property on which they are charged. However, the methods for evaluating land value differ considerably between and even within jurisdictions. For instance, municipal rates in New South Wales and Queensland are usually based on the unimproved value of the land, while in Victoria municipal rates are typically based on a differential assessment, which is dependent on the principal use of the land (DITRDLG, 2010).

3.3.2 Other local government non-grant revenue sources

The sale of goods and services comprises any revenue derived by local authorities in the direct provision of goods and services, including 'user fees and charges', such as parking and the use of recreational facilities, 'water and sewerage charges, fees for regulatory services, rental income, and revenue for acting as an agent on behalf of other levels of government' (PC, 2008, 23). Table 3.7 shows that in 2010/11 local authorities received $8,466 million or 25% of their total revenue from the sale of goods and services. On a per capita basis, Table 3.8 demonstrates that revenue attributable to the sale of goods and services varied significantly between jurisdictions, from a high of $573 per capita for Queensland to a low of $180 for South Australia.

In 2010/11, local government authorities received $1,192 million or 3.5% of their total revenue in the form of interest from council investments, which include 'revenue derived from owning financial assets, such as interest on bank account balances and government securities' (PC, 2008, 23). On a per capita basis, local government revenue attributable to interest income also varied considerably between jurisdictions, ranging from a high of $115 per capita for Queensland to a low of $18 per capita for South Australia.

The 'other income' category reported in Tables 3.7 and 3.8 includes 'fines, contributions and donations' (PC, 2008, 23). Local authorities are often authorised through development and planning legislation to 'raise revenue from developer charges and contributions for economic and social infrastructure' (PC, 2008, 21). However, while many local government authorities received contributions from developers, the Australian Bureau of Statistics unfortunately 'does not produce statistics on this source' (McNeil, 1997, 37).

Table 3.9. Special Purpose Payments Direct to Local Government by Jurisdiction 2006/07

	NSW	*VIC*	*QLD*	*WA*	*SA*	*TAS.*	*ACT*	*NT*	*Total*
Direct payments – current	$'000	$'000	$'000	$'000	$'000	$'000	$'000	$'000	$'000
Disability services	194	607	688	0	0	0	0	0	1,489
Children's services	13,588	14,887	5,757	2,090	1,409	2,093	5,852	0	45,676
Regulation Reduction Fund	3,549	3,064	9,637	566	1,676	0	177	1,178	19,847
Strengthening Tasmania	0	0	0	0	0	1,420	0	0	1,420
Total current	**17,331**	**18,558**	**16,082**	**2,656**	**3,085**	**3,513**	**6,029**	**1,178**	**68,432**
Direct payments – capital									
Auslink (R2R)	90,200	64,950	60,000	49,780	22,750	10,350	5,000	0	303,030
Development of sewerage schemes	0	0	0	0	0	200	0	0	200
Local sporting infrastructure	0	667	0	0	0	0	0	0	667
Victorian road project	0	2,000	0	0	0	0	0	0	2,000
Total capital	**90,200**	**67,617**	**60,000**	**49,780**	**22,750**	**10,550**	**5,000**	**0**	**305,897**
Total direct payments	**107,531**	**86,175**	**76,082**	**52,436**	**25,835**	**14,063**	**11,029**	**1,178**	**374,329**

Source: Department of Infrastructure, Transport, Regional Development and Local Government, *2007-08 Local Government National Report* (DITRDLG, 2010), 21.

3.3.3 Local government revenue from grants

The Commonwealth financially supports local government authorities by means of (i) untied Financial Assistance Grants (FAGs) and (ii) tied Specific Purpose Payments (SPPs) direct to local government. FAGs - which are discussed in detail in section 3.4 - comprise two components: (i) a general purpose component which is distributed to states on a per capita basis and (ii) an identified local road component that is allocated to states on a historical fixed shares basis. In 2008/09, the Commonwealth Government provided $2.34 billion in FAGs to local government authorities (DITRDLG, 2012).

SPPs from the Commonwealth are made directly to local governments in accordance with the current *Intergovernmental Agreement on Federal Financial Relations.* Under this arrangement, the Commonwealth provides continuing financial assistance to local governments through (i) SPPs to be spent in key service delivery areas and (ii) national partnership payments (NPPs) to maintain the delivery of specific projects, facilitate reforms, or reward those jurisdictions which actually deliver those reforms (Commonwealth of Australia, 2012a). By way of example, Table 3.9 reports the SPPs from the Commonwealth Government direct to local government jurisdictions for 2006/07. These include direct Commonwealth payments to local government authorities for disability and children's services.

By far the most significant SPP from the Commonwealth direct to local government has been the *Roads to Recovery (Auslink) Program,* which is considered in detail in Chapter 7. In 2006/07, this program accounted for $303,030 or 80% of all Commonwealth direct payments to local government authorities. Furthermore, in the May 2012 Budget, the Gillard government announced a fifth extension of the *Roads to Recovery Program,* which will run from 2014 to 2019. Over this period, the Commonwealth has committed to funding $350 million per annum directly to local government authorities.

While the Commonwealth makes SPPs directly to local government authorities (most notably *Roads to Recovery* grants), state governments also provide a range of grants to local governments from their own funds (DITRDLG, 2012). For example, Table 3.10 shows that in 2007/08 state governments provided

$2.06 billion to local government, sourced directly from their own funding. On a per capita basis, state grants varied significantly from a low of $34.77 per capita in Tasmania to a high of $315.53 per capita in the Northern Territory. However, caution needs to be exercised when considering these figures as 'state grants may increase or decrease from time to time' (DITRDLG, 2012, 9).

Table 3.10. Grants from States to Local Government by Purpose 2007/08

	NSW	***Vic.***	***Qld***	***SA***	***WA***	***Tas.***	***NT***	***Total***
Purpose	$m	$m	$m	$m	$m	$m	$m	$m
Agriculture, forestry, fishing and hunting	–	1	2	1	1	–	–	5
Education	10	32	1	1	–	–	–	44
Fuel and energy	–	–	1	–	4	–	–	5
General public services	31	12	69	11	1	–	29	153
Health	5	12	5	2	2	2	4	32
Housing and community amenity	102	46	192	12	14	3	22	391
Mining, manufacturing and construction	3	–	7	–	–	–	2	12
Public order and safety	41	3	12	16	1	–	4	77
Recreation and culture	54	96	68	52	20	4	7	301
Social security and welfare	59	362	24	31	19	1	4	500
Transport	209	225	248	186	63	34	10	975
Other economic affairs	11	11	8	3	1	1	3	38
Other purposes	493	319	225	124	96	29	2	1,288
Total	**1,019**	**1,120**	**862**	**438**	**223**	**75**	**86**	**3,823**
Less FAGs								
General purpose grants	406	306	245	123	93	29	13	1,215
Local road grants	159	113	103	84	30	29	13	530
Supplementary local road funding	–	–	–	–	14	–	–	14
Net state grants	**453**	**701**	**514**	**231**	**86**	**17**	**60**	**2,064**
Net state grants per capita	**64**	**138**	**127**	**113**	**55**	**35**	**305**	**101**

Source: Department of Infrastructure, Transport, Regional Development and Local Government, *2007-08 Local Government National Report* (DITRDLG, 2010), 10.
Notes: The figures in Table 3.10 may not sum to the totals due to rounding. Data for Victoria include Commonwealth Grants as the Victorian Grants Commission data do not discriminate between Commonwealth and state government grants revenue.

3.4 Financial Assistance Grants

The *Commonwealth of Australia Constitution Act 1900* specifies that the Commonwealth is bestowed powers to provide financial assistance to any state for any purpose on such terms and conditions that the parliament considers fit. Nonetheless, Commonwealth 'assistance to local government did not effectively commence until 1974/75 when united grants were distributed on the basis of recommendations made by the Commonwealth Grants Commission (CGC), operating under the Grants Commission Act (1973)' (Worthington and Dollery, 2000b, 29). This was the first time that the CGC was required to review and assess local government finances. Prior to this, its principal role (and that pursued subsequently) had been the allocation of Commonwealth general purpose grants to the states and territories.

However, notwithstanding the 'allocation of local government assistance being subsequently taken up by separate state Grant Commissioners, the basic principles and procedures were established at this time' (Worthington and Dollery, 2000b, 29). More specifically, the allocation of these funds was based on the principles of *horizontal equalisation* and the assessment of local government's ability to raise revenue exclusively from municipal rates.

Table 3.11 shows that in 2008/09 the Commonwealth Government provided $2.34 billion in Financial Assistance Grants (FAGs) to 566 local government authorities and the Australian Capital Territory Government. FAGs to local government comprised (i) a general purpose grant and (ii) a local roads grant. In 2008/09, the general purpose grant was $1.62 billion and the local roads grant $0.72 billion. These grants are paid to the states and territories, which are, in turn, passed onto local authorities. Since these grants are untied, local governments are permitted to spend them in accordance with local needs and local priorities. The overarching objective of the general purpose grant is to improve the capacity of local government to 'provide their communities with an equitable level of services' and increase the level of 'efficiency and effectiveness of local government' (DITRDLG, 2012, 14).

Table 3.11. Allocation of Financial Assistance Grants 1974/75 to 2009/10

Year	*General purpose grants ($)*	*Local road grants ($)*	*Total grants ($)*
1974/75	56,345,000	n/a	56,345,000
1975/76	79,978,000	n/a	79,978,000
1976/77	140,070,131	n/a	140,070,131
1977/78	165,327,608	n/a	165,327,608
1978/79	179,426,870	n/a	179,426,870
1979/80[a]	222,801,191	n/a	222,801,191
1980/81	302,226,347	n/a	302,226,347
1981/82	352,544,573	n/a	352,544,573
1982/83	426,518,330	n/a	426,518,330
1983/84	461,531,180	n/a	461,531,180
1984/85	488,831,365	n/a	488,831,365
1985/86	538,532,042	n/a	538,532,042
1986/87	590,427,808	n/a	590,427,808
1987/88	636,717,377	n/a	636,717,377
1988/89	652,500,000	n/a	652,500,000
1989/90	677,739,860	n/a	677,739,860
1990/91	699,291,988	n/a	699,291,988
1991/92[b]	714,969,488	303,174,734	1,018,144,222
1992/93[c]	730,122,049	318,506,205	1,048,628,254
1993/94	737,203,496	322,065,373	1,059,268,869
1994/95	756,446,019	330,471,280	1,086,917,299
1995/96[d]	806,748,051	357,977,851	1,164,725,902
1996/97	833,693,434	369,934,312	1,203,627,746
1997/98	832,859,742	369,564,377	1,202,424,119
1998/99	854,180,951	379,025,226	1,233,206,177
1999/2000	880,575,142	390,737,104	1,271,312,246
2000/01	919,848,794	408,163,980	1,328,012,774
2001/02	965,841,233	428,572,178	1,394,413,411
2002/03	1,007,855,328	447,215,070	1,455,070,398
2003/04	1,039,703,554	461,347,062	1,501,050,616
2004/05	1,077,132,883	477,955,558	1,555,088,441
2005/06	1,121,079,905	497,456,144	1,618,536,049
2006/07	1,168,277,369	518,399,049	1,686,676,418
2007/08	1,234,986,007	547,999,635	1,782,985,642
2008/09	1,621,289,630	719,413,921	2,340,703,551
2009/10[e]	1,006,820,860	446,756,045	1,453,576,905
Total	**24,980,443,605**	**8,094,735,104**	**33,075,178,709**

Source: Department of Infrastructure, Transport, Regional Development and Local Government, *2008-09 Local Government National Report* (DITRDLG, 2012), 24.

Notes to Table 3.11: (a) Grants to the Northern Territory commenced in 1979/80. (b) Prior to 1991/92 local road grants were provided as tied grants under different legislation. (c) In 1992/93 part of the road grant entitlement of the Tasmanian and Northern Territory governments was reallocated to local government in these jurisdictions. (d) Grants to the Australian Capital Territory commenced in 1995/96. (e) Estimated entitlement for 2009/10.

Under current legislative arrangements, general purpose grants are delivered in accordance with the *Local Government (Financial Assistance) Act 1995* (Cth), which replaced the *Local Government (Financial Assistance) Act 1986* (Cth), and came into effect on 1 July 1995 (DITRDLG, 2012). At the Special Premiers Conference in 1990, it was decided that road grants for local government authorities be provided in addition to the existing general purpose grants (which are shown in Table 3.11). These local roads grants, which came into effect from July 1991, were 'intended to help local government with the cost of maintaining their local roads but, as they are also untied, local governing bodies are not specifically required to spend them on local roads' (DITRDLG, 2012, 14). In 2002, the House of Representatives Standing Committee on Economics, Finance and Public Administration commenced an inquiry into 'cost shifting onto local government by state governments and the financial position of local government' (Hawker Report, 2004, xii). In the final report, *Rates and Taxes: A Fair Share for Responsible Local Government*, it was 'identified that South Australia was disadvantaged in the interstate distribution of the local road grant' (DITRDLG, 2012, 14). In response to this finding, the Commonwealth Government introduced supplementary local roads funding for South Australian local government authorities to run for three years from 2004/5 to 2006/07. The Commonwealth Government subsequently extended this additional funding for another four years from 2007/08 to 2010/11 (DITRDLG, 2012).

3.4.1 Determining the delivery of Financial Assistance Grants to local government

The current arrangements for determining the distribution of FAGs to local governments are summarised as follows (DITRDLG, 2012):

- The Commonwealth estimates the 'quantum of general purpose and local road grants that local government is entitled to nationally' (DITRDLG, 2012, 15).
- The states and territories are advised of their estimated share of the general purpose grant and the local roads grants.
- Local government grants commissions recommend to their respective ministers the allocation of the general purpose grants and local road grants.
- Local government ministers then forward the recommendations of the local government grants commission (LGGC) in their jurisdiction to the responsible Commonwealth Minster for Local Government (DITRDLG, 2012). Subject to satisfactorily meeting all legislative requirements, the Commonwealth Minster then approves payment of the grants.
- The Commonwealth Government then pays these grants to the states and territories on the understanding that these grants are passed onto local governments as untied grants.

The Commonwealth Treasurer uses a formula specified under section 8 of the *Local Government (Financial Assistance) Act 1995* (Cth) to determine the quantum of local government FAGs. The formula itself explicitly takes into account changes in inflation and population, so that the 'value of the grants is maintained in real per capita terms' (DITRDLG, 2012, 16). This formula is applied to both the general purpose grant and the local roads grant. However, it is important to note that the allocation of the general purpose grant among the states and territories is provided on a per capita basis. The allocation itself is derived from the Australian Bureau of Statistics 'estimate of each jurisdiction's population and the estimated population of all states and territories as at 31 December of the previous year' (DITRDLG, 2012, 16). On the other hand, the allocation of local grants among the states and territories is fixed and it is based largely on prior historical arrangements.

Financial assistance grants can only be paid to jurisdictions that have 'established local government grant commissions' (DITRDLG, 2012, 26). Local government grants commissions (LGGC) are subsequently responsible for making recommendations, in line with National Principles, on the quantum of FAGs distributed to local governments (DITRDLG, 2012). The National Principles governing the distribution of general purpose grants cover:

- *Horizontal equalisation.* General purpose grants will be allocated to local government authorities on the basis of full horizontal equalisation. This approach is designed to ensure that each local government body 'is able to function, by reasonable effort, at a standard not lower than the average standard of other local governing bodies in the state or territory. It takes account of differences in the expenditure required by those local governing bodies in the performance of their functions and in the capacity of those local governing bodies to raise revenue' (DITRDLG, 2012, 63).
- *Effort neutrality.* An effort-neutral approach will be employed when assessing the 'expenditure requirements and revenue-raising capacity of each local governing body', which means that individual local government expenditure and revenue policies 'will not affect grant determination' (DITRDLG, 2012, 63).
- *Minimum grant.* The minimum general purpose grant distribution for a local government authority in a year 'will be not less than the amount to which the local governing body would be entitled if 30 per cent of the total amount of general purpose grants to which the state or territory is entitled … were allocated among local governing bodies in the state or territory on a per capita basis' (DITRDLG, 2012, 63).
- *Other grant support.* This includes any other relevant grant support provided to local government authorities. This support should be taken into account when assessing the expenditure needs of local governments (DITRDLG, 2012).
- *Aboriginal peoples and Torres Strait Islanders.* Financial assistance grants shall be distributed to local government authorities in such a way that recognises the needs of Aboriginal peoples and Torres Strait Islanders residing in their areas.
- *Council amalgamations.* In the event where two or more local government authorities are consolidated into a single entity,

the general purpose grant provided to the new local government body for each of the four years following consolidation 'should be the total of the amounts that would have been provided to the former bodies in each of those years if they had remained separate entities' (DITRDLG, 2012, 64).

The National Principle governing the distribution of the local roads component of financial assistance holds that grants should be allocated to local government authorities on the 'basis of the relative needs of each local governing body for roads expenditure and to preserve its road assets' and, in assessing local road needs, 'relevant considerations include length, type and usage of roads in each local governing area' (DITRDLG, 2012, 64).

3.4.2 Methods employed by local government grants commissions

Each local government grants commission (LGGC) has its own method for distributing grants to local authorities within its jurisdiction. While methods differ between jurisdictions, the allocation of funding is essentially guided by the following core set of principles: (i) funding allocation based on horizontal equalisation; (ii) the functioning of each local government set at a standard not lower than the average standard of other local government entities in the jurisdiction; (iii) the evaluation of revenue and expenditure needs and disabilities; and (iv) effort (or policy) neutrality (Worthington and Dollery, 2000b). The most important consideration is that the distribution of grants is based on the LGGC's impartial assessment of local government revenue and expenditure needs and disabilities. Expenditure needs are defined as the 'differential costs, relative to standard, that a council needs to provide a standard level of service', while revenue needs are defined as the 'differential revenues a council would raise if the standardised revenue effort was applied to its revenue base' (Worthington and Dollery, 2000b, 30). Expenditure disabilities usually take into account socioeconomic, demographic and geographic factors while 'revenue disabilities are largely proxied by variance in rateable property value' (Worthington and Dollery, 2000b, 30).

Revenue-raising capacity

As noted earlier, municipal rates accounted for 37% of total revenue across local government in Australia in 2010/11. It is thus not surprising that property values form the cornerstone for assessing the revenue-raising capacity of local councils. While property values may provide a useful indicator of the relative economic strength of a local government area, there has been considerable debate on the efficacy of using rateable property values as a means of assessing local council's revenue-raising capacity (Worthington and Dollery, 2000b). This is because the methods by which rates are charged vary considerably between jurisdictions. For example, in local government in New South Wales and Queensland, rates are typically based on the unimproved value of the land, while Western Australia uses 'gross rental value of the land' for non-rural rates, which is the 'amount that could be charged should it be made available for rent', whereas rural land is largely assessed on the unimproved value of the land (DITRDLG, 2010, 16). Local government in Victoria, however, can use: (i) the capital improved value, (ii) the net annual value or (iii) the site value. In South Australia, local government authorities can use: (i) the capital (improved) value, (ii) the site (unimproved) value or (iii) the annual (gross rental) value. There is 'no differentiation for rural property' although it needs to be borne in mind that '85 per cent of the state is unincorporated' (DITRDLG, 2010, 16). In Tasmania, local government rates are also based on the three criteria employed by Victoria and South Australia, although recent 'agreements in Tasmania between the state government and councils means councils are now able to charge rates on selected state government-owned land', which will 'increase the amount of revenue local governments can realise from rates' (DITRDLG, 2010, 16). However, in the Northern Territory, the recent radical local government amalgamation has resulted in 'eight new shire councils providing services almost exclusively to Indigenous communities' and given that land trusts 'own the land in most Aboriginal communities' it is difficult to determine 'distinct properties and values for assessing rate revenue raising capacity' (DITRDLG, 2012, 189).

However, the assessment of revenue-raising capacity in each jurisdiction will also depend on additional provisions relating to revenue-raising practice. The four primary considerations include: (i) the use of minimum council rates, (ii) pensioner concessions, (iii) differential rates and (iv) rate pegging (exclusively in New South Wales) (Worthington and Dollery, 2000b). The first main difference between jurisdictions is whether limits are set on the percentage of total general municipal rates to be raised from a flat charge per property. Second, discounts for pensioner concessions also differ across jurisdictions. Third, in all jurisdictions there is significant discretion in the different rates for residential and commercial properties. Finally, rate pegging – the percentage limit that councils may increase total income from municipal rates – also affects the revenue-raising capacity of local council in New South Wales.

The quantum of revenue assistance that is given to local government authorities will also depend on the method employed by the LGGC. For example, local government in New South Wales, Victoria, South Australia and Tasmania relies heavily on the valuation tax base to calculate revenue-raising capacity (Worthington and Dollery, 2000b; DITRDLG, 2012), whereas local government in Western Australia also assesses the 'revenue capacity for recreation and culture' (DITRDLG, 2012, 189). How closely these approaches approximate the underlying revenue-raising capacity of local governments will critically depend on the property valuation technique employed.

Expenditure needs and disabilities

While roads account for the largest category of expenditure for many local government authorities, the LGGC in each jurisdiction assesses between 7 and 21 classes of expenditure (DITRDLG, 2012). Local government's principal expenditure falls on general public services, recreation facilities, sanitation and environmental protection. For each class of expenditure, the LGGCs estimate how much each local authority 'would have to spend to provide service of average standard' (Worthington and Dollery, 2000b, 33). These estimates are guided by the impartial assessment of expenditure 'disabilities' (or disability factors) for each type of expenditure. In keeping with the principle of effort neutrality, LGGCs do not compensate for expenditure differences that arise as a result of council policy or management decisions. A range of factors are usually taken into account when assessing disabilities, including population growth and the proportion of the population from a low socioeconomic background.

These different disabilities are then combined to estimate an overall disability factor for each council. The overall disability factor is then used to estimate 'standardised expenditure', which is illustrated below by the following general formula:

$$\text{Standardised expenditure} = \text{Number of units} \times \text{standard cost} \times \text{disability factor}$$

In the formula, the 'number of units' is a measure of council service use (usually population size), the 'standard cost' represents the state average expenditure, and the 'disability factor' is a measure of council disadvantage. Thus, if an LGGC estimates that it would cost a council 10% more than the standard for the provision of library services because of population growth in the local government area, then the disability factor would be 10% (DITRDLG, 2012). In other words, disability factors measure the underlying factors that may lead councils to spend more (or less) per capita on service provision than the state average.

3.4.3 Efficiency and grant distribution

The Commonwealth does not explicitly request that LGGCs pay specific attention in grant allocation to the productive efficiency with which local government authorities operate. Three reasons for this have been identified by Worthington and Dollery (2000b). First, the principle of horizontal equalisation under the *Local Government (Financial Assistance) Act 1995* (Cth) has been the pre-eminent policy goal. Second, the expression 'by reasonable effort' in the legislation has 'largely been interpreted to refer solely to the rating effort of councils, and does not take into account any matters concerning reasonable efforts to ensure economic efficiency' (Worthington and Dollery, 2000b, 33). Finally, the principle of 'effort neutrality', which relates to policy decisions made by local government authorities, has been 'interpreted to mean that councils should not be able to act in a manner which affects their grant' and thus grants to local government authorities only reflect a range of factors that are beyond the control of a local government authority and 'therefore the LGGC grants process neither rewards nor penalises councils with differing levels of efficiency' (Worthington and Dollery, 2000b, 33).

However, it has been argued that the LGGC methodologies have, in fact, both positively and negatively influenced the efficiency of local government authorities. For example, it has been claimed that 'by providing the highest per capita support to those councils with revenue raising difficulties and expenditure needs in regard to size, sparcity, location and cost disabilities, [the grants system] may not be conducive to an efficient allocation of resources' (AURDR, 1994, 55). On the other hand, it has been argued that 'councils which are cost effective may be rewarded through unit cost adjustments up to the standard if their operations are cost effective' (AURDR, 1994, 14).

In essence, the use of local government expenditure to estimate a state 'standard cost' for each class of expenditure serves to mask the impact that several efficient or inefficient councils may have on grant allocation. For example, assume that a local council's expenditure in a particular area is efficient. Thus, in the 'case of industry wide efficiency this would infer [sic] a lower standard cost for that function, irrespective of factors beyond managerial control, thereby putting strong pressure on councils to improve efficiency to the state standard' (Worthington and Dollery, 2000b, 34). On the other hand, if 'the industry standard is broadly inefficient, thereby implying a higher standard expenditure cost, the incentive for councils to improve their inefficiency is removed' (Worthington and Dollery, 2000b, 34). These examples serve to highlight that the level of efficiency in a particular function may become institutionalised over time. However, despite the principle of effort neutrality, there is some evidence in the Australian context that the grants process may, in fact, influence local government authorities to become more efficient (Worthington and Dollery, 2000b).

3.5 Concluding remarks

Chapter 3 has sought to provide a broad overview of local government expenditure with particular reference to local government expenditure on new non-financial assets (ie, local government infrastructure). We saw that by far the largest purchases made by local governments were in the area of construction and buildings. We also examined the major source of local government revenue including taxation, grants from higher tiers of government, the sale of goods and services, and interest received from local government investments. While local government's taxation revenue accounted for only approximately 3.5% of all taxation revenue raised across all levels of government in Australia, it needs to be borne in mind that municipal rates are the only source of taxation for Australian local government. Moreover, local authorities raise approximately 90% of their own revenue with grants and subsidies accounting for the remaining source of revenue.

The nature of Financial Assistance Grants and the role that local government grants commissions (LGGCs) play in the allocation and distribution of funds was also investigated in this chapter. While the Commonwealth Government provides the requisite funding, the actual allocation and distribution of these funds to local government is made through these LGGCs. The allocation of these grants is essentially guided by the following core set of principles: (i) funding allocation based on horizontal equalisation; (ii) the functioning of each local government at a standard not lower than the average standard of other local government entities in the jurisdiction; (iii) the evaluation of revenue and expenditure needs and disabilities; and (iv) effort (or policy) neutrality. In the allocation of grants to councils, the LGGC's methodological approach explicitly takes into account local needs and disabilities independently of policy and managerial decisions made by councils including those related to efficiency. There is, however, some partial evidence to suggest that the LGGC methodological approach may, in fact, influence local government efficiency and thus comprise the primary objective of horizontal equalisation.

Finally, it is worth taking stock of the current trends in local government expenditure and revenue. Between 2001/02 and 2010/11, the share of local government expenditure devoted to housing and community amenities, social security and welfare, and general public services remained fairly constant. However, the share of local government expenditure on recreation and cultural activities slightly increased from 13% to 15%. By contrast, the share of local government expenditure on transport and communication decreased from 28% to 23%. The modest increase in expenditure on recreation and culture suggests that local governments are increasingly playing a larger role in the development of cultural and social capital. On the other hand, the decline in expenditure on transport and communications (eg, road and bridge construction and maintenance) is perhaps, in part, a result of the Commonwealth Government's direct investment in local roads under the banner of the *Roads to Recovery* program.

Local government finances its activities from the following revenue sources: (i) taxation on property, (ii) grants and subsidies, (iii) the sales of goods and services, and (iv) interest received. In 2010/11, local government raised approximately 90% of its own revenue, with grants and subsidies accounting for the remaining 10%. The heavy reliance by local government on its own revenue sources has remained relatively stable between 2007/08 and 2010/11. However, as Australian local government is increasingly taking on a broader range of 'services to people', there is a need to consider alternative revenue streams, especially given the differential capacity of local authorities to raise revenue. Furthermore, many of the new responsibilities inherited by local government have been met with limited, if any, financial assistance. As a result, Australian local government has become victim to worsening financial sustainability and the emergence of a massive infrastructure backlog.

PART B

Financial Sustainability and Australian Local Government

Chapter 4
Public Perspectives on Financial Sustainability

4.1 Introduction

As we saw in Chapter 1, Australian local government is afflicted by severe fiscal distress, the result of at least three factors. In the first place, inexorable and intensifying financial pressures mean that the *status quo* simply cannot be sustained indefinitely (Worthington and Dollery, 2000b; Dollery, Crase and Byrnes, 2006). Given these monetary pressures, it is no exaggeration to stress that existing arrangements have only been maintained at the cost of steadily depreciating physical infrastructure (Byrnes, Dollery, Crase and Simmons, 2008). Second, state and territory governments across Australia remain concerned over the operational efficiency of municipalities, particularly small regional, rural or remote councils (Dollery and Crase, 2004). This concern has engendered a heavy emphasis on compulsory council amalgamation as the primary engine in the drive for more cost-effective local services. Thus, during the 1990s, South Australia, Tasmania and Victoria all underwent episodes of compulsory consolidation of differing degrees of intensity. Similarly, over the past decade, forced amalgamation has occurred in New South Wales, Queensland and the Northern Territory. Finally, changes in the respective enabling acts of the different Australian local government systems have witnessed a significant expansion in the role of local government and growing complexity in its relationships with state and federal governments (Dollery, Wallis and Allan, 2006). Moreover, differences in the functions and responsibilities of the various state and territory municipal systems have widened over time, and the state government oversight mechanisms are now often quite dissimilar, severely diminishing the prospects of a uniform national approach to local governance (Dollery, O'Keefe and Crase, 2010). An uneven devolution of additional functions to local government within and between the different states and territories further complicates an already incoherent network of intergovernmental relations.

Against this background, it is thus most fortunate that the past decade has witnessed a host of national and state inquiries into local government which have not only provided valuable insights into the problems experienced by the sector, but also generated a range of policy recommendations for tackling these problems. Beginning with the Commonwealth Grants Commission's *Review of the Operation of Local Government (Financial Assistance) Act 1995* (CGC, 2001) early in the new millennium, at the national level, the inquiries include the House of Representatives Standing Committee on Economics, Finance and Public Administration *Rates and Taxes: A Fair Share for Responsible Local Government* (Hawker Report, 2003, the PriceWaterhouseCoopers report *National Financial Sustainability Study of Local Government* (PWC Report, 2006) and the Productivity Commission's report *Assessing Local Government Revenue Raising Capacity* (PC, 2008).

In an analogous vein, at the state level, we have seen the South Australian Financial Sustainability Review Board's *Rising to the Challenge Report* (FSRB, 2005), the Financial Sustainability of NSW Local Government inquiry *Are Councils Sustainable?* (Allan Report, 2006), the Local Government Association of Queensland inquiry *Size, Shape and Sustainability* (LGAQ, 2006), the Western Australian Local Government Association *Systemic Sustainability Study* (WALGA, 2006), the Local Government Association of Tasmania *Review of the Financial Sustainability of Local Government in Tasmania* (LGAT, (2007), the Queensland Local Government Reform Commission *Report of the Local Government Reform Commission* (QLGRC, 2007), the Queensland Treasury Corporation report *Financial Sustainability in Queensland Local Government* (QTC, 2008) and the NSW Independent Pricing and Regulatory Tribunal's *Review of the Revenue Framework for Local Government* (IPART, 2009).

Taken together these documents present a wealth of material on the problems in contemporary Australian local government which can not only provide analytical insight into the complexities of modern local government, but also inform public policy making. It is thus important for the Australian local government community to give the work of these inquiries careful consideration. This chapter seeks to examine the findings of these inquiries into local government on financial sustainability, determine the common issues raised, identify patterns of policy recommendations and uncover recurring unresolved matters. It then attempts to draw some general conclusions on the policy and practice implications of these public inquiries for local government policy makers and practitioners alike.

A useful way of organising the analysis of local government and associated recommendations for local government reform in the inquiry reports is to follow the fivefold typology developed by Dollery, Garcea and LeSage (2008) in their comparative study of the local government systems in Australia, Britain, Canada, Ireland, New Zealand and the United States. They distinguished between financial reforms, functional reforms, jurisdictional reforms, organisational and managerial reforms, as well as structural reforms.

In terms of the Dollery, Garcea and LeSage (2008) taxonomic system, financial reform consists of changes to the financial circumstances of local government, including any changes to revenue sources (ie, 'own-source' revenue and intergovernmental transfers), expenditure (ie, financial responsibilities and financial restrictions) and financial management. Functional reforms involve changes in the number or types of functions performed by local government, including the realignment of functions between local government and other tiers of government. Jurisdictional reforms consist of changes to the authority and autonomy of local government, including general competency powers, specific by-law making powers and the like. Organisational and managerial reforms involve changes to the administrative, executive and management processes of local council. Finally, structural reforms consist of changes to the boundaries, numbers and types of local authorities. While the five categories in the Dollery, Garcea and LeSage (2008) typology are analytically discrete, in practice there is often some overlap between them.

All five types of reform have vital significance for the smooth functioning of Australian local government. However, given the focus of this book, this chapter will concentrate exclusively on the problem of financial reform and financial sustainability in Australian local government.

The chapter is divided into two main sections. Section 4.2 deals with financial sustainability and financial reform in local government, which was by far the major concern of the bulk of the 12 inquiries under consideration. Section 4.3 tackles the findings of the inquiries, determining the common issues raised, patterns of policy recommendations and recurring unresolved matters, and it then draws some general conclusions on the policy and practice implications for local government.

4.2 Financial reform and financial sustainability

4.2.1 Commonwealth Grants Commission report (2001)

The genesis of contemporary concern with Australian local government sustainability can be traced back to the Commonwealth Grants Commission (CGC) annual report (2001) *Review of the Operation of Local Government (Financial Assistance) Act 1995*. In this pioneering document, the CGC (2001, 52–3) identified five main reasons for the acute level of financial stress faced by many local authorities, especially in non-metropolitan areas:

- 'devolution' – where a higher sphere of government gives local government responsibility for new functions;
- 'raising the bar' – where a higher tier of government, through legislative or other changes, raises the complexity and/or standard at which local government services must be provided, thereby increasing the cost of service provision;
- 'cost shifting' – either where a local council agrees to provide a service on behalf of a federal or state government (with funding subsequently reduced or stopped) or where some other tier of government ceases to provide an essential service, thus obliging a local authority to take over;

- 'increased community expectations' – where a local community demands improvements in existing municipal services or the provision of a new service; and
- 'policy choice' – where specific local councils voluntarily expand and/or enhance their services.

This analysis is by no means complete. For example, as Johnson (2003) has observed, the CGC (2001) list did not include local council policies which can exacerbate financial problems, such as holding rates and charges at artificially low levels. Moreover, the CGC (2001) list also ignored 'internal' governance and management factors which can play an important role. However, the CGC (2001) report did set the scene for succeeding analyses of financial sustainability.

4.2.2 Hawker Report (2003)

Although originally established to examine cost-shifting in Australian local government, the Hawker Report (2003) expanded its initial terms of reference and ultimately considered virtually the entire spectrum of local government activity. The Final Report consisted of six substantive chapters dealing with: the roles and responsibilities of local government; cost shifting; the preservation of local infrastructure; capacity building, including performance monitoring and structural reform; local government funding and intergovernmental financial relations; and the need for a 'summit'.

The Hawker Report (2003) made 18 specific recommendations dealing with 'roles and responsibilities' (three recommendations); 'cost shifting' (five recommendations); 'infrastructure' (two recommendations); 'capacity building in our regions' (four recommendations); 'Commonwealth funding of local government' (two recommendations); and the 'way forward' (two recommendations).

Several of these recommendations dealt with financial sustainability and financial reform. For instance, Recommendation 6 tackled cost-shifting and called for additional funding to meet additional responsibilities, as well as the removal of state restrictions on council revenue-raising. Similarly, Recommendation 15 focused on ameliorating the impact of the

GST and Recommendation 16 considered a new methodology for Financial Assistance Grants (FAGs). Only a few recommendations have been indirectly acted upon.

Despite its lack of original research, heavy reliance on submissions by interested parties and an unfortunate degree of politicisation, the Hawker Report (2003) nonetheless reiterated many of the problems raised in the CGC (2001). Furthermore, it served to underline the acute extent of financial distress in Australian local government.

4.2.3 South Australian Financial Sustainability Review Board report (2005)

At the state level, South Australia instigated the first public inquiry when the Financial Sustainability Review Board (FSRB) was established by the South Australian Local Government Association on 14 February 2005 to examine 'the financial position and prospects of councils in South Australia' by considering three main questions:

- Does local council expenditure on service provision and local infrastructure meet with current and future revenues flows?
- What is the optimal method of remedying any 'mismatch' between expenditure and revenue?
- Should grants from state and federal government be directed at diminishing the financial mismatch?

In its Final Report *Rising to the Challenge: Towards Financially Sustainable Local Government in South Australia,* the FRSB (2005) considered the problem of defining 'financial sustainability' as a means of assessing the long-term solvency of South Australian councils. The FRSB (2005, 7) argued that no universal agreement existed on the meaning and content of 'financial sustainability' for Australian local government. Consequently, the FRSB (2005, 10) proposed the following definition:

> A council's long-term financial performance and position is sustainable where: (i) continuation of the council's present spending and funding policies; (ii) likely developments in the council's revenue-raising capacity and the demand for and costs of its services and infrastructure; and (iii) normal

financial risks and financial shocks, altogether are unlikely to necessitate substantial increases in council rates (or, alternatively, disruptive service cuts).

The FRSB (2005, 15) advanced four financial indicators 'for assessing a council's financial sustainability':

- net financial liabilities as the chief financial indicator of a council's 'indebtedness to other sectors of the economy';
- operating surplus or deficit as the key financial indicator of the 'intergenerational equity of the funding of the council's operations';
- net outlays on the renewal or replacement of existing assets as the chief financial indicator of the 'intergenerational equity of the funding of the council's infrastructure renewal or replacement activities'; and
- net borrowing or lending as the key financial indicator of the 'impact of the council's annual transactions – both operating and capital – upon the council's indebtedness to other sectors of the economy'.

The central conclusion of the FSRB (2005b, 19–20) came in the form of Recommendation 2.3(1) which set out in a 'statement of principles' governing 'key financial sustainability indicators', comprising six factors:

- A local council is financially sustainable if 'its net financial liabilities are at levels at which the associated interest payments (less interest income) can be met comfortably from a council's annual income (ie, by current ratepayers) without the prospects of rates increases which ratepayers would find unacceptable (or disruptive service cuts)'.
- The net financial liabilities of a specified local authority 'can be too low where they are (a) associated with current ratepayers being asked to bear an inequitable proportion of the cost of future service potential or (b) below levels that include more than enough room to absorb unexpected financial risks or financial shocks'.

- Annual operating financial performance of a local council is sustainable 'if operating deficits will be avoided over the medium to long term, because such deficits inevitably involve services consumed by current ratepayers being paid for either (a) by borrowing and so by future ratepayers or (b) by deferring funding responsibility for the renewal or replacement of existing assets onto future ratepayers'.
- A local authority's operating surplus can be too high 'where it (a) is associated with current ratepayers being asked to bear an inequitable proportion of the cost of the council's future service potential or (b) is above a level that includes more than enough room to absorb unexpected financial risks or financial shocks'.
- The annual capital financial performance of a municipality is sustainable 'if capital expenditure on the renewal or replacement of existing assets on average approximates the level of the council's annual depreciation expense, because any shortfall of such capital expenditure against annual depreciation expense would involve future ratepayers being left with an excessive burden when it comes to replacing or renewing the council's non-financial assets'.
- Finally, net borrowing of a local council can be too low 'where, over the planning period, it results in the council's net financial liabilities as a ratio of non-financial assets falling well below the targeted ratio'.

These principles formed the benchmarks that the FSRB employed to assess South Australian councils. In its application of these principles, the FSRB (2005, Rec 6.4(1)) established that 33 councils were either 'unsustainable' or 'vulnerable', which accounted for about 50% of South Australia's population, 30% of metropolitan councils and 40% of country councils.

The FSRB (2005, 11–21) proposed 62 recommendations, almost all focused on improving financial management and financial record keeping. Many of these recommendations have been adopted in local government financial practice in South Australia.

Table 4.1. Allan Report (2006) Key Financial Aggregates

Income items	Expense items	Capital flows	Asset items	Liabilities items
Rates revenue	Operating costs (employee expenses, superannuation, other non-employee expenses, current grant expenses, subsidy expenses and capital grant expenses)	Capital expenditure, distinguishing between capital expenditure on: (i) the renewal or rehabilitation of existing assets; and (ii) new or enhanced assets	Cash and investment securities – externally restricted	Interest-bearing liabilities
Fees and charges	Borrowing costs	Grants from other governments for capital purposes	Cash and investment securities – other	Other liabilities (provisions, other)
Grant from other governments for non-capital purposes	Loss from the disposal of assets	Other grants and contributions provided for capital purposes	Other financial assets (receivables, investments accounted for using equity method, other)	Memo item: infrastructure renewal backlog
Other operating revenues	Loss from interests in joint ventures/ associates	Assets donations	Non-financial assets (property, plant and equipment, inventories)	
Interest	Depreciation	Revenue from disposals of non-financial assets		
Gain from the disposal of assets				
Gain from interests in joint ventures/ associates				
Gain on revaluation of non-financial assets				

Source: LGI 2006, Table 11.1, 267.

4.2.4 Independent Inquiry into NSW Local Government report (2006)

Chronologically, the Independent Inquiry into the Financial Sustainability of NSW Local Government (Allan Report, 2006), instituted by Local Government and Shires Associations of NSW (LGSA), represented the second state-based public inquiry. The aims of the Inquiry were fourfold:

- to determine the current financial position and performance of the NSW local government sector;
- to gauge the adequacy of existing NSW local government physical infrastructure and service delivery;
- to assess the financial capacity of local government to meet its statutory obligations, expected functions and likely future challenges; and
- to identify possible financial, administrative, governance and intergovernmental reforms that could address any problems.

In essence, the Allan Report thus represented a much wider investigation than the South Australian FSRB report since its ambit extended far beyond financial sustainability *per se*. However, the Allan Report did stress that financial sustainability lay 'at the heart of this Inquiry' (Allan Report, 2006, 267). In Chapter 11, the Allan Report set out the 'key financial aggregates necessary for the analysis of a council's financial position and performance' (Allan Report, 2006, 267). These are reproduced in Table 4.1.

After consideration of the 'practical realities' of financial reporting by NSW councils, the Inquiry (LGI, 2006, 271–2) concluded that 'each council's financial reports should be accompanied by disclosure of relevant key financial performance indicators (financial KPIs)' (LGI, 2006, 271), and must provide information on the following financial dimensions of a council's operations:

- 'A council's financial position, which involves the state of its balance sheet, and so the relative level and composition of its assets and liabilities'; and

- 'A council's annual financial performance, which involves the state of its annual operating statement, and especially the size of relevant annual surpluses or deficits'.

Financial KPIs should bear 'a strong predictive relationship with the degree to which a council's finances are likely to be sustainable in the long term, being based upon generally accepted key analytical balances'. The 'principal choices' of KPIs identified by the Inquiry are reproduced in Table 4.2.

Table 4.2. Allan Report (2006) Key Analytical Balances

Analytical balances	Definition	Denominator for comparative ratio
Net debt	Interest-bearing financial liabilities less holdings of cash and securities other than externally restricted cash and securities	Total operating revenue
Net financial liabilities	Total liabilities less financial assets net of holdings of externally restricted cash and securities	Non-financial assets plus holdings of externally restricted cash and securities
Net interest expense	Annual interest expense less interest earnings on holdings of cash and securities other than externally restricted cash securities	Total operating revenue
Operating surplus/ (deficit)	Operating revenue before capital amounts less operating expenses less depreciation expense less net interest expense	Own-source revenue
Net borrowing/ (lending)	Capital expenditure less capital revenues less depreciation expense less operating surplus/ (deficit)	Annual capital expenditure on renewal or rehabilitation of existing assets
Annual renewals deficiency	Annual depreciation expense less annual capital expenditure on existing assets	Annual capital expenditure on renewal or rehabilitation of existing assets
Renewals backlog	Cumulative past annual renewals deficiencies	Non-financial assets

Source: LGI, 2006, Table 11.2, 272.

The Allan Report (2006, 273) then prescribed 'benchmark values' based on the 'average' NSW council, with upper and lower 'safe' limits, and the caveat that 'these values should be adjusted on account of each council's individual circumstances', depending whether the local council under review is 'developed' or 'developing' and whether it is 'growing' or 'declining'. These 'indicative benchmark values' are reproduced in Table 4.3.

Table 4.3. Allan Report (2006) Indicative Benchmark Values for Council Financial KPIs

Financial Key Performance Indicators	Average Council Actual	Proposed Council Target	Proposed Upper Limit	Proposed Lower Limit
Net debt as % of total revenue	10.5%	100%	150%	50%
Net financial liabilities as % of total capital employed	2.2%	10%	15%	5%
Net interest expense as % of total revenue	0.6%	15%	20%	7%
For general govt activities: operating surplus as % of own-source revenue	–4.5%	%%	10%	0%

Source: LGI, 2006, Table 11.3, 273.

In respect of Table 4.3,the Allan Report (2006, 274) stressed that 'if used, each of these ratios should be adhered to, not just some of them'. In addition, Allan Report (2006, 276) prescribed the conditions that must be met should a council wish to be classified as 'currently healthy' in financial terms: the council should be 'a modest net debtor' with borrowings or debt making up only 'a minority of the total capital invested in the council's infrastructure and other assets', and at the same time 'the associated expense burden should not be a substantial proportion of the council's annual operating revenues'. While this represented a minimum requirement, 'for a council's financial performance to be assessed as "currently healthy" ' and to 'involve a margin of comfort to cope with the usual assortment of financial risks and financial shocks' the council must meet three further criteria:

- the council in question should 'generally be running an operating surplus rather than an operating deficit';
- the local authority should not exhibit a 'significant infrastructure renewal backlog' and its capital expenditure over the financial year on infrastructure renewal and replacement should 'on average over time be about the same level as the council's depreciation expenses'; and
- annual net borrowing should not be 'putting any pressure on the council's targeted net financial liabilities ratio'.

Despite these stipulations, the Allan Report (2006, 283) conceded that financial sustainability is a 'controversial' concept, but nevertheless concluded that 'a council's finances should be considered sustainable in the long term only if its financial capacity is sufficient – for the foreseeable future – to allow the council to meet its expected financial adjustments over time without having to introduce substantial or disruptive revenue (and expenditure) adjustments'.

Bearing in mind the conclusions of the South Australian FSRB Final Report on financial sustainability, its definition and the Allan Report definition are very close, which may be explained by the fact that Access Economics (2006a) worked as a key consultant in both inquiries. It should thus not be interpreted as indicative of a consensus on financial sustainability in the Australian local government milieu.

Of the 48 recommendations of the Allan Report (2006), five have special significance in the context of financial reform and financial sustainability. For example, in Recommendation 7 on infrastructure funding, the Allan Report suggested an additional $900 million per annum be available to councils through a combination of increased Commonwealth and state grants ($200 million), council expenditure savings ($200 million), and higher rates, fees and charges ($500 million). In order to facilitate this change, in Recommendation 21 the LGI advised that rate-capping be abolished, as well as limitations removed on some fees and charges, in return for councils adopting longer-term strategic and financial planning with outcome targets. Furthermore, in Recommendation 27 the LGI proposed that the Commonwealth Government set its Financial Assistance Grant (FAG) to local government at a fixed percentage of gross domestic product (GDP), preferably at 0.22% of GDP. In Recommendation 38 the Allan Report suggested that key accounting and reporting policies be standardised across all councils. Finally, in Recommendation 39 the Allan Report endorsed its financial KPIs and the associated range of lower and upper benchmarks for each KPI. None of these recommendations was subsequently adopted.

4.2.5 Queensland Size, Shape and Sustainability Review Framework (2006)

In 2004, the Local Government Association of Queensland (LGAQ) resolved to consider the pressures confronting councils in Queensland and the consequent need for reform to ensure the long-run viability of local councils. As a consequence of this decision, a *Discussion Paper* was released on 3 March 2005 and a Special Conference was held in June 2005, which led in turn to the *Size, Shape and Sustainability* (SSS) Review Framework. The resultant reform program was set out in the *Size, Shape and Sustainability: Guidelines Kit* (LGAQ, 2006) which held that, as part of the overall reform program, local councils must 'assess their current and future sustainability against a number of key indicators'. In particular, SSS indicators would 'help identify where there might be present or future vulnerabilities, opportunities, and strengths'. These latter three terms are defined in some detail: 'vulnerabilities' consist of 'risks or weaknesses within specific areas of council operations'; 'opportunities' focus on 'areas within council operations that could be improved'; and 'strengths' consider excellence in council operations and areas where a given council could 'provide assistance/benefit to other councils'.

The Guidelines Kit (LGAQ, 2006, Chapter 3) advanced five criteria that indicators should fulfill: indicators should be 'relevant' and 'limited' in number; 'capable of relating to other indicators'; 'easy to understand' 'reliable'; and based on 'accessible information'. Four categories of indicators were prescribed: (1) 'financial and resource base'; (2) 'community of interest'; (3) 'planning'; and (4) 'standards of governance'. Category (1) is pertinent in the realm of financial sustainability and financial reform. It contained seven indicator groups: 'financial forecasts'; 'revenue base'; 'rating capacity'; 'asset sustainability'; 'levels of service'; 'human resourcing'; and 'cross border use of council services'.

These seven indicator groups derived from the Queensland Treasury Corporation's (QTC) 2005 financial sustainability review process offered to local councils and therefore had to form part of the overall SSS exercise. It is worth noting some of the salient characteristics of these indicator groups:

- Two indicator groups contained more than a single indicator. For example, 'revenue base' included three specific indicators dealing population growth, age dependency and population size. An aggregate score for revenue base was obtained by averaging the score for each of these specific indicators. This was unfortunate since population growth, population age structure and population base all have quite different effects on council service, expenditure and revenue patterns.
- Whereas some indicators required subjective judgment, others simply reported ratios taken from 'objective' data. This meant that the scores obtained for different indicator groups were not directly comparable, since they were based on completely different assessment criteria.
- In contrast to both the South Australian FSRB (2005) and the Allan Report (2006), the scores represented absolute and not relative perceptions of financial sustainability since the data were not expressed in comparative terms.
- Insufficient justification was provided for the selection of the indicator groups. For instance, unlike the Allan Report (2006), no distinction was drawn between a council's financial position (ie, the state of its balance sheet and the level and composition of its assets and its liabilities) and a council's annual financial performance (ie, the state of its annual operating statement and the magnitude of relevant annual surpluses or deficits). This has serious implications for the usefulness of the data gathered through the exercise.
- The indicator groupings confused inputs into council operations with the outputs from council activities. For example, 'asset sustainability' clearly deals with council assets employed to produce serve outcomes, whereas 'service levels' obviously represents a final output. Economists always separate inputs from outputs for fear of comparing 'apples with oranges'.

With respect to local government reform, the SSS review process outlined four main 'options for change': 'resource sharing through service agreements'; 'resource sharing through joint enterprise'; 'significant boundary change'; and 'merger/amalgamation of adjoining councils'. It is significant that none of these options included the possibility of either (i) 'business as usual' or (ii) that amalgamation could occur on a strictly voluntary basis. By the latter half of 2006, a number of councils across Queensland had undergone financial assessment by the QTC and were in the process of conducting the SSS review for their respective areas.

This process was still under way when the Queensland Government made the shock announcement on 17 April 2007 that it had abandoned its collaboration with the LGAQ SSS process and decided instead to embark on a radical program of compulsory amalgamation. Under its new Local Government Reform Program, the Queensland Government appointed a seven-member Reform Commission to recommend local council amalgamations by August 2007 for the election of new councils on 15 March 2008. Submissions by councils and other affected individuals and organisations to the Reform Commission had to be lodged by 25 May 2007, thereby effectively curtailing consultation and severely limiting opportunities to make considered submissions to the Reform Commission.

4.2.6 Western Australian Systematic Sustainability Study (2006)

In January 2006, the Western Australian Local Government Association (WALGA) commissioned a wide-ranging review of local government in that state. This process culminated in December 2006 with the Final Report of the WA Systematic Sustainability Study group entitled *In Your Hands: Shaping the Future of Local Government in Western Australia* (WALGA, 2006). Although this document deliberately considered the entire gamut of local government activity in Western Australia, it nevertheless devoted significant attention to financial reform and financial sustainability; two of nine chapters examined this issue.

The Final Report's assessment of financial sustainability in Western Australia is based largely on the Access Economics report (2006b) commissioned by WALGA, a feature in common with the South Australian, New South Wales and PriceWaterhouseCoopers (PWC) reports (see, for example, Access Economics, 2006a). It is thus not surprising that the WALGA definition of financial sustainability shares a great deal with these other three reports. Access Economics (2006b, 55) defined financial sustainability thus: 'a council's finances are sustainable in the long term only if its financial capacity is sufficient – for the foreseeable future – to allow a council to meet its expected financial requirements over time without having to introduce substantial or disruptive revenue (and expenditure) adjustments'.

This definition of financial sustainability involves comparing long-term fund-raising ability with long-term expenditure needs. In this context, 'financial capacity' refers to the operating and capital finance which can be raised using existing 'revenue-raising and financing policies' as well as 'any additional funding were the council to increase its revenue-raising efforts to levels commensurate with those displayed with higher-effort councils'. By contrast, 'financial requirements' has two components: capital and operating expenditure sufficient to meet statutory requirements and 'expected spending pressures' (both of which imply asset maintenance and renewal); and a 'margin of comfort' adequate to meet any 'future financial shocks'.

This approach to financial sustainability requires an analysis of individual council accounts. It is made operational by examining a council's 'underlying operational deficit' as a proportion of its 'own-source' revenue. According to Access Economics (2006b, 56), 'persistent operating deficits' thus imply a council's revenue-raising efforts are 'too low', whereas 'excessive operating surpluses' mean that a municipality's revenue-raising efforts are 'too high'. A 'benchmark' deficit of 10% of the operating debt ratio was arbitrarily set; councils with a ratio in excess of 10% were assessed as 'financially unsustainable'.

However, Access Economics (2006b, 56–7) advanced four caveats against the blanket application of the underlying operational deficit criterion of 10% of the operating debt ratio:

- Councils failing to meet this cut-off mark are not necessarily unsustainable 'on the grounds that a 10 per cent deficit could be eliminated if necessary by "manageable" increases in rates and other charges' since this deficit could be eliminated by a one percentage point increase in rates and charges over the 'no-policy change' option in 10 years.

- Current operating deficits do not take into account the 'spending pressures that will arise as councils address their infrastructure backlogs'. Operating debt ratios should thus be adjusted on the understanding that deferred infrastructure maintenance and renewal has effectively subsidised current consumption by councils. Nominal interest rates on the accumulated backlog should therefore be notionally charged to account for this historic subsidy.
- Current operating deficits do not 'allow for the additional financial capacity available to those councils with below-par revenue-raising efforts'. Thus councils which have 'under-charged' with rates and charges require adjustment to their operating deficits to the extent of this imputed under-charging.
- Finally, 'another candidate for the adjustment of currently-observed operating deficits when assessing the financial sustainability of councils would be the impact of likely expenditure trends on a no-policy change basis on account of population shifts and ageing along with environmental imposts'. This latter category is sometimes termed 'non-discretionary' variables in the literature since it refers to costs over which councils have no control!

On this basis Access Economics (2006b, 57–8) constructed a summary table and chart depicting all WA local councils, adjusted to reflect the caveats outlined above, according to their financial sustainability. This information was subsequently employed in WALGA (2006, 33, Table 5.1) in a table of financial sustainability by type of council, reproduced as Table 4.4 here.

Table 4.4 shows that 83 (out of 142) WA councils (or 58%), serving around 21% of the WA population, are unsustainable according to the Access Economics (2006b) methodology. Access Economics (2006b, 58) compared this outcome with its earlier calculations for the SA and NSW inquiries based on broadly the same technique: 'In NSW, 25 per cent of that state's councils were assessed as financially unsustainable, with such councils serving 17 per cent of the state's population' whereas 'in SA, 50 per cent of that state's councils were assessed as financially unsustainable, with such councils serving 50 per cent of the state's population'.

Table 4.4. WALGA (2006) Financial Sustainability by Type of Councils

Type of council	Councils with unsustainable long-term finances:			
	Number	% of total	% of type	% of state pop.
Metropolitan	3	4%	10%	5%
Regional, with large towns	19	23%	70%	11%
Regional, without large towns	61	73%	71%	5%
Above-average growth	13	16%	45%	8%
Declining population	53	64%	75%	9%
Largest 25%	11	13%	31%	12%
Smallest 25%	24	29%	69%	1%
All WA councils	**83**	**100**	**58**	**21**

Source: WALGA, 2006, Table 5.1, 33.

WALGA (2006, 33, Table 5.1) presented 48 recommendations, of which only some are relevant to financial reform and financial sustainability. For example, Recommendation 4 called for revision of the escalation methodology for FAGs to a new formula based on local government cost movements. Recommendation 14 advocated increasing the use of developer charges to fund new community infrastructure and Recommendation 26 urged local government to adopt 10-year asset management plans integrated with business and financial plans. As yet, these recommendations have not been adopted.

4.2.7 PriceWaterhouseCoopers Report (2006)

The PriceWaterhouseCoopers report *National Financial Sustainability Study of Local Government* (PWC Report, 2006) was commissioned by the Australian Local Government Association (ALGA) to determine 'key financial issues' affecting financial sustainability and to develop recommendations for improving sustainability. The PWC Report was made public in November 2006. In contrast to the earlier state-based inquiries, the PWC Report (2006) took a national perspective on financial reform and financial sustainability.

The PWC Report (2006, 6–7) stressed the difficulties involved in assessing the 'financial viability' of local councils across Australia, with three main problems preventing the use of a common sustainability index: 'mixed approaches to measuring and recording financial data' and 'inconsistencies between states'; 'infrequent' asset valuations and differences in assumed asset lives; and 'incomplete' financial and asset management records, especially in smaller councils. These difficulties forced the authors of the PWC Report to adopt two techniques in their assessment of financial sustainability:

- The PWC Report applied financial ratio analysis to a sample of 100 local councils, appropriately weighted by state and stratified in proportion to the number of councils in each of the Department of Transport and Regional Services (DOTARS) seven categories.

- The PWC Report 'extrapolated' from the Access Economics and Municipal Association of Victoria (MAV, 2005) approaches using the KPIs in the FSRB (2005), the Allan Report (2006) and WALGA (2006) state inquiries and the MAV 'viability index'.

The PWC Report (2006, 95) defined 'financial sustainability' thus: 'financial sustainability of a council is determined by its ability to manage expected financial requirements and financial risks and shocks over the long term without the use of disruptive revenue or expenditure measures'. This involves two elements:

- Councils should maintain 'healthy finances', given current expenditure and revenue policies and foreseeable future developments.
- Councils must ensure infrastructure expenditure 'matches' asset planning.

This definition was applied to a stratified sample of 100 local authorities drawn from all state and territory local government jurisdictions using five financial KPIs:

- 'Operating surplus', representing 'total operating revenue less total operating expenses'. If an operating deficit exceeds 10% of total revenue, then it places the council at financial risk. In the PWC sample of 100 Australian local councils, 16% of all councils were unsustainable.

- 'Interest coverage', measuring a council's ability to pay interest on its debt and calculated as the ratio of 'Earnings Before Interest and Tax' (EBIT) to 'borrowing costs'. A ratio value below 3 indicates unsustainability. Almost 36% of the PWC sample failed on this KPI.

- 'Sustainability ratio', or the ratio of capital expenditure to depreciation which measures changes in the asset base of councils. If the ratio exceeds 1, then the asset base is increasing. In the sample, the median ratio was 1.8, with only 8% of councils falling below 1. However, the PWC Report (2006, 97) stressed that the sustainability ratio must be 'interpreted with care' due to infrequent and inconsistent asset valuation procedures.
- 'Current ratio', or the ratio of current assets to current liabilities. This is intended to measure a council's capacity to meet its short-term debt obligations. A sustainable council must have a current ratio at least equal to 1, and 21% of the sample fell below this level.
- 'Rates coverage', or total rates revenue as a proportion of total costs. An arbitrary 'benchmark' of 40% was taken to indicate 'adequate self-funding', and 48% of all councils exceeded this figure. However, a significant majority of rural councils fell short.

In its evaluation of these findings, the PWC Report (2006, 114) stressed that 'these results must be assessed with a caveat on their accuracy' due to data deficiencies. However, the PWC Report (2006) drew three main conclusions from its work on the sample of 100 local councils, spelt out in terms of the seven DOTARS council categories:

- Most 'large' metropolitan councils were 'generally viable', with some 'stretched' owing to 'service expansion', and 'internal reform' is necessary.
- 'Urban fringe' councils have 'mixed' sustainability, 'internal reform' is needed, and 'only some' councils need 'additional' funding.
- 'Rural remote' and 'rural agricultural' councils exhibited 'pronounced' sustainability problems, required 'internal reforms', and most should receive 'extra funding' for the 'renewal of existing community infrastructure'.

The second approach adopted in the PWC Report involved extrapolation using the KPIs in the FSRB (2005), the Allan Report (2006) and WALGA (2006) state inquiries and the MAV (2005) 'viability index' to all Australian local councils in order to ascertain infrastructure sustainability. While we have already considered the FSRB (2005) and LGI (2006) KPIs, the MAV 'viability index' comprises three elements:

- 'cumulative long-term debt' relative to annual rate income;
- 'cumulative underlying operating surplus/debt'; and
- 'rate effort, rates affordability and population growth'.

The PWC Report (2006, 111) summarised the findings as follows:

- 20–40% of all Australian councils 'could be unsustainable'.
- In monetary terms, NSW has the most acute 'financial viability issues'.
- The average annual per council 'underspend' on 'existing infrastructure renewals' lies between $1.3 million and $1.7 million.
- In order to remedy the annual infrastructure shortfall plus the accumulated infrastructure backlog, the 'average' council would need to spend an additional $2.6–$3.3 million per year.

In its overall assessment of the findings from both its evaluation exercises, the PWC Report (2006, 117) concluded:

- around 40% of all Australian local councils 'are currently not sustainable'; and
- a 'significant proportion' of all councils – 'say 10% to 30%' – face 'sizeable sustainability challenges'.

4.2.8 Local Government Association of Tasmania Review (2007)

Private consulting firm Access Economics was requested by the Local Government Association of Tasmania (LGAT) to conduct an inquiry into the financial sustainability of Tasmanian local government, which produced a Final Report entitled *Review of the Financial Sustainability of Local Government in Tasmania* (LGAT,

2007). In particular, Access Economics was requested to investigate seven matters in detail (LGAT, 2007, i):

- Take stock of local government finances, including financial position, financial performance and infrastructure-related financial obligations, in terms of key financial indicators and applicable benchmark values.
- Consider the 'outlook for council finances over the next 10 years under present and alternative infrastructure and service provisioning scenarios'.
- Examine 'the financial capacity of councils to fund their service and infrastructure obligations, and the additional own-source financial capacity available under alternative revenue raising options'.
- Evaluate 'the present standard of council financial governance policies and processes relative to good practice'.
- Assess 'the financial sustainability of individual councils'.
- Consider any 'adjustments that may be necessary to current policy directions, including how any deficits – current or emerging – might be addressed'.
- Outline 'possible improvements to financial governance'.

A complicating factor in this analysis was that the Tasmanian Government had initiated steps to remove water and sewerage activities from local councils. Data constraints prevented Access Economics from excluding sewerage and water from its statistical deliberations, but it nonetheless held that 'we are comfortable that including water and sewerage activities within our analysis will not invalidate our broad conclusions were a decision eventually made to transfer such activities out of local government in Tasmania' (LGAT, 2007, ii).

In its deliberations, Access Economics considered the definition of financial sustainability in some detail and contrasted it with the concept of 'financial viability' (LGAT, 2007, 23–5). In so doing it observed that 'it is important to note that a council being classified as financially "unsustainable" does not imply the council's financial viability is necessarily in question'. In other words, 'financial unsustainability' in the long term refers only to the unsustainability of a council's current revenue-raising and expenditure policies, since council finances can 'almost always' be adjusted with increases in rates and/or expenditure reductions, even if this comes at 'a considerable cost to ratepayers and the community'. Access Economics argued that 'there can be no doubt that the local government sector is, and will always be, financially "viable" in the sense that it will always be able ultimately to meet its debt service obligations' because 'ratepayers are bound to meet all outstanding obligations under the Local Government Act' and therefore the ability of a local authority to levy property taxes means that it cannot go bankrupt in the usual commercial manner.

As a consequence of this line of reasoning, Access Economics defined financial sustainability in local government as 'the extent to which a council's financial capacity is sufficient – for the foreseeable future – to allow the council to fund the spending that is necessary to meet both its existing statutory obligations and any associated spending pressures and financial shocks without having to introduce substantial or disruptive revenue (and expenditure) adjustments infrastructure assets means non-financial assets excluding any holdings of land' (LGAT, 2007, vii). It is immediately evident that this definition echoes earlier definitions developed by Access Economics for the SA, WA and NSW inquiries discussed earlier, a view verified by a corresponding observation in the Final Report (LGAT, 2007, 24).

Drawing on this definition and earlier work for the SA, NSW and WA inquiries, Access Economics set out six financial KPIs and associated benchmark values, which are reproduced in Table 4.5.

The Final Report of the LGAT Review (LGAT, 2007, 1) noted that 'each of these financial indicators is based upon a generally accepted key analytical balance with a strong predictive relationship to the degree to which a council's finances are likely to be sustainable in the long term'. It observed further that 'a council should set target values for these financial indicators based upon the following broad principles':

- A local council's financial situation is in 'a healthy state if its net financial liabilities (and associated debt) and any infrastructure backlog are at levels where the resultant and prospective net interest expense can be met comfortably from annual income (ie, by current ratepayers) at the existing rating effort'.

- A local council's operating financial performance is 'satisfactory if it is running a modest operating surplus before capital revenues, indicating that costs incurred in the year in question (including both routine maintenance and annual depreciation of non-financial assets) are at least being met by today's ratepayers and not being transferred to tomorrow's ratepayers, with revenues sufficient to finance current operations'.
- A local council's capital financial performance is satisfactory if both (a) its actual renewals capex broadly matches the annual desired levels of such expenditure and (b) its annual net borrowing does not put any long-term pressure on achievement of the council's targeted net financial liabilities ratios.

Table 4.5. Key Financial Indicators and Benchmark Values for Tasmanian Councils

Indicator	Denominator	Target Range low	high
Net financial liabilities ratio	Capital employed	3%	12%
Net interest expense ratio	Operating revenue	2%	5%
Operating surplus ratio	Own-source operating revenue	22%	71%
Net borrowing ratio	Enhancement capex	25%	50%
Annual renewals gap ratio	Desired renewals capex	−10%	10%
Infrastructure backlog ratio	Infrastructure assets	0%	5%

Source: LGAT, 2007, Table 1.1.

With respect to the benchmark values in Table 4.5, the LGAT Review's Final Report (LGAT, 2007, 2) noted that these values were taken from the Allan Report (2006), and had been 'adapted to Tasmanian circumstances' and then applied 'depending upon a council's general circumstances (growth, size, grants dependency)'.

Against this background, the Final Report supplied the material in Table 4.5 to individual Tasmanian local authorities to create financial sustainability rankings generated by algorithms using a methodology developed by Fiscal Star Services (2007), which extended and refined the earlier approach used by Access Economics in the SA, NSW and WA inquiries. This methodology combines the KPI outcomes into an 'equivalent overall financial shortfall' expressed as a percentage of a council's annual revenue from rates and charges, with 'persistent shortfalls … indicative of a council's revenue-raising effort being too low'; 'overall financial shortfalls cannot persist over the long term, as they involve services consumed by current ratepayers being paid for by future ratepayers either by borrowing or by avoiding essential renewal of existing assets'.

The results of this exercise demonstrated that six Tasmanian councils (about 20%), serving 8% of the population, could be classified as 'unsustainable' on the benchmark values. This implied that these councils faced 'substantial or disruptive revenue (or expenditure) adjustments' to correct imbalances in the long-term finance. This can be compared with the following results from the Access Economics analysis of SA, NSW and WA, which established that:

- 50% of SA councils were financially unsustainable, serving about 50% of the population;
- 25% of NSW councils were financially unsustainable, serving 17% of the population; and
- just over 50% of WA councils were financially unsustainable, serving 21% of the population.

In Tasmania, an additional five councils (some 17%), serving 14% of the population, were classified as 'vulnerable'.

In its analysis, the LGAT Review's Final Report (LGAT, 2007, 27) argued that 'the Tasmanian Councils which we assess to be either financially unsustainable or vulnerable have a range of structural characteristics'. Chief among these are that 'small sized and declining population councils are disproportionately represented among the unsustainable or vulnerable councils', and 'larger councils and/or above-average growth councils' under represented. Moreover, in common with the WA outcome, but in contrast to the SA and NSW inquiries, 'structural factors are at work in explaining the sustainability of a council's long-term finances in Tasmania as well as financial governance and policy deficiencies'.

In terms of its policy implications, the Final Report (LGAT, 2007, 66) advanced a number of recommendations for local councils to develop long-term spending, asset management, revenue as well as borrowing policies to meet local infrastructure and service obligations within sustainable financial limits. In particular, Access Economics recommended councils adopt a 'rolling 10-year financial plan' aimed at:

- dealing with the local infrastructure backlog;
- investing in the new infrastructure required for residential and business growth;
- developing service provision to accommodate population growth and changing community needs;
- generating additional resources from revenue measures, operational savings, re-ordering of expenditure priorities, infrastructure enhancement deferrals;
- arranging asset leases or disposals and extra borrowings; and
- ensuring that sustainable financial targets are met.

As yet, these recommendations have not been implemented.

4.2.9 Queensland Local Government Reform Commission Report (2007)

As we have seen in section 4.2.5, in 2005 the LGAQ launched its SSS program into the sustainability of local government in collaboration with the Queensland Government, which provided financial assistance. Despite subsequent assurances by the Queensland Government that the SSS process had proceeded satisfactorily, on 17 April 2007 the Queensland Government unilaterally abolished the SSS program and established a Local Government Reform Commission (QLGRC) to consider compulsory council amalgamation. In its Final Report entitled *Report of the Local Government Reform Commission* (QLGRC, 2007), the Reform Commission recommended a forced amalgamation program to reduce the number of local councils from 157 to just 73 entities (Dollery, Ho and Alin, 2008).

While the Final Report had little comment on financial reform and financial sustainability, with only one of its six criteria concerned with 'financial sustainability' and 'boundaries', the fourth main criterion guiding the QLGRC was 'financial sustainability'. However, the QLGRC Final Report (2007, 42) did not define 'a minimum level of financial sustainability for local government in Queensland'. Instead, the QLGRC observed that it relied on the Queensland Treasury Corporation's (QTC) *Financial Sustainability Reviews*, despite the fact that not all councils had undergone QTC scrutiny prior to the Final Report. Moreover, as we can see from Tables 4.5 and 4.7 in section 4.2.11, of the 109 councils that had been reviewed by the QTC, 57 councils (52%) were classified as 'moderate' in terms of financial sustainability, where moderate implies a 'high capacity to meet its financial commitments', and 28 (25.6%) were designated as 'weak', where weak means an 'acceptable capacity to meet its financial commitments' (QLGRC, 2007, 71). In other words, in the view of the QTC, these two groups of councils were not perceived as financially unsustainable.

4.2.10 Productivity Commission Report (2008)

The threefold terms of reference (TOR) for the Productivity Commission's (PC) study into assessing the capacity local government to raise revenue were provided to the Commission on 5 April 2007. The TOR obliged the Commission to investigate:

- the capacity of different types of councils (eg, capital city, metropolitan, regional, rural, remote and indigenous) to raise revenue and the factors contributing to capacity and variability in capacity over time;
- the impacts on individuals, organisations and businesses of the various taxes, user charges and other revenue sources available to local government; and
- the impact of any state regulatory limits on the revenue-raising capacity of councils.

In addition, the Commission was expressly forbidden from investigating the scope for local government to borrow. It is thus apparent that the Commission had to investigate hypothetical capacity to raise revenue rather than real-world revenue accrual.

This severely limited the usefulness of the Commission's Final Report *Assessing Local Government Revenue Raising Capacity*, published in April 2008 (PC, 2008).

Against this background, the Commission was to assess specifically (i) the revenue-raising capacity of local government and (ii) the factors contributing to such capacity. It identified two methods of determining the capacity of local authorities to raise revenue:

- The fiscal capacity of a local government, which is measured as the aggregate income net of tax of its local community. In terms of this approach, aggregate income represents the ability of a community to purchase local government and private goods and services. Accordingly, the higher the fiscal capacity of a local government, the higher its potential to raise revenue.
- The willingness of the local community to pay for services provided by local governments. In practice, the amount of revenue that a local government can actually raise from its local community depends on what the local community requires by way of services. Thus, the higher the level of desired services, the greater the willingness to pay.

The Commission (PC, 2008) found that fiscal capacity differed by category of local government. Thus capital city CBD councils had the highest fiscal capacity, due to high business income, parking and traffic fine revenue and comparatively small resident populations. By contrast, most remote councils, without mining and petroleum activity, had low fiscal capacity, particularly indigenous councils. On average, 'urban developed', 'urban regional' and 'rural' councils had intermediate levels of fiscal capacity, whereas 'urban fringe' councils generally had lower levels of fiscal capacity. The Commission (PC, 2008) found that revenue-raising effort, measured as the ratio of own-source revenue to fiscal capacity, also differed by the category of local government.

Recognising that the effective operation of local government is important in the promotion of local community well-being, the Commission prescribed several principles to guide revenue-raising decisions of local government. These principles dealt with sustainable financial management, evaluation and priority setting, core functions, identifying costs of service delivery, prudent borrowings, rate setting and pricing of services, responsibility and accountability, openness and transparency, and the provision of services on behalf of other tiers of government.

The Commission Report (PC, 2008) advanced 29 formal findings, a few of which are relevant in the present context. For example, Finding 2.1 held that at the national level, the ratio of local government rates revenue to GDP decreased over the period 1990/91 to 2005/06. Finding 3.2 established that there is considerable variation per capita in both own-source revenue raised and grants received by Australian local governments. Finding 3.3 observed that, for the majority of local governments, own-source revenue is the main source of revenue. However, for 20% of councils, which represent only 1% of the population, grants account for 48% or more of total revenue. Finding 5.6 noted that, given the differences in the scope to raise additional revenue across different classes of councils, Commonwealth Government general purpose grants should be reviewed.

4.2.11 Queensland Treasury Corporation Report (2008)

Following an invitation from the LGAQ and the Queensland Department of Local Government, Sport and Recreation (DLGSR), the Queensland Treasury Corporation (QTC) assessed the financial sustainability of local council participating in the LGAQ SSS Program. The QTC assessment process had three main aims:

- to provide each local authority with a financial sustainability rating as part of the SSS Program;
- to provide each council with a report analysing its finances with recommendations for improving financial sustainability; and
- to provide a more general analysis of the financial problems in Queensland local government and recommendations for enhancing the overall effectiveness of local government.

The QTC completed this assessment process by July 2007 and submitted a Final Report containing financial ratings, observations and analysis of 109 local councils. This required, *inter alia,* defining financial sustainability, selecting suitable financial indicators, and developing an assessment methodology and a rating scale. Its definition of financial sustainability drew heavily on the South Australian FRSB (2005) examined above in section 4.2.3. Financial sustainability in local government means that a given council is able 'to manage likely developments and unexpected financial shocks in future periods without having at some time to introduce economically significant or socially destabilising revenue or expenditure adjustments' (QTC, 2008, 16).

In its analysis, the QTC (2008) broke this definition down into several different elements, such as operating performance sustainability and depreciation sustainability, and then developed specific indicators for each of them and normative values for these indicators. For example, 'fiscal flexibility' was defined by the QTC (2008, 42) as 'the capacity of a local government to respond to changing circumstances (including unforeseen financial shocks) by adjusting revenue and/or expense levels or by maximising balance sheet management'. Fiscal flexibility was deemed to have three core aspects: own-source revenue, self-generated revenue and debt capacity. The QTC (2008, 44) defined self-generated revenue as 'net rates, utilities and charges plus sales (contract and recoverable works) and other fees and charges as a percentage of total operating expenditure (including interest and depreciation'. For self-generating revenue, the QTC prescribed the following normative minimum value, described as the 'self-generated revenue ratio minimum indicative measure' set thus: 'the QTC minimum benchmark ratio for self-generated revenue is a contribution of at least 60.0 per cent of operating expenses'. A similar approach was adopted for each of the other areas of the financial operation of councils. The QTC (2008) therefore adopted the reasonable view that there is no single ideal indicator for financial sustainability.

In essence, the QTC (2008) financial sustainability review assessed financial sustainability in terms of the capacity of a given council to:

- meet its commitments in the short, medium and long term;
- manage unforeseen financial shocks and adverse changes in its economic environment; and
- manage 'core business risks'.

In its assessment, the QTC (2008) considered the council in question's past financial performance and a long-term (10-year) financial forecast, an evaluation of the council on several quantitative and qualitative indicators, discussion with senior council officers on strategic objectives, as well as more general macroeconomic considerations.

Using this methodology, the QTC (2008) ranked councils on a six-dimensional scale: very strong, strong, moderate, weak, very weak and distressed, which referred to the generic capacity of a council to meet its financial commitments in the short, medium and long term, its ability to manage unforeseen financial shocks and any adverse changes in its business and general economic environment without the need for significant revenue or expense adjustments, and its capacity to manage core business risks. The results of the financial sustainability review exercise are outlined in Table 4.6.

Table 4.6. QTC (2008) Financial Sustainability Review Rating Outcomes

RATING DISTRIBUTION					
Very Strong	**Strong**	**Moderate**	**Weak**	**Very Weak**	**Distressed**
1	11	55	28	12	2
0.9%	10.1%	50.5%	25.7%	11.0%	1.8%

Source: QTC, 2008.

From Table 4.6 we can see that 61.5% of the 109 councils reviewed were rated Moderate and above, whereas 38.5% of councils were rated Weak, Very Weak or Distressed.

These results are decomposed into outcomes for particular indicators under each of the five groups of indicators in Table 4.7.

The QTC (2008, 7–9) drew 13 findings from its analysis, some of which are relevant in the current context:

- A significant number of local governments routinely recorded operating deficits (annual operating expenses).
- A large number of councils depreciated their assets too quickly.
- Liquidity levels were generally sound.

Table 4.7. QTC Historical Financial Indicator Distribution by Ratings

QTC RATING	RATING DISTRIBUTION										
Rating	Number rated	Operating margin > –4%		Self-generated income > 60%		Interest cover > 6 times		Cash holdings > 3 months		Asset replacement > 1.1 times	
Very Strong	1	1	100%	1	100%	1	100%	1	100%	1	100%
Strong	11	7	64%	11	82%	9	82%	11	100%	10	91%
Moderate	55	39	71%	43	71%	39	71%	55	100%	47	85%
Weak	28	4	14%	17	68%	19	68%	26	93%	9	32%
Very Weak	12	2	17%	4	58%	7	58%	8	67%	6	50%
Distressed	2	0	0%	0	50%	1	50%	0	0%	0	0%
Total	109	53	49%	76	70%	76	70%	101	93%	73	67%

Source: QTC, 2008.

- About 57% of the Review Group did not have sound Asset Management Plans.
- Many local authorities were repatriating funds from their commercialised business activities to the detriment of these businesses.
- The financial focus of most councils lay in the cash accounting approach which emphasised the current financial year.
- Many councils were basing revenue increases on the Consumer Price Index rather than on a better measure of actual costs.
- Asset maintenance funding was often sacrificed under tight budgetary conditions.
- Councils were not using adequate debt to fund capital works.

The QTC (2008, 9–11) made 17 formal recommendations for policy change, some of which are relevant in the terms of financial reform and financial sustainability:

- Councils should target a balanced or surplus operating result, and if this is not feasible, then operating deficits should not be greater than 4% of annual operating revenue.
- Increases to net rates, utilities and charges should be determined as a function of service provision costs rather the Consumer Price Index.
- Annual depreciation expenses should be realistic and an industry-wide review of the depreciation methodology should be initiated and guidelines developed.
- A common industry policy should be developed for taxation and dividend policy principles to be used in local government commercial business activities.
- Tax equivalent amounts should be paid as a consequence of capital grants, subsidies and contributions, and should be immediately reinvested in the business as equity contributions, and dividend payments should be made as a percentage of operating profits after tax, adjusted for capital grants, subsidies and contributions.

- Each council should develop and have in place approved policies and processes to manage and monitor liquidity.
- Councils should consider an optimal and prudent funding mix for capital investment and borrow where appropriate.
- Asset Management Plans should be completed and linked to a long-term financial forecasting model.
- Each council should develop, maintain and regularly review a 10-year financial forecasting model which incorporates an income statement, cash statement and a balance sheet to assist strategic planning and decision making.
- When developing long-term financial forecasts, councils should include estimates for asset revaluation.

In its overall assessment of financial policy in Queensland local government, the QTC (2008, 11) bemoaned that 'of some concern is that many of these issues have remained unattended for years despite there being a general industry awareness of their existence. Indeed, evidence from the FSR process shows that a number of formerly financially sound local governments have, over time, failed to react in a timely manner to the erosion of their financial capacity'. The result has been that 'this has ultimately resulted in an increased financial cost to ratepayers as local governments subsequently attempted to address their deteriorating financial position by approving large ad hoc rate increases'.

4.2.12 NSW Independent Pricing and Regulatory Tribunal Review (2009)

The problem of financial reform and financial sustainability in New South Wales is made much more complicated than in other Australian local government jurisdictions due to the longstanding application of rate-pegging in that state (Dollery and Wijeweera, 2010). However, on 27 October 2008, (then) Premier Rees said that the New South Wales Government was considering removing rate-pegging. This followed an earlier instruction to the NSW Independent Pricing and Regulatory Tribunal (IPART) in May 2008 to investigate the operation of rate-pegging and report on its findings. In July 2009, IPART released a Draft *Review of the Revenue*

Framework for Local Government report (IPART, 2009a). While this document did canvass various matters, its overwhelming focus fell on rate-pegging. After a period of public submissions on the Draft Review, IPART handed a Final Report of the *Review of the Revenue Framework for Local Government* to the NSW Government in December 2009 (IPART 2009b). This subsequent report proposed two alternative approaches for a revised system:

- Option A would retain rate-pegging for all councils, but link it to a new local government cost index and establish a 'medium-term' cap on rates to allow for some revenue certainty.
- Option B would add to Option A: under Option B councils which demonstrated sound financial performance (as measured in accounting terms) would be exempted from rate-pegging altogether for periods of up to four years.

As part of the 2010/11 NSW budgetary process, (then) NSW Premier Kenneally announced 'sweeping changes to local government charges on new housing development' which involved some modification in the manner in which rate-pegging would be applied in NSW local government in future. As part of its $44 million *Comprehensive Housing Supply Strategy,* aimed at securing 'additional land releases, lower levies and faster planning decisions', the NSW Government set out the following measures:

- a 'hard cap' of $20,000 per lot for council developer charges, known as Section 94 contributions in New South Wales, imposed on new developments, and
- a constraint on council Section 94 developer charges to be limited to 'essential infrastructure' which was 'necessary for the development to happen', like road works and stormwater management.

Since (i) and (ii) would inevitably intensify financial distress in local government, the NSW Government recognised that they would place upward pressure on rate-peg variation claims from local authorities. As a consequence, it retained the practice of rate-pegging but modified the process:

- The NSW Government transferred the determination of the rate-peg to IPART, which would devise a new Local Government Cost Index to employ in setting the annual rate-peg
- IPART was also placed in charge of deciding 'special rate variation requests' by councils, as well as 'variations for essential and community infrastructure'. These requests, through which councils sought permission to levy rates above the rate-peg, had hitherto been considered by the Minister for Local Government directly.
- As at the time of writing, no further detail has been forthcoming from the NSW Government on the mechanics of the new process, and it remains to be seen how it will work in practice.

With its heavy emphasis on rate-pegging, the IPART Report (2009a) has limited relevance for Australian local government as a whole. However, in its assessment of financial sustainability, IPART (2009a, 112) found that claims of 'widespread problems of unsustainability' in NSW local government was 'not supported by the evidence'. Moreover, financial sustainability in NSW local government was not 'vastly different to the situation faced by councils in other states' (IPART, 2009a, 104).

4.3 Policy and practice implications for financial sustainability

Of the five types of local government reform in the Dollery, Garcea and LeSage (2008) taxonomy, this chapter has focused exclusively on the problem of financial sustainability and financial reform, since the bulk of the 12 public inquiries we have examined devoted most of their attention to financial sustainability.

With respect to the findings of these 12 inquiries, five general conclusions can be drawn on financial reform and financial sustainability in terms of the evaluation of financial sustainability, common issues raised, patterns of policy recommendations and recurring unresolved matters, as well as some general conclusions on the policy and practice implications for local government.

4.3.1 Evaluating financial sustainability assessment

Financial sustainability in local government is a thorny question since it inevitably involves developing methods of evaluating the financial performance of individual councils. In addition, the conceptual and measurement difficulties revolving around the development and implementation of satisfactory financial performance evaluation are formidable. For example, despite a voluminous literature on this problem, summarised in Honadle, Costa and Cigler's (2004) *Fiscal Health for Local Governments*, there is no agreed definition of 'financial sustainability'. Indeed, there is not even 'consensus about the terminology surrounding fiscal health' (Honadle, Costa and Cigler, 2004, 18). Definitions abound. For instance, in the United States, writers use a wide range of terms, including 'fiscal health' (Berry, 1994), 'financial condition' (Lin and Raman, 1998), 'fiscal stress' (Pagano and Moore, 1985), and 'fiscal capacity' (Johnson and Roswick, 1991). By contrast, in Australia the term 'financial sustainability' has recently become fashionable and acquired widespread usage, even though it still lacks agreed meaning.

This lack of consensus should not be surprising given the complexities of defining financial sustainability in a democratic non-profit local public service environment. For example, should the financial circumstances of a council be judged exclusively on financial magnitudes, such as operating expenditure, operating revenue, indebtedness and the like, or should the yardstick be standards of service provision, operational efficiency and community expectations? Similarly, inherent tensions between local government democracy and local government efficiency further complicate matters (Aulich, 2005; Dollery, 2010).

In addition to these conceptual difficulties surrounding the definition of financial sustainability, further intractable problems exist in measuring financial performance. The first attempt at evaluating the fiscal standing of local government was undertaken by the American Advisory Commission on Intergovernmental Relations (ACIR) (1973) which devised six 'early warning signs' in the form of financial indicators, thereby initiating a literature on KPIs in US local government which culminated in the construction of comparative indicators, typically in terms of financial ratios (Brown, 1993, 1996).

Parallel developments have occurred in Australian local government. Woodbury, Dollery and Rao (2003, 7) analysed Australian local government performance measurement systems. They observed that 'a key strategy in improving local government performance over the past decade has been the development of performance measures for use in the benchmarking'. In effect, the methodologies developed in the South Australian, New South Wales, Western Australian, Tasmanian and PriceWaterhouseCoopers inquiries follow in this tradition, since they all seek to find elusive comparative measures of local government financial performance.

While the aim of constructing comparative financial indicators to assess local government system is laudable, since it strives to develop an 'objective' measurement tool to generate unbiased policy recommendations in a highly charged political environment, numerous problems afflict comparative financial indicator indexes (Kloha, Weissert and Kleine, 2005, 316–7). These specific problems are amplified when we consider wider anomalies. For instance, in reference to Australian financial KPIs, Worthington and Dollery (2000b) have stressed the significance of 'nondiscretionary variables' in performance indicators, which cannot be changed by councils. Nondiscretionary variables include pensioner rate rebates, non-rateable properties, the proportion of Aboriginal people, and a host of other economic, environmental and social factors beyond individual council control.

A notable feature of this chapter's analysis of the 12 national and state inquiries into local government financial sustainability is that 5 of the 12 reports (ie, FSRB, IPART, WALGA, LGAT and PWC) relied heavily on the methodology of Access Economics. As we have seen, Access Economics defined financial sustainability in terms of accounting measures by employing financial KPIs and associated benchmark values to distinguish between financially sustainable and unsustainable councils.

Several unfortunate aspects of excessive reliance on the methodology of a single commercial consulting firm appear evident:

- In contrast to the Access Economics-dominated reports, the QTC report (2008), which developed its own KPIs and benchmark values, augmented with interviews with council senior management, found the degree of financial unsustainability much less acute. This surely serves to underline how easily even basic KPIs can be modified through the politicised process of public inquiries to reach dramatically different conclusions. It is also striking that the Queensland *Size, Shape and Sustainability* (LGAQ, 2006) inquiry generated a much broader view of sustainability without Access Economics' input and much less weight on KPIs.

- The uncritical acceptance of the 'accounting' approach to financial sustainability has allowed 'ideology' to masquerade as objective 'analysis' in some instances. For example, if we use operating deficits to proxy financial capacity, then this will inevitably mark small rural councils as unsustainable due to their low rate base, an artifact of non-discretionary factors such as demographic trends, and not council discretionary policy. After all, state local government grants commissions were established precisely to compensate for disability factors outside council control.
- The Access Economics and other KPI-based approaches have ignored the academic literature on the uncertain predictive capacity of KPIs in Australian local government unsustainability. This literature has shown that KPI benchmark values are not always reliably correlated with financial stress since other factors, like governance failure, can play an even larger role (Murray and Dollery 2005, 2006).

4.3.2 Common findings of public inquiries on financial sustainability

Despite the problems associated with excessive reliance on accounting measures in many of the inquiries, a common theme runs through the findings of all the 12 reports considered in this chapter: all Australian local government jurisdictions are afflicted by severe financial distress and the primary symptom of ongoing financial unsustainability resides in a large and growing local infrastructure backlog. Moreover, the degree of financial distress differs by type of council, with the problem more acute in rural and remote councils. These results emerge from all of the inquiries which assessed financial sustainability and therefore are not dependent on the methodology employed. It follows that there is thus an immediate and compelling case for policy intervention aimed at alleviating the problem. Policy intervention will have to take two main forms: (i) policy designed to fund tackling the existing infrastructure backlog and (ii) policy structured to reduce ongoing financial problems. These weighty questions are taken up in Part C of this book.

4.3.3 Common policy recommendations and patterns in policy implementation

As we have seen, all 12 of the reports we have examined have advanced some or many recommendations for improving financial sustainability in local government. These policy recommendations have ranged from proposed changes to Commonwealth Government financial relations with local government (Hawker Report, 2003) to enhanced financial governance by council management. Despite the plethora of recommendations, it is possible to identify at least one common theme in most of the state-based inquiries. This centres on the urgent need for local authorities to improve asset and financial management, with several reports prescribing long-term financial planning, common approaches to asset depreciation, and a need for uniform financial practice and record-keeping across state jurisdictions and the like.

Unfortunately, the major common pattern in the implementation of these recommendations is that federal and state policy makers have by and large simply ignored proposals emanating from inquiries. A partial exception to this general rule resides in piecemeal changes to improve asset and financial management practice in many state jurisdictions, generally obliging councils to engage in long-term financial planning, although it is by no means clear whether the state governments in question have acted independently or in accordance with inquiry recommendations. For instance, while both the Allan Report (2006) and the IPART Report (2009a, 2009b) recommended long-term planning, and the NSW Government enacted the *Local Government Amendment (Planning and Reporting) Act 2009*, which introduced an Integrated Planning and Reporting framework, forcing local councils to prepare a minimum 10-year Community Strategic Plan and a 4-year Delivery Program, it is not obvious that the Act flowed from these recommendations.

4.3.4 Unresolved problems in local government financial sustainability

While the widespread application of long-term asset and financial planning represents a most welcome finance reform, which will undoubtedly assist in improving financial sustainability, core problems remain unresolved. By far the most important of these problems is the immense local infrastructure backlog, the scale of which far exceeds the capacity of local government alone to remediate. While the federal government has taken some steps to assist through the *Roads-to-Recovery Program* and the more recent *Regional and Local Community Infrastructure Program*, the size of the problem demands Commonwealth infrastructure funding on the scale outlined in the PWC Report (2006). Second, despite numerous recommendations in the 12 inquiries, nothing has been done to provide local government with additional adequate and reliable sources of recurrent funding. Finally, intergovernmental coordination and service provision arrangements, with their attendant cost-shifting, remain unsatisfactory, notwithstanding many recommendations to ameliorate this state of affairs.

4.3.5 Lessons from public inquiry financial sustainability reviews

At least four general policy and practice lessons can be drawn from the 12 inquiries as they pertain to financial sustainability in local government:

- It is not possible to define sustainability with any degree of precision and thus it cannot be captured adequately using financial KPIs. This means that other techniques are needed to augment accounting measures, including public opinion surveys aimed at soliciting the views of the local community in question. For example, a local council may be sustainable if the local community is reasonably content with its performance. This 'holistic sustainability' approach is considered in Chapter 5.

- Data inconsistencies and deficiencies mean that financial KPI ratios and other numerical indexes are at best only broadly indicative of the actual financial situation facing individual councils. The very fact that the national PWC Report (2006) was obliged to construct its own weighted sample of 100 councils has demonstrated that state differences in data and regulation mean that no coherent national set of financial KPIs can be employed with confidence.
- Where financial indicators are employed, effort should be taken beforehand to determine the predictive capacity of the proposed KPIs. Put differently, to what extent in the past have a particular set of KPIs predicted good, bad or indifferent financial performance? This evaluative type of 'pretest' or 'trial program' should be used before embarking on expensive system-wide performance measurement programs.
- Immense diversity between councils in any given local government jurisdiction precludes the use of a 'one-size-fits-all' method of assessing local authorities. Not only are the expectations and needs of residents of metropolitan, regional, rural and remote councils quite different, but the problems faced by these different categories of councils also vary. A given and fixed set of KPIs cannot hope to cope with these subtleties.

Chapter 5
Holistic Sustainability in Australian Local Government

5.1 Introduction

Chapter 4 presented an exhaustive analysis of the problem of financial sustainability in Australian local government through the prism of the host of national and state inquiries conducted over the past decade. One of the many lessons which emerged from this analysis was that it is not possible to adequately define financial sustainability in local government. This implies *inter alia* that financial Key Performance Indicators (KPIs) represent an imperfect means of assessing financial viability and should be augmented by additional instruments, such as surveys of resident satisfaction, aimed at securing a broader perspective on the performance of particular local authorities. For instance, if a local community is content with its local council performance, despite adverse financial measures, can it be concluded that the local government entity in question is in some sense 'sustainable'? Put more generally, should the performance of a given council be judged exclusively on financial magnitudes, such as operating expenditure, operating revenue, indebtedness and the like, or should the yardstick be quality of standards and mix of service provision, affordability, operational efficiency, community expectations and so forth? Similarly, the inherent tensions between local democracy and organisational efficiency in democratically elected local authorities suggest that local government sustainability is far broader than simple financial sustainability. The thorny question of 'holistic sustainability' in local government is considered in detail in this chapter.

Holistic sustainability has been examined in other comparable local government systems. For example, although the

Lyons Inquiry into local government in England was formally restricted to seeking 'a sustainable solution to the problems of local government finance' (Lyons, 2005, 3), in fact the Inquiry considered a far wider range of matters, including the role of local government, devolution and decentralisation, and relationships between central and local government (Lyons, 2005, 7–10). Grant and Dollery (2011) have argued that the Inquiry's subsequent recommendations, and especially its focus on 'place-shaping' (Lyons, 2007), implied that financial sustainability embraced not only factors such as local governments' own revenue-raising capacity, but also strategic planning where sustainability is place-based and where involvement in local politics plays an important part in overall sustainability. Along analogous lines, in New Zealand the Local Government Rates Inquiry Report (NZ Rates Inquiry, 2007) *Funding Local Government* initially defined sustainability according to terms derived from the Government's *Fiscal Responsibility Act* (1994), or what it described as 'the affordability of expenditure and equity of funding over the long term', noting that 'in general, local government is paying insufficient attention to these issues' (NZ Rates Inquiry, 2007, 3), and integrating 'environmental sustainability' into its recommendations.

Against this comparative context, in this chapter we pursue the question: Aside from direct financial considerations, what other factors determine the broader long-term sustainability of Australian local councils? In other words, can we identify 'holistic sustainability' in local government, define its characteristics and explain its origins?

This chapter is divided into six main sections. Section 5.2 provides a synoptic description of the genesis of the term 'sustainability' in policy analysis by way of background. Section 5.3 sketches the inherent tensions which complicate the question of sustainability in Australian local government. Section 5.4 briefly outlines the academic literature on the problem of 'sustainability' in Australian local government. Section 5.5 discusses the taxonomic 'government failure' approach to sustainability. Section 5.6 examines the main elements of 'holistic sustainability' in Australian local government. The chapter ends in section 5.7 with some brief concluding comments.

5.2 Meaning of sustainability

In its generic sense, sustainability as a concept in public policy analysis first emerged in the literature on economic development through the efforts of the World Commission on Environment and Development ('Brundtland Commission') (1987, 8), which defined 'sustainable development' as a process which 'meets the needs of the present without compromising the ability of future generations to meet their own needs'. In contrast to earlier work in this field, which juxtaposed environmental objectives against economic growth, a key feature of the Brundtland Commission definition is the manner in which it conflates environmentalism and growth into a synergistic whole (Romero-Lankao, 2000). The Brundtland Commission (1987) definition was swiftly adopted by scholars from not only across the ideological spectrum, but also from a wide range of natural and social sciences, since it served as a helpful umbrella term for a diversity of perspectives on development. However, the compromise embodied in this definition, which served to minimise conflictual views, came at the price of ambiguity (Adger and Jordan, 2009; Leuenberger and Bartle, 2009). As a consequence, the demands of logical precision have generated 'dozens of definitions [which] are being passed around among experts and politicians, because many and diverse interests and visions hide behind the common key-idea' (Sachs, 1995, 8).

The collapse of the common consensus on the meaning of sustainability into a mishmash of conflicting, value-laden usages is evident in its application to local government. This should not be surprising given the complexities of local government with its myriad of democratic, economic, environmental and sociological characteristics. While the disintegration of accord on sustainability is understandable, the fact that there is presently no agreed universal definition of sustainability in local government is unfortunate. For instance, explicit recognition of the significance of sustainability would oblige local government policy makers to give consideration to the future consequences of current decisions and therefore address important questions, such as intergenerational equity. It is thus worth investigating the nature of sustainability in the local government environment.

In this chapter we contend that local government sustainability should extend beyond financial sustainability of the kind proposed in the national and state inquiries examined in Chapter 4. In contrast to the narrow confines of financial viability, local government sustainability should embrace wider economic, political and sociological attributes, as well as administrative and technical capacity. In its broader connotation, holistic sustainability is the ability of a local authority to function effectively over the long term. It should be stressed that this definition does not embrace environmental concerns directly for the twin reasons that (i) local government seldom has the legislative authority to make a decisive contribution to long-term environmental sustainability and (ii) environmental sustainability has as yet no uncontested meaning.

5.3 Tensions between local government democracy and local government efficiency

In comparison with private for-profit firms and public utilities, which characteristically pursue a few well-defined goals such as profit and revenue maximisation and other readily identifiable maximands that render them amenable to standard economic analysis, a complicating factor in local government derives from its dual role as both a democratic organisation and a service provider. As a consequence, in addition to the common conceptual and empirical difficulties involved in defining financial sustainability in any public sector entity, the inevitable tensions in local government between democracy and efficiency exacerbate these difficulties. Aulich (2005) has described this dual role in some detail.

In its democratic function, local government 'provides a voice to local aspirations for decentralised governance' (Aulich, 2005, 198). This 'local democracy approach' places fundamental value on 'local differences and system diversity' and it encourages activities directed at enhancing 'local choice and local voice'. Spatial variation in community preferences and the consequent need for decentralised decision-making imply that local authorities 'can and will make choices that will differ from those made by others'. Under this democratic imperative, 'a premium is placed upon traditional democratic values' which incorporate 'access', 'accountability', 'representativeness' and 'responsiveness' (Stewart, 1997). The 'vibrancy' of local democracy thus becomes a desired outcome in its own right.

Aulich (2005, 198) has argued that the local democracy imperative entails support for 'collaborative or pluralist processes of reform' rather than top-down 'technocratic' policy intervention which can contravene local opinion. In this view, rather than a financial impost on the local resources, representative local government is a worthy policy goal in its own right. Accordingly, the pecuniary costs of local governance, including local elections, consultation processes, community participation, elected councillors, and the whole administrative panoply of local democratic autonomy, are justified in the same way as financial outlays on any other worthwhile council service. It follows that public policy making should not focus only on efficient service provision, but also on effective local democracy. In other words, political process is as important as economic outcome.

The second primary role of local government in a Westminster-type system concentrates on local municipalities as 'a mechanism for [the] efficient delivery of local services to local communities' (Aulich, 2005, 199). Tucker (1997) has observed that local government should focus on efficient service delivery above all else as a provider of local public and quasi-public goods and services. According to this view, local government is not regarded as a representative entity in its own right, but simply as an instrument for meeting local needs through local services in the most cost-effective manner possible. This instrumentalist perspective on the function of local government in a federal system emphasises public policy reform aimed exclusively at enhancing the efficiency of local government, regardless of the effects this may have on local democracy. Put differently, Aulich (2005, 199) has noted that 'fiscal and economic issues override other social and political concerns' and 'tradition-bound or value-orientated forms of political and social organisation are replaced by purely instrumentally rational institutions'. Economic outcomes thus take precedence over political processes.

The chief implications of the 'local service delivery approach' have been described by Aulich (2005, 199). In the first place, Commonwealth and state government policy intervention in local government focuses overwhelming on operational efficiency. Second, policy intervention typically invokes legislative and regulatory criteria which promote uniformity in processes and outcomes across the local government sector, regardless of differences between local authorities. Finally, deliberative and participatory processes are thereby devalued, 'with top-down technocratic processes being more typical' (Aulich, 2005, 199).

It is clear that strong tensions exist between the two principal roles of local government, and these are exemplified in the diametrically opposed policy implications which flow from the local democratic and local service perspectives. For instance, Steyvers, Reynaert, De Cuerninck and Valckew (2006, 429) underscored this tension by distinguishing between 'output legitimacy' and 'input legitimacy'. In terms of their dichotomy, output legitimacy is achieved by providing 'effective and efficient public services', whereas input legitimacy derives from 'responsive government' attained by 'integrating citizens and providing space for participatory input' into local government decision-making. This dichotomy is illustrated in Figure 5.1.

Figure 5.1 serves to illustrate the contrasting value systems of the local democracy approach and the local service approach. The instrumentalist nature of the local service approach is apparent in its end-state objective of achieving greater economic efficiency, notwithstanding any negative impact on democratic process. For instance, even if clear local community preferences favour 'closer-to-the-people' small local councils, despite more costly service provision, according to the local service approach, 'top-down' state government intervention in the form of forced mergers would still be justified if it can deliver more cost-effective local services. By contrast, if full participatory democratic processes yield a collective preference for the provision of more costly local services, then this would be warranted under the local democracy approach, despite the additional cost.

Although Aulich (2005) juxtaposed the local democracy and the local service approaches as competing and mutually exclusive roles for Australian local government, it is possible to identify

Figure 5.1. Models of Local Government Reform

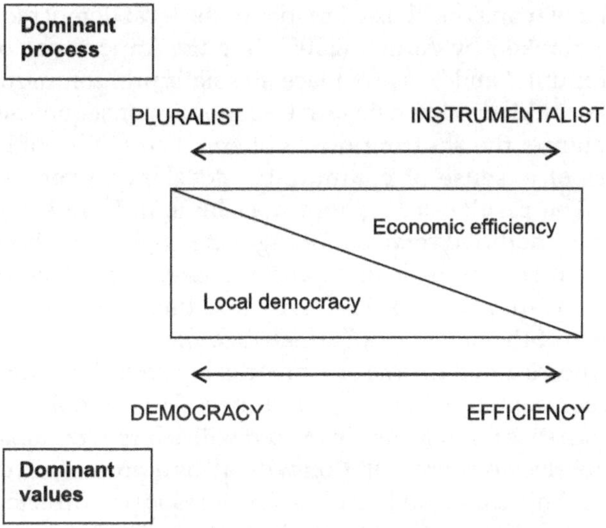

Source: Adapted from Aulich, 1999, 20.

characteristics of these approaches which embody overlapping and reciprocally reinforcing elements in contemporary local councils. For example, suppose a proposed forced amalgamation of several small councils with a single large municipality in a regional setting would result in lower per capita service provision costs across the new merged entity. Moreover, assume that the compulsory consolidation would shift council expenditure and employment away from the small councils towards the new large municipality. This would stimulate feedback loops between local democracy and the local service approaches. Thus, since small country councils are frequently a major employer in their respective local government areas, any move by council employees to the new amalgamated council centre would then induce powerful negative multiplier effects which could reduce population and decrease economic activity. This would in turn undermine the viability of public services and private firms, such as public schools and banks. In sum, equity concerns expressed through local democratic preferences can have deleterious efficiency consequences if they are ignored.

Second, if we consider characteristics of the local democracy approach overlooked by Aulich (2005), like the importance of 'sense of community' and 'sense of place' to small rural communities, then this could also have negative economic consequences. Thus, for instance, the shutting down of small councils could induce a loss of a 'sense of community' developed over the generations. The results of this loss may be manifested in a variety of ways: modified retail shopping patterns, lower school enrolments, sporting club closures and the like. These factors could negatively affect economic activity and thus the strength of the rate base of the newly amalgamated council.

Third, process and outcome are inextricably bound through democratic representation in local government. For example, if a small local council is forcibly amalgamated with a larger regional centre, then its elected representation will fall as a proportion of all councillors. This could well result in fewer resources directed towards the small council than towards the larger regional city. In addition, if local service preferences vary between the people of small and large councils, then the pattern of service provision can also shift, to the detriment of residents of small towns. These effects will be even more acute if electoral wards are abolished, since this may mean no representation at all for minority ratepayers living in sparsely populated areas on the outskirts of the new local government structure.

Finally, and perhaps most importantly, decisions regarding the use of scarce local government resources fall ultimately upon the shoulders of elected councillors. This means that any dysfunctionality in the process of decision-making by these elected representatives could have serious consequences in terms of resource allocation. For instance, council chambers riddled with conflict between individuals and groups sometimes result in gridlocked decision-making processes with dire economic effects. Similarly, corrupt conduct by councillors can subvert council decisions and result in the misappropriation of council funds. In these cases there is thus a direct link between political process and economic outcome.

In essence, it is thus clear that the local democracy and the local service approaches can overlap, which may affect the nature of trade-offs between the two perspectives. It follows that single-minded pursuit of economic gain, regardless of political process, can have unintended and negative economic effects. Political process thus cannot be entirely divorced from economic outcome.

The tensions between input legitimacy and output legitimacy, stressed by Steyvers, Reynaert, De Cuerninck and Valckew (2006), highlight the complexities involved in defining, identifying and promoting sustainability in local government compared with other organisational entities that do not have a dual role, such as private for-profit firms and public utilities. As we shall see, it implies that any meaningful approach to holistic sustainability must include both economic and political attributes (Kersting and Vetter, 2003).

5.4 Academic approaches to sustainability in local government

As we saw in Chapter 4 the various national and state inquiries into local government over the past decade focused almost exclusively on financial sustainability, with the partial exceptions of the Financial Sustainability of NSW Local Government Inquiry *Are Councils Sustainable?* (Allan Report, 2006) and the Local Government Association of Queensland *Size, Shape and Sustainability* Inquiry (LGAQ, 2006). It was argued that this proved problematic; it is not possible to define financial sustainability in local government with any degree of precision, and such an approach is far too reductionist, ignoring many other aspects of local government which can have decisive effects on its functioning, such as the inevitable tensions between local democracy and the imperatives of efficient local service provision. By contrast, the academic literature on sustainability in Australian local government is much more rounded, although still far from settled in its conclusions.

This small but growing academic literature on sustainability in Australian local government has three main strands. In the first place, some writers have critically examined the methods employed in the various national and state-based inquiries, rejecting the heavy emphasis on financial sustainability and instead proposing broader definitions of sustainability in local government (see, for example, Dollery and Crase, 2006). The major conclusions of this strand hinge on the argument that the accounting approach to sustainability adopted in the public inquiries is too narrow.

Second, scholars have considered the predictive capacity of KPIs as a means of diagnosing local council unsustainability adopted by some Australian local government jurisdictions (see, for example, Woodbury, Dollery and Rao, 2003). For instance, Murray and Dollery (2006, 59) investigated the approach used by the NSW Department of Local Government to classify individual councils as 'at risk' in that state. They concluded that while 'monitoring lists within NSW are created through an analysis of financial and corporate results', which purport to measure 'financial soundness', these lists were compiled on a 'subjective basis' and thus should be 'treated with a considerable degree of caution'. Moreover, many of the elements used in the lists represented discretionary factors over which councils could exercise little or no control, including rate capping and the 'application of restrictive regulations and statutes over user charges and fees'. Murray and Dollery (2005) argued that the Department employed KPIs drawn from its comparative performance tables constructed from information supplied by individual local authorities. In its assembly of 'monitoring lists', the Department assessed these indicators, as well as other information, to determine whether a council should be classified as 'at risk' or 'not at risk'.

Using statistical estimation, Murray and Dollery (2005, 332) assessed whether local councils deemed to be 'at risk' by the NSW Department of Local Government were really 'at risk' or whether have they had been classified as 'at risk' in error. Their results undermined claims for the accuracy of KPI analysis of local government viability and this led them to conclude that 'the findings of our paper suggest that those councils that have been publicly identified as "at risk" may in fact not be in a parlous financial state at all' (Murray and Dollery, 2005, 342–3).

The Murray and Dollery (2005, 2006) analysis has some interesting implications for the analysis of sustainability in local government. For instance, if KPI analysis is a poor predictor of actual council financial performance, then what factors can explain local government financial failure? Murray and Dollery (2005, 343) have contended that 'governance issues' appear to have been the most 'critical factors' in most recent NSW local government 'failure episodes'. These included 'failed entrepreneurial projects by councils or councils in partnership with private organizations; factional "infighting" amongst elected councillors and the attendant resignation of frustrated experienced professional staff; a preponderance of ill-informed and unwise elected councillors; poor quality professional staff, especially in rural and remote areas; and a lack of adequate internal controls'.

The analysis presented by Murray and Dollery (2005, 2006) attracted two main criticisms from Walker and Jones (2006). First, Walker and Jones (2006) argued that, in presuming published KPIs had formed the basis of the NSW Department of Local Government (DLG) 'watch list' of 'at risk' local authorities, Murray and Dollery (2005, 2006) had attacked 'a straw man', since the DLG had not relied exclusively on published KPIs, but in addition had used other sources of information. This proposition was accepted by Dollery (2006) in a rejoinder to Walker and Jones (2006). Second, Walker and Jones (2006) set out various technical criticisms of the econometric analysis by Murray and Dollery (2005).

While Walker and Jones (2006) had served to qualify the conclusions drawn by Murray and Dollery (2005, 2006), their major contribution lay in the development of an alternative approach to financial sustainability in Australian local government. The essence of the Walker and Jones (2006, 352) approach can be summarised as follows: 'if the basic operating objectives of local councils are to provide services to the community', then 'it follows that a relevant concept of council distress' would be 'an inability to deliver services at pre-existing levels'. In essence, financial sustainability can therefore be defined as the capacity of councils to continue the current level of service provision to their residents in the future. From the discussion in Chapter 4, it is apparent this definition differs from that deployed in the state-based inquiries based on the Access Economics approach. Dollery (2006, 360) argued that the Walker and Jones (2006) definition is defective since it assumes that '"yesteryear's" levels of service will be acceptable to "tomorrow's" local government community'. He noted further that 'it is easy to think of instances where this procedure will fail', citing the environmental regulation of local authorities and the continual 'raising the bar' that has taken place.

The third strand in the academic literature on sustainability in local government, which derives from welfare economics, has centred on the 'government failure' approach, which we examine below in section 5.5. In general, 'government failure' can be defined as the inability of a governmental entity or public agency to achieve allocative and productive efficiency. Numerous taxonomies of government failure have been proposed. For example, an early contemporary typology of government failure was advanced by O'Dowd (1978), who argued that there are three types of government failure: 'inherent impossibilities', 'political failures' and 'bureaucratic failure'. Along analogous lines, Dollery and Wallis (1997) set out a taxonomy containing three major forms of public sector failure: 'legislative failure', 'bureaucratic failure' and 'rent seeking'. Weisbrod (1978) advanced a quadrilateral classification which embraces 'legislative failure', 'administrative failure', 'judicial failure' and 'enforcement failure'. However, the most significant taxonomic contribution was made by Charles Wolf (1989) in his pioneering book *Markets or Governments* with his theory of 'non-market failure'.

Wolf (1989, 66) developed a four-fold taxonomy of non-market failure. First, 'internalities and private goals' refers to 'intra-organisational allocation and evaluation procedures' which determine distributional outcomes for public agencies and agency personnel alike. Although both market and non-market firms must perforce employ an 'internal version of the price system' for intra-firm resource allocation, market forces ensure that the 'internal standards' of private firms are strongly linked to the 'external price system', while non-market organisations may have internalities mainly unrelated to optimal performance. Examples of internalities are easy to find within the public sector and include the 'more is better' approach and the 'more complex is better' yardstick – both instances of Wolf's (1989) contention that 'Cadillac quality' is encouraged in public agencies.

Second, 'redundant and rising costs' denote that while market processes impose a relationship between production costs and output prices, this relationship is generally absent in non-market activity since at least part of the revenues of public entities may derive from non-commercial sources, like tax income. Wolf (1989, 63) has contended that 'where the revenues that sustain an activity are unrelated to the costs of producing it, more resources may be used than necessary to produce a given output, or more of the non-market activity may be provided than is warranted by the original market-failure reason for undertaking it in the first place'. Generous subsidies to 'elitist' performing arts far in excess of their popularity are a common example of this form of government failure.

'Derived externalities' refer to the 'side effects that are not realized by the agency responsible for creating them, and hence do not affect the agency's calculations or behavior' (Wolf, 1989, 77). Finally, Wolf (1989) incorporated adverse distributional consequences as a category of non-market failure. Hypothesising that there is 'an identifiable process by which inequities can result from non-market activities similar to inequalities flowing from market outcomes', Wolf (1989, 84) argued that non-market inequities characteristically occur in terms of power and privilege, whereas distributional market failures typically appear in income and wealth differences. Thus politicians and senior civil servants may secure preferential treatment in the administration of regulations compared with the general public.

5.5 Local government failure

In contrast to the substantial and predominantly public choice literature on government failure at state and federal levels (Mueller, 2003), little effort has been expended on governmental failure in local government. Despite this comparative neglect, it is possible to identify at least three taxonomic approaches to local government failure. British scholars Bailey (1999) and Boyne (1998) have advanced separate approaches to local government failure, premised on the belief that the problem of government failure is less apparent at the local government level than with state and central governments. By contrast, Dollery and Wallis (2001, 54–72) have argued that government failure is more widespread in local governance. They proposed a fourfold taxonomic classification of local government failure based on this presumption, comprising 'voter apathy', 'asymmetric information and councillor capture', 'iron triangles' and 'fiscal illusion'. Byrnes and Dollery (2002, 60) extended this taxonomy to include 'political entrepreneurship', applied it using evidence from NSW local government and found significant empirical support for the typology.

Voter apathy

An axiomatic proposition in public choice theory holds that, as a general rule, voting by citizens in elections does not represent rational conduct, in the sense that whereas the voting process is costly to the individual voter, the benefits associated with voting to that voter are negligible. Dollery and Wallis (2001) have identified five factors which contribute to higher voter apathy at the local level. In the first place, in local government systems such as the Australian state jurisdictions, voters do not view council elections as politically important events because local government conduct is severely constrained by state and Commonwealth governments. Second, even where local government elections occur along political party lines, with the attendant informational benefits for residents, many political candidates do not have a party affiliation at all, and party affiliations are typically much weaker than at higher levels of government. Third, local council elections often get scant attention from the news media. Fourth, Dollery and Wallis (2001, 57) have observed that 'because of their lower public profiles and complicated interface, governance and management roles are often confused in the eyes of many citizens, who cannot readily distinguish between elected representatives and professional public servants, making it difficult to assign responsibility for previous policy outcomes'. Finally, it is difficult to determine accountability in local government owing to the strong influence of higher tiers of government.

Asymmetric information and councillor capture

Dollery and Wallis (2001) have identified four factors which contribute towards the acute agency problem in local government. They contend that 'since the hands-on nature of their jobs means managers are bound to be much better informed than councillors, it seems likely that by manipulating the asymmetry of information to their advantage, managers can capture councillors and thereby achieve the policy outcomes they desire' (61). In contrast to state and Commonwealth politicians, local council representatives generally almost never have policy advisers, who can 'filter' information from senior managers. Well-informed bureaucrats can thus readily exercise 'agenda control'. Finally, 'selective behaviour' can play a significant role, where 'selective efficiency' represents a means by which 'bureaucrats control their master's choices by being efficient at the things they want to do, and inefficient at those they do not' (Wintrobe, 1997, 251).

Iron triangles

Iron triangles refer to the establishment of colluding relationships (or 'triangles') which can affect the disbursement of a local council's budget. Byrnes and Dollery (2002) argued that three factors make the problem of 'iron triangles' more acute at the local government level. First, given the comparatively sharp asymmetry of information at the local government level, as well as the tendency for local authorities to rely on standing committees to manage their operations, rent seekers can easily identify councillors with powers over specific functions and attempt to form alliances with them. Second, because council income is largely unrelated to the consumption of local public services, interest groups have an incentive to attempt the redistribution of service provision in their favour. Finally, due to the fragmented nature of local government, iron triangles might be expected to have a more decisive impact on expenditure, since small local authorities attract little scrutiny from the media.

Fiscal illusion

Fiscal illusion refers to the possibility that the costs and benefits of government activity may be consistently misconstrued by residents of a given fiscal jurisdiction. Of the five main types of fiscal illusion, Dollery and Wallis (2001) argued that two may apply especially strongly to local government: the 'fly-paper effect' and 'renter illusion'. The flypaper effect denotes the tendency for grants from higher tiers to increase council expenditure by a greater amount than an equivalent increase in revenue from other sources. This occurs as a consequence of the fact that ratepayers tend to view these grants as 'gifts' and ignore their associated tax liability increases. By contrast, renter illusion hinges on the proposition that, since local government revenue derives in substantial part from property taxes, only residents who own properties and pay rates will correctly estimate the tax-price of local public goods and services, in contrast to people who rent accommodation and thus do not pay rates directly. Since local government depends on rate revenue, it is thus especially susceptible to this kind of fiscal illusion.

Political entrepreneurship

The extravagant use of resources by 'political entrepreneur' councillors to capture the attention of voters to further their own political careers may lead to systematic allocative inefficiency in local government expenditure. Byrnes and Dollery (2002, 57) have contended that 'councils can be conceived of as breeding grounds for political entrepreneurs to not only capture the attention of political party officials at higher levels of government, but also of prospective voters in federal and state seats'. Three factors purportedly explain the greater magnitude of political entrepreneurship at the local government level. First, since local government typically has the largest number of elected representatives in a given polity, political entrepreneurship is likely to be correspondingly higher. Second, given voter apathy and media inattention to local government, politically ambitious councillors may embark on expensive and conspicuous projects to 'catch the eye' of voters. Finally, since national and state jurisdictions are typically spatially larger than local government areas, political entrepreneurs may need to provide public goods and services which benefit regions much larger than the local government area they represent.

While it provides some insights into the phenomenon of 'local government failure' and hence sheds at least some light on the broader question of holistic sustainability in local government, the Byrnes and Dollery (2002) typology has been criticised on the grounds that it considers only 'internal' factors, to the exclusion of the 'external' environment facing local authorities. For example, key fiscal considerations, such as the value of grants, revenue from rates and the like are ignored. In addition, demographic, spatial and other influences are entirely neglected. These weaknesses in the Byrnes and Dollery (2002) approach led Dollery, Byrnes and Crase (2008b) to develop a more comprehensive taxonomic system. They offered an instructive justification for pursuing a typological approach to sustainability in local government (Dollery, Byrnes and Crase, 2008b, 53):

> One way of approaching the design of a comprehensive conceptual framework for analysing the question of local government sustainability is to invoke the methodology developed in welfare economics. The famous market failure paradigm has long served as a fruitful technique for diagnosing the ills of competitive markets and an analogous conceptual framework in the form of the theory of government failure has performed essentially the same role in the analysis of public sector organisations (see, for example, Wallis and Dollery 1999)...What is therefore required is a typology of local government sustainability that simultaneously embraces both internal factors and external forces that impinge on the long-run sustainability of municipal authorities. A taxonomy of this kind could prove most useful in not only diagnosing the problems of contemporary Australian local government, but also in developing a prognosis and possible policy remediation.

The Dollery, Byrnes and Crase (2008b) taxonomy advances five main pillars of local government sustainability: demographic factors, council revenue, council expenditure, council financial management and council governance. In contrast to Byrnes and Dollery (2002), this approach combines elements of both the 'external' and 'internal' council environment.

Demographic factors

Dollery, Byrnes and Crase (2008b, 58) have contended that population trends have significant repercussions for the mix of local council services, income, infrastructure requirements and expenditure, as well as 'almost all other aspects of local governance'. They observed further that although 'local councils can exert some influence over population flows and population density directly and indirectly through efforts to attract or deter new residents (via planning regulations, local economic growth strategies and so forth), in the main, demographic characteristics should be considered "non-discretionary" variables in the sense that they lie beyond the control of individual municipalities'. The pervasive effects of demographic composition and population trends are obvious. For example, infrastructure needs are directly dependent on population, with changing population composition and size the critical factors determining infrastructure investment. Similarly, population density and population growth are key determinants of local government financial sustainability, an empirical reality demonstrated in the Allan Report (2006). Dollery, Byrnes and Crase (2008a, 58) noted that 'this report establishes that regardless of whether a given council was located in a metropolitan zone or a regional area in South Australia, the rate of growth in population appears to determine the extent of its operating deficit', with 'net financial liabilities also closely related to population growth', as well as population density.

Council revenue

Three main sources of income sustain Australian local government: property taxes, fees and charges, and intergovernmental grants. Compared with many other countries, this is a relatively limited range of revenue streams. In addition, Dollery, Crase and Johnson (2006) have pointed out that legislative restrictions exist on both revenue raising – in terms of property taxes and fees and charges – and developing new sources of funding, and they concluded that Australian local government finance has strong 'non-discretionary' elements over which local authorities have little control. In New South Wales these problems are compounded by the long-standing practice of rate-pegging.

As a major source of revenue for local councils, especially remote, rural and regional municipalities, the magnitude and nature of intergovernmental grants from higher tiers of government obviously falls entirely outside the control of local government. The phenomenon of cost shifting has relevance in this context, since hypothecated 'specific purpose' grants designed to encourage local council activity deemed beneficial by higher tiers of government are frequently either insufficient to cover the full costs of a given program or cease after a designated initial time period.

As we saw in Chapter 2, intergovernmental grants will doubtless continue to represent an important source of revenue as long as Australian federalism is characterised by vertical fiscal imbalance (VFI), under which a majority of taxation income is accrued by the Commonwealth Government but substantial expenditure occurs at lower levels of government. Over the recent past, direct Commonwealth grants to local government have emerged as an increasingly important source of revenue for local government, especially through the *Roads to Recovery (R2R)* Program (Lopez, Dollery and Byrnes, 2009). However, it has also become increasingly tied to specific projects.

The trend towards greater use of hypothecated grants reduces local government autonomy and raises questions about local democracy. In essence, tied grants weaken local government by diminishing its decision-making power, thereby undermining subsidiarity in Australian fiscal federalism.

Finally, all local government systems, including Australian local government, exhibit some degree of horizontal fiscal imbalance (HFI). HFI refers not only to different local authorities having different revenue-raising abilities, but also to the costs of local service provision varying between councils. As a consequence, striking differences in local service provision between different councils will emerge unless HFI is addressed. In the Australian milieu, this almost invariably means that people in remote, rural and regional local council areas will experience lower levels of service provision than their metropolitan cousins. In Australian local government systems, HFI has long been tackled through 'equalisation grants' by state-based local government grants commissions. However, Brooks (2006) has observed that the declining real value of these grants has threatened this system and engendered a growing differentiation in local service provision.

Council expenditure

The third element in the Dollery, Byrnes and Crase (2008a) local government sustainability taxonomy focuses on local government expenditure. In all Australian state local government jurisdictions, Departments of Local Government impinge upon council outlays in at least two ways. First, a great deal of expenditure is effectively mandated through state government regulation, not only requiring councils to deliver a range of specified services, but also stipulating service quality and mix standards. A second related problem in the cost structure of contemporary Australian local government resides in cost-shifting, a factor recognised by the CGC Review (2001), Hawker Report (2003) and Allan Report (2006). Although the pecuniary magnitude involved in cost-shifting is difficult to estimate with any degree of precision, it is undoubtedly significant. In the context of NSW local government, for example, the Allan Report (2006, 69) commissioned a survey which was found the impost of cost-shifting to be substantial.

Dollery, Johnson and Byrnes (2008) have argued that the central problem with cost-shifting is not the shifting of expenditure functions *per se* but rather inadequate accompanying funding. Indeed, it is often objectively rational for local government to conduct designated functions, like managing the local Rural Fire Service, given that local authorities usually possess more accurate information on local service preferences. The problem, however, is that sufficient matching funding is typically not transferred along with the functional responsibilities. It follows that unfunded or partial cost-shifting by higher levels of government results in many local councils being financially unsustainable over the long term.

Financial management

As we saw in Chapter 4, all of the state-based inquiries, as well as the national PWC Report (2006), documented an acute backlog in local infrastructure maintenance and investment in Australian local government. In the present context, it is worth stressing two dimensions of the problem. In the first place, these inquiries established that inadequate financial management, especially asset management, was a significant cause of this problem. Various recommendations were made. For instance, the Allan Report (2006) prescribed in detail the requisite characteristics of a satisfactory financial management system and how it should be implemented. The problems involved are onerous and include the thorny matter of valuing assets which cannot be sold. Second, the magnitude of the Australian local infrastructure problem is such that many local authorities will never be able to rectify it using 'own-source' revenue. This has stimulated a search for alternative methods of financing local infrastructure renewal, which are examined in detail in Part C of this book.

An accurate perspective on the genesis of the local infrastructure crisis must recognise that much local infrastructure was simply inherited by local government in the immediate post-WW2 era. This can explain why the local government revenue model was never designed to pay for its renewal. It can also explain why a substantial proportion of the current stock of local government infrastructure is reaching the end of its effective life at about the same time. While the size of the infrastructure renewal task is the subject of continuing debate, the much more important question of implementing systems to prevent future crises seems to have been neglected. The long-term sustainability of local government should thus rest on the management of renewed local infrastructure and not only on the funding of current asset renewal.

Governance

Whereas local government demographics, revenue and expenditure focus largely on the 'external' environment facing the local government sector, financial management combines features of both the 'internal' and 'external' context. By contrast, 'governance' is concerned mainly with the internal dynamics of local councils. This is warranted by the fact that the overwhelming majority of local council 'failure' cases – defined by the dissolution of local authorities by their state Departments of Local Government – are caused mostly by internal factors, in particular conflict-wracked elected councils. As we have seen, the Byrnes and Dollery (2002) fivefold typology of 'voter apathy', 'asymmetric information and councillor capture', 'iron triangles', 'fiscal illusion' and 'political entrepreneurship' encompasses many of the internal sources of local government unsustainability. In addition, Dollery, Crase and Grant (2011) have identified three critical dimensions of holistic local government sustainability: local democracy, local social capital and local capacity.

First, according to Dollery, Byrnes and Crase (2008b), local democracy refers to the manner in which local government can be differentiated from other levels of government. Thus, the very existence of local government itself implies that it will make policy decisions differently from higher tiers of government since it will accord much greater weight to local preferences. By contrast, if a given local authority fails to act on local preferences, then its fundamental *raison d'être* disappears and its ongoing sustainability as an 'independent' governmental entity comes into question.

Second, despite the conceptual problems plaguing the concept of 'social capital' (see, for instance, Quibria, 2003), in the municipal context Dollery, Byrnes and Crase (2008b, 62) have contended that social capital 'engenders a local civic awareness that manifests itself in community projects, ranging from local social associations and sports clubs to local business initiatives'. In addition, local social capital 'breeds a "sense of community" and a "sense of place" that derive from living in a small and distinctive local government area, with community size and community social capital therefore intrinsically linked'. They argued further that 'if a council does not play a positive role in facilitating the formation of social capital, its long-term sustainability must be called into question'.

Third, Dollery, Byrnes and Crase (2008b, 63) have observed that local government capacity affects local council sustainability. They argued that 'local government cannot command the respect of its constituents if it is unable to formulate agreed policy and implement decisions effectively'. In essence, local government capacity thus has three essential characteristics: 'functioning elected leadership', 'adequate administrative and technical expertise' and the facility to make 'autonomous decisions'. Taken together, these attributes of local government capacity are central to holistic local council sustainability.

5.6 Holistic sustainability in local government

At least two features of the evolution of the literature on local government sustainability and local government failure (see, for example, Dollery, Byrnes and Crase, 2008b, 63) are noteworthy in the present context. In the first place, it is instructive to observe the manner in which the concept of local council 'failure' has been gradually broadened from its initial emphasis on financial viability to a much wider array of factors. Second, it exemplifies a steady progression away from an exclusive concentration on 'internal' considerations, as displayed by Byrnes and Dollery (2002), towards a broader focus which includes 'external' variables, as shown by Dollery, Byrnes and Crase (2008b). This latter trend has continued. In particular, the tripartite constellation of local democracy, local social capital and local capacity was proposed by Dollery, Crase and Grant (2011) under their category of 'governance'. We now consider this in some detail.

Dollery, Crase and Grant (2011, 5) began their analysis by defining local government sustainability, observing that 'the concept of local government sustainability should extend beyond the narrow confines of financial sustainability or financial viability to include the vibrancy of local democracy, local social capital and local council administrative and technical capacity', where 'sustainability is taken to broadly refer to the ability of a local authority to function effectively over the long term'. However, they deliberately excluded 'environmental concerns' from this definition, since local government 'seldom has the legislative authority to make a decisive contribution to long-run environmental sustainability nor does environmental sustainability itself have an uncontested meaning'.

Dollery, Crase and Grant (2011, 11) set the scene for their subsequent discussion by posing the question: 'What are the chief elements of "community sustainability" (as distinct from financial sustainability) that comprise the essence of the local democracy approach?' In an attempt to answer this question they noted that 'several clusters of factors suggest themselves' and then pursued the Dollery, Crase and Grant (2008) trinity of factors by investigating local democracy, local social capital and local capacity.

Local democracy

Dollery, Crase and Grant (2011, 11) concentrated on the 'vibrancy of local democracy' since it 'engages maximum public participation' through 'local democratic processes' such as 'access', 'accountability', 'representativeness' and 'responsiveness'. They examined the various meanings which contemporary scholars have ascribed to the term 'governance', including Stoker (1998), Goodin (1996) and Keohane and Nye (2000), and concluded that governance is not the 'exclusive domain of governments themselves', but it 'also involves private organizations, nonprofit institutions, and a host of other social structures'. In addition, they pointed to the difficulties presented by the Denters and Rose (2005a, 6) 'dual challenge', which referred to 'an increase in citizen involvement' in local government at the same time as 'party-political links' have declined. This has seen the rise of 'different avenues for decision-making and citizen involvement'.

The measurement of 'local democratic vibrancy' yields substantial conceptual and empirical problems not yet fully resolved. In an effort to determine how these problems could be surmounted in practice, Dollery, Crase and Grant (2011, 13–14) considered the deliberations of two of the state-based public inquiries into Australian local government systems. For instance, in its *Systemic Sustainability Study,* WALGA (2006, 1–2) underscored the significance of 'good governance', which it defined as the 'ability of local government to operate with integrity and to assure the community that efficient and effective management is applied in the community interest'. By contrast, the Queensland *Size, Shape and Sustainability: Guidelines Kit* (LGAQ, 2006, Chapter 3, 20–1) provided various 'implicit measures of good governance', such as Indicator Category 4 (dealing with 'standards of governance') which had two specific indicators: (i) 'Decision Making and Management' which measured the 'level of competence' in 'corporate planning', 'risk management' and 'delegations' and (ii) 'Accountability' (concerned with how 'key activities' are accounted for and what systems and processes sustain this accountability), which also had two indicators: 'performance management' and the 'internal audit processes'. With respect to 'community of interest', it suggested the use of 'community surveys', 'current community engagement plans' and a 'community complaints register'.

Local social capital

Following Quibria (2003, 19), social capital refers to the process which 'creates social networks, fosters trust and values, sustains norms and culture and creates community'. Dollery, Crase and Grant (2011, 15–17) observed that, whereas 'little is known about the genesis of social capital', it bears a close relationship to a 'sense of community' and a 'sense of place'. While Coleman (1990, 302) perceived social capital as an instrumental variable in the sense that it made 'possible the achievement of certain ends that would not be attainable in its absence', Putnam (1993, 7) conceived of social capital as 'features of social organization, such as trust, norms, and networks, that can improve the efficiency of society by facilitating coordinated actions'.

At least two links exist between the performance of local councils and social capital. First, Putnam (1993) argued that local government performance was stimulated by high levels of social capital through the monitoring of council employees by members of the local community. This process proved effective since council employees interacted frequently with community members and cared about their own reputations. Put differently, social capital assists in overcoming free riding. Second, Putnam (1993, 2000), Aarts (1995), Knack and Keefer (1997) and other scholars have argued that various social forces, notably greater urbanisation, have induced a fall in civic participation and a consequent decline in the linkages between citizens and local government.

Some Australian empirical work has focused on social capital in regional and rural areas. For example, Woodhouse (2006) undertook a study of two regional centres and established that high levels of social capital boosted local economic development. Onyx and Bullen (2000), Sobels, Curtis and Lockie (2001) and Leigh (2006) have arrived at similar conclusions. However, as yet no Australian study has directly examined the relationship between local council performance and social capital.

Local government capacity

Dollery, Crase and Grant (2011, 17–19) have contended that local government capacity has two attributes. First, 'well-functioning elected leadership' is essential since 'anecdotal evidence suggests that the primary cause of the failure and ultimate dissolution of local councils by state governments lies in dysfunctional elected councils rather than financial distress and other problems'. In cases where local authorities are inundated by 'bitter personal animosities', ' "infighting" between councillors', 'intransigent factionalism' and 'disruptive meetings', the outcome can be 'policy gridlock', which can 'effectively stall the smooth running a local authority'. This results in a 'loss of public confidence' and a 'diminution of collaborative partnerships between community organizations and local government'. It follows that an evaluation of the long-term sustainability of local government must determine whether 'sound relations exist between both mayors and elected councillors and amongst elected representatives themselves'.

Second, 'sufficient administrative and technical expertise' is also vital. Whether or not an individual local authority has adequate administrative and technical expertise is obviously an empirical question and it is therefore amenable to measurement by means of performance indicators. For example, the proportion of vacancies for professional and technical staff provides a good basic yardstick. The Queensland *Size, Shape and Sustainability: Guidelines Kit* (LGAQ, 2006, Chapter 3) has sought to provide measurable estimates of council sustainability in human resources and its 'Human Resourcing' indicator included 'staff turnover rates'.

5.7 Concluding remarks

This chapter has presented the case for a broader conception of local government sustainability than the narrow and inadequately defined notion of financial sustainability hitherto adopted in Australian local government. In canvassing the evidence for a more inclusive definition of sustainability, the chapter has provided a synoptic review of the various strands of the literature on Australian local government which point to a wider 'holistic sustainability'. To this end, the chapter has considered the genesis of the term 'sustainability' in policy analysis in general, it has sketched the inherent tensions between local democracy and local government efficiency which complicate the question of sustainability in local government, and it has outlined the academic literature on the problem of 'sustainability' in Australian local government, the 'local government failure' approach to the problem and its various typologies of local government failure, as well as the three main components of holistic sustainability in Australian local government. While these arguments are far from conclusive, they nonetheless present a compelling case for moving beyond the confines of finance as a measure of sustainability.

A common theme running through the discussion of financial sustainability in Chapter 4 and holistic sustainability in this chapter has been the 'non-discretionary' nature of the external environment in which Australian local government is obliged to operate. This serves to illustrate a dismal truth about Australian local government: to a significant extent, its fate lies outside its own control. However, perhaps a silver lining in this otherwise rather bleak conclusion is that it obliges policy makers to recognise that, due to the predominantly 'non-discretionary' nature of the local government environment, there are distinct limits on the extent to which individual local authorities can be held responsible for their own long-term sustainability. In particular, given the acute vertical fiscal imbalance in Australian fiscal federalism, it is inevitable that higher tiers of government will always have to assist local councils financially, and in the short term this means that immediate local infrastructure crises will have to be resolved by means of extensive intervention by Commonwealth and state governments. Section C of this book thus concentrates on intergovernmental cooperation as the best means of resolving the infrastructure backlog.

PART C

Financing Australian Local Government Infrastructure

Chapter 6
Australian Local Government Finance

6.1 Introduction

Part B of this book considered the problem of financial sustainability in great detail from both conceptual and empirical perspectives. The analysis of financial sustainability in Australian local government shed a great deal of light on the policy conundrums facing local government policy makers, not least the existence of an immense and growing local infrastructure backlog. Part C of the book is devoted to an investigation of the various policy instruments which have been proposed as methods of tackling the local infrastructure shortfall. This chapter sets the scene for this discussion by providing a synoptic account of Commonwealth funding of local government in the era following the Second World War (WW2) up to the end of the Hawke/Keating period in the mid-1990s.

The chapter is divided into two main sections. Section 6.2 describes financial relationships between the Commonwealth and local government during the immediate WW2 and post-WW2 Labor administrations of John Curtin and Ben Chifley, through to the Whitlam, Fraser, and Hawke and Keating governments. Drawing on the work of the Commonwealth Grants Commission (CGC) and the National Office of Local Government (NOLG), as well as Mathews and Jay (1972) and Mathews and Grewal (1997), we find that the Australian local government sector has been treated to acts of largesse – especially under the Whitlam administration of the 1970s, for example – as well as comparative neglect under the Hawke and Keating governments. It is argued that funding for local government during this extended historical period has been unpredictable. The chapter ends with some brief concluding remarks in section 6.3.

6.2 Commonwealth infrastructure funding of local government

The Commonwealth Grants Commission (CGC) (1995, 108) has summarised the relationship between the Commonwealth and local government in the immediate post-WW2 era as follows:

> Ever since 1947, local government associations had been making approaches to the Commonwealth Government seeking access to direct federal funding. But the Government had consistently declined to accede to their requests, arguing that local government was a state responsibility in which the Commonwealth should not be involved.

The CGC (1995) was technically correct in asserting that the immediate post-WW2 Commonwealth administrations did not entertain *direct* financial transfers from the Commonwealth to local government bodies. Nevertheless, it is misleading to suggest that these administrations - specifically under Prime Minister John Curtin (1941–45) and then under Ben Chifley (1945–49) - as well as future governments, did not have an interest in the funding of local governments in any other way than through the states. On the contrary, the history of post-WW2 Commonwealth-local government financial relations is a partisan-political one, with Labor governments pursuing a strengthening of fiscal relationships between the first and third tiers of the Australian federation, primarily through the creation of regional governance structures within which local government representatives played varying, but sometimes important, roles and within which infrastructure funding, as a part of regional and national development, formed a significant part.

Kelly, Dollery and Grant (2009) characterised post-WW2 Commonwealth initiatives directed at the regions, and by implication at local government, in terms of what they labelled three 'generations'. The first of these was the 'Nation Building' initiative of the 1940s. The institutional core of this policy thrust lay in the Department of Post-War Reconstruction and Development (DPWR), first headed by Ben Chifley, then under Chifley's Prime

Ministership from July 1945 to the defeat of the Labor Party in 1949 by John Dedman. *Regional Planning in Australia*, the defining policy document of the DPWR, was published in 1949. It is instructive on the aims of the policy. Post-war reconstruction was to be 'directed toward the full development of the regions' resources in order to maintain the maximum population', with the accompanying policy objectives of natural resource utilisation and urban decentralisation aimed not just at economic growth, but also at resituating industry away from Australia's vulnerable coastline. The Preface to *Regional Planning* did not mince words in this regard:

> When, during 1942, invasion of Australia seemed imminent, plans for the organisation of government to meet the emergency revealed many difficulties, which showed that a regional organisation of government machinery was essential for strategic and defence needs' (DPWR, 1949, vii).

To achieve these goals, the Australian continent was divided into 100 administrative 'regions', represented by Regional Development Committees (RDCs). However, local government still formed the basis for these new administrative structures. Spatially adjacent local governments comprised the regions' boundaries and local government representatives made up approximately half of all RDC membership. Kelly, Dollery and Grant (2009, 175) observed that 'the number of council delegates reflected Commonwealth's belief that councils could break out from their straightjacket "wastebin" functions to regional cooperation on broader issues'.

Infrastructure was not perceived as a discrete category of policy development and funding. Rather, the DPWR (1949, 22–4) conceived of the regions in terms of three broad categories: (i) 'Physical Resources', further delineating these into specific types (climate, physiography, water, soils, minerals, vegetation, fisheries and land-use); (ii) 'Economic Resources', which included the demographic characteristics of the regions as well as economic indicators, such as employment, income and finance, and primary and secondary industries, and (iii) 'Social Resources', including residential housing stock, social facilities (hotels and halls, for example) and important items of infrastructure ('Public utilities and institutions'; 'Educational and cultural facilities' and services associated with health). These classifications were designed to form an inventory, or 'schedule of resources', rather than being the basis of any funding *per se*. Furthermore, if we examine Commonwealth Government outlays at the time (see, for example, Mathews and Jay, 1972), it is difficult to determine to any precise extent the quantum of funding directed toward this policy initiative.

However, despite this enthusiasm for regional economic development grounded in local government structures, and which clearly had as one of its goals the development of infrastructure (albeit broadly conceived), Kelly, Dollery and Grant (2009, 175–6) noted that the policy initiative foundered for three main reasons. First, there was a distinct lack of clarity and detail concerning the roles of regional plans themselves, in particular the relationships between regional planning bodies on the one hand and state and local authorities on the other. Second, local government simply did not have the capacity to move from the limited functions it had historically undertaken to incorporate broader activities, such as regional planning. Third, both local government and conservative elements of the Australian polity were suspicious of the role of the federally initiated regional authorities and their potential towards contributing to the further centralisation of the Australian federation, in an era of what Mathews and Jay (1972, 184–237) characterised as being marked by the 'consolidation of Commonwealth fiscal supremacy'. Following the 1949 federal election, the Menzies Government returned all regional policy to the states, and along with it the possibility that the Commonwealth would by-pass state governments to fund local authorities through regional structures (Kelly, Dollery and Grant, 2009, 175).

Two important characteristics of intergovernmental fiscal relations that emerged in the immediate post-WW2 era were to have lasting effects upon the fiscal capacity of Australian state and local government. The first of these was the appearance of high levels of vertical fiscal imbalance (VFI) in this era. To a significant degree this was a consequence of the enactment of uniform income taxation by the Commonwealth in May 1942, through which it assumed sole power to impose taxes on income for the duration of the war (plus an additional year), but which the Chifley Government extended indefinitely in 1946 (Dollery,

2002, 35). For example, Mathews and Jay (1972, 191) noted that in the financial year 1948/9 the Commonwealth collected 88% of total taxes levied, the states 8% and local government 4%. This contrasts starkly with the pre-WW2 era, especially measured as a proportion of national income. For instance, in 1938/9 the Commonwealth garnered 8.3% of national income, and state and local government together 7.2%. By 1948/9, the quantum had shifted to 21.8% and 2.9% respectively, with a concurrent increase in grants from the Commonwealth to state governments from 1.6% to 3.6% of gross national product (GNP) over the same period. However, this increase in grants to states still did not compensate for the loss of income tax. Mathews and Jay (1972, 193) argued that the increased VFI could be partly justified on the basis that the Commonwealth was still paying for Australian involvement in the war, principally through debt servicing and social service benefits. However, it did have the effect that 'state and local authorities increased their net indebtedness by a good deal more than the amount required to finance capital expenditure on public enterprises' (Mathews and Jay, 1972, 197). In other words, the states – and by implication, local governments – were "chasing their tails", particularly in terms of 'the war-time backlog of works and deferred maintenance expenditures and rapidly rising costs of government', a situation which, despite the continued operation of the National Works Council (which co-existed alongside the Loans Council and whose members were drawn from the participants in the Premier's Conferences) was not rectified until the 1970s (Mathews and Jay, 1972, 197).

The second element of the overall intergovernmental fiscal portrait at this time which was to affect future relations was that finance available on capital markets fell dramatically short of that required by the states (and thereby local government) for infrastructure spending. As a result, they became reliant upon 'special loans' from the Commonwealth which, together with Financial Assistance Grants (previously called tax reimbursement grants) and Specific Purpose Payments (defined arbitrarily by the Commonwealth and used frequently to provide infrastructure funding, formed the basis of state funding for approximately two decades. In this regard, Mathews and Jay (1972, 204) observed that 'in this way was established a pattern of borrowing which has continued virtually unchanged'. Furthermore, Dollery (2002, 35) noted that both special loans (which constituted 27–69% of public works and housing programs for all states between 1951/2 and 1957/8) and Specific Purpose Payments were tied grants.

The wholly secondary role that local government found itself playing in relation to state governments was reinforced during the entire period of the Liberal-Country Party Governments from 1949 to 1972, dominated by the 16-year Prime-ministership of Robert Menzies. In 1950 the first Menzies Government introduced significant reform to the personal income tax system, which Mathews and Jay (1972, 191) chose to characterise as 'tend[ing] to benefit higher-income taxpayers to a greater extent than low and middle incomes … also placing wages and salaries and other earned incomes at a disadvantage relative to other income recipients'. Nevertheless, due to indexed tax rates, tax receipts rose faster than GNP and the fiscal dominance of the Commonwealth continued, with the states finding it politically convenient not to seek own-source revenue and instead rely on the Commonwealth. The federal budget of 1951/2 did plan for a large surplus aimed at funding state public works programs, however this plan was thwarted by a subsequent collapse in commodity prices (Mathews and Jay, 1972, 200).

The main battleground of Australian fiscal relations continued to be fought over Commonwealth-state financial relations. Alongside continued dominance of the Loans Council by the Commonwealth, monies known as Special Grants, which existed alongside Specific Purpose Payments, increased in the areas of education (inclusive of those for universities), housing, and welfare and resource development. A significant recalibration of Commonwealth-state fiscal relations was implemented in 1959, with the introduction of Financial Assistance Grants (FAGs) (Mathews and Jay, 1972, 240) which was subsequently modified following the 1965 Premiers' Conference (Mathews and Jay, 1972, 243). Yet Special Grants continued to increase, from $16,652 million in 1959/60 to $23,680 million in 1970/71 (Mathews and Jay, 1972, 260).

It is striking from this synoptic portrait of intergovernmental financial relations from 1949 through to the 1970s to note that local government played a wholly secondary role in relation to state governments. During this time, all local governments were utterly reliant upon transfers from the states, alongside own-source revenue. For example, for the years 1948/9 and 1958/9, the *Australian National Accounts 1948-9 to 1964-5* recorded no direct transfers from the Commonwealth to local government. Furthermore, *National Income and Expenditure 1970/71* recorded no specific payments to local government, although in this iteration of national accounts figures the (former) categories of 'State Government' and 'Local Government' are aggregated to 'State and local authorities' (Mathews and Jay, 1972, 194, 230, 282 respectively). Writing at the end of this period, Mathews and Jay (1972, 291-2) reminded us of the plight of local government during this time:

> This problem of vertical fiscal imbalance relates not only to the division of powers and responsibilities between the top two layers of the Australian federal system, but extends to local governments. In many ways, local governments are beset by all the problems of the States as well as having special problems of their own. Because their actions are governed by the often outmoded provisions of State local government legislation, they lack even the nominal independence of the States themselves. Furthermore, their financial resources are to a very large extent confined within the limits of the revenues that can be obtained from property taxes and borrowing, which in turn are effected by legislative or executive decisions over which the local authorities have no control.

To this situation – which, as we have seen, crystallises the central problem of our discussion here – Mathews and Jay (1972, 292) added the observations that at that time, as now, local governments laboured with limited borrowing powers; that wholesale contractions in the economy could significantly affect their revenue base; and that rapid increases in demand for a range of services, to both property and people, impact upon them in conditions of horizontal fiscal imbalance.

Yet, as Megarrity (2012, 12) has recently documented, it was at this time that the Australian local government sector *writ large* was prompted into collective action in the face of these challenges. The Australian Local Government Association (ALGA) was formed in 1947. In a meeting with Prime Minister Menzies in 1959, the then ALGA President, RS Luke, argued that the

Commonwealth's post-war immigration policies, of both political persuasions, had burdened local government most and that the Commonwealth, with its position of fiscal supremacy, ought to assist. To this Menzies was quizzical, stating 'To go on involving the Commonwealth in matters over which it has no authority ... was in fact a great challenge to federalism because it would encourage concentration of power' (cited in Megarrity, 2012, 12). Megarrity (2012, 13) concluded that '[b]y the end of its time in office in 1972 ... the conservative Coalition had failed to develop clear local government policies'.

However, significant attempts at reform were afoot. In the second edition of its *History*, the CGC (1995, 108–9) took the story up in some detail:

> In the late 1960s the Leader of the Opposition, E. G. Whitlam, had adopted the idea of providing funds direct to local governing bodies to encourage developments which the states were unwilling to undertake. In 1971, the Australian Labor Party's Federal Conference adopted a policy of 'balancing the functions and finances of the Commonwealth, state and Local Governments to ensure adequate services and development of resources'. Part of this policy was to provide Commonwealth financial assistance to local government on the recommendation of the Grants Commission 'to remove inequalities in servicing proposed and developing suburbs, cities and regional centres'. Whitlam expounded the Party's policy in 1971 and 1972, emphasising that in providing access to the Commission for local government, the policy was also expected to encourage the formation of regional groups of local governing bodies.

This succinctly captures the nature of the ensuing Whitlam Government's approach to intergovernmental fiscal relations: namely that a reconfiguration of fiscal federalism, based on the identification and direct funding of regions by the Commonwealth, would aim to foster economic development, reduce inter-regional inequality of service provision and promote self-governance. Moreover, the funding was to be allocated on the basis of applications from individual regional groups, thereby seeking to foster cooperation at a regional level.

The final form of the legislation, which comprised an element of *The Commonwealth Grants Commission Act 1973* (and which superseded *The Commonwealth Grants Commission Act 1933*), saw approval for the registration of suitable regional organisations reside with the federal Minister for Urban and Regional Development, in consultation with the state Ministers of Local Government. Approved organisations could then apply for funding from the Minister overseeing the CGC (CGC, 1995, 109–10). Following consultation by the CGC in all state capitals and the drafting of its *First Report 1974 on Financial Assistance for Local Government* from late October 1973, the Minister for Urban and Regional Development approved a total of 68 groups of local governing bodies, including 889 councils, as eligible for direct funding. All these organisations then applied for funding by the end of 1973. These applications were followed with 'on site' hearings conducted by the CGC, during which applicants argued the case for funds, usually in front of one Commissioner (CGC, 1995, 111–14). Equity principles formed the basis for considering applications,[1] while a 'direct assessment' method was used which measured a region's taxable capacity, a 'standard' taxable capacity

1 A brief consideration of the equity principles underlying the allocation of financial assistance provides the flavour of the policy. According to the CGC (1995, 114), recommended financial assistance was designed to enable:

(i) All local governing bodies in a region to function, by reasonable effort, at a standard not appreciably below the standards of the local governing bodies in other regions;

(ii) A local governing body in a region to function, by reasonable effort, at a standard not appreciably below the standards of the other local governing bodies in that region or of the local governing bodies kin other regions; or

(iii) An approved regional organisation to function, by reasonable effort, at a standard not appreciably below the standards of other approved regional organisations or of the local governing bodies in other regions.

These horizontal equity principles have been designed to limit inter-regional differences. These principles also serve to demonstrate that while much has been made of the Whitlam Government's establishment of regional organisations as the basis of funding (see, for example, Kelly, Dollery and Grant, 2009), the policy came to rely upon local government bodies as the key point of comparison in measuring inequality, as well as being the key node of service delivery from which inequalities could be addressed.

and the expenditure differential that was necessary 'to enable the region to provide a "standard" range and level of services and amenities' (CGC, 1995, 115).

The vast majority of regional organisations which were formed in order to access Commonwealth monies, alongside several other programs implemented during the Whitlam period, faltered quickly after the ascendancy of the Fraser Government following the landslide federal elections in 1975. Local councils were suspicious of these organisations' claims to represent regions, and the states were also suspicious of them as a competing (albeit nascent) basis of authority, despite the fact that all monies derived from the Commonwealth under the scheme had to be channelled through state agencies in order that the legislation conformed to the Constitution (Kelly, Dollery and Grant, 2009, 178–9). However, Kelly, Dollery and Grant (2009, 177) argued that, while the entities initially responsible for funding applications disappeared, 'a new financial nexus between municipal and Commonwealth governments via the state governments provided a foundation for local government's maturity'. Further, as we shall see, while this nexus has been altered by various Commonwealth administrations, Financial Assistance Grants (FAGs) inclusive of a general purpose (or unallocated) component have remained an important component of local government revenue.

Table 6.1. Economic Transactions of Commonwealth, State and Local Governments 1969/70 to 1972/73 ($ million; select data)

	1969/70	1970/71	1971/72	1972/73
Commonwealth Government outlays:				
To state governments	1324	1671	1769	2065
To local governments	0	1	1	1
Total	**1324**	**1672**	**1770**	**2066**
Capital grants to other governments	312	555	627	707
Local government capital outlays:				
Total capital outlays	476.3	496.6	543.4	601.8
Total outlays	745.4	802.5	888.4	995.1
Outlays by purpose:				
Transport and communications	275	285	319	345
Total outlays as a % of GDP	**2.3**	**2.3**	**2.3**	**2.2**

Source: Compiled from Mathews and Grewal, 1997, Tables 1.3 (8), 1.9 (15) and 1.10 (16).

In chronological terms the change in funding arrangements has been marked. For example, Table 6.1 demonstrates the aptness of the 'poor cousin' designation of local government compared with state government before the changes introduced by the first Whitlam administration came into effect.

Table 6.1 demonstrates the negligible monies accrued directly by local government from the Commonwealth over the period 1969/70 to 1972/73 ($3 million), compared with $6829 million to the states. This was despite Commonwealth capital grants to other tiers of government growing steadily in nominal terms, from $312 million to $707 million over this time. Furthermore, the rate of increase of capital outlays by local government was less than the rate of increase in capital grants to other tiers of government by the Commonwealth: approximately 21% against approximately 56%, a rate slightly bettered by the rate of increase in expenditure on transport and communications by the local government sector itself over the same period (around 30%).

This picture alters radically when we consider figures spanning the period after the changes introduced by the Whitlam Government came into effect to include all payments for the period of his administration, summarised in Table 6.2. From the table we observe that the value of Commonwealth direct funding to local government increased from $2.2 million to $189.87 million over a period of four years. Second, the quantum of other payments through the states to local government also increased in nominal terms from $115.23 million to $157.65 million. Third, funding for 'human services' (ie, child care, aged care, employment grants and monies for Aboriginal advancement, for example) enjoyed significant growth during the period. Fourth, funding for roads increased and funding for other types of capital expenditure (including urban flood mitigation programs, the national sewerage program, funding for growth centres and area improvement programs, as well as regional organisations) expanded significantly, from zero in 1972/73 to $48.31 million in 1975/76, along with an increase in General Purpose Assistance Grants. It is here that we first see the genesis of Commonwealth infrastructure funding for local government, with a political sentiment directing this funding toward 'regions', inclusive of urban and rural areas.

Table 6.2. Commonwealth Payments to or for Local Authorities 1972/73 to 1975/76 ($ million; select and aggregated data)

	1972/73	1973/74	1974/75	1975/76
General purpose assistance for local government (paid through States)	--	--	56.34	79.91
Direct payments (various purposes[a])	2.20	5.96	53.86	109.96
Total	**2.20**	**5.96**	**110.2**	**189.87**
Other payments through the states				
Assistance for Exmouth Shire	--	--	--	0.15
Pre-schools and child care	--	0.28	2.59	7.34
Home care services	0.39	0.37	2.48	2.16
Senior citizens centres	0.38	0.69	1.47	3.41
Employment Grants	45.29	14.66	14.84	14.89
Aboriginal advancement	2.91	0.14	.15	0.60
Growth centres	--	0.30	2.54	3.66
Area improvement program	--	6.49	13.78	15.00
Urban flood mitigation	--	--	--	2.16
National sewerage program	--	2.00	25.55	25.15
Community facilities, Townsville	0.06	0.30	0.07	--
Capital assistance for leisure facilities	--	0.41	1.98	5.51
National estate	--	--	1.72	0.98
Roads	**65.00**	**67.45**	**68.06**	**75.28**
Urban public transport	--	--	0.14	0.62
Tourism development	--	0.05	0.40	0.60
Regional organisations assistance program	--	--	0.31	0.14
Total, other payments through states	**115.23**	**93.14**	**136.07**	**157.65**
Australia Assistance Plan	--	0.06	0.24	0.29
Northern Territory	1.34	1.62	.99	1.75
Total, all transfers	**117.79**	**100.78**	**247.50**	**349.55**
% of GDP	**0.26**	**0.19**	**0.38**	**0.46**

Source: Adapted from Mathews and Grewal, 1997, Table 4.8 (114).
Note: (a) These direct payments comprised very small amounts spent on a variety of human services, such as child care, aged care, employment, homelessness and Aboriginal advancement. They are aggregated for the purposes of Table 6.2.

Table 6.3. Economic Transactions of Commonwealth, State and Local Governments 1975/76 to 1982/83 ($ million; select data)

	1975/76	**1976/77**	**1977/78**	**1978/79**	**1979/80**	**1980/81**	**1981/82**	**1982/83**
Commonwealth Government outlays:								
To *or through* State governments	5415	6104	7217	7857	9079	10290	11382	13195
To local governments	97	4	7	12	12	17	19	25
Total	**5512**	**6108**	**7224**	**7869**	**9091**	**10307**	**11401**	**13220**
Capital grants and advancements to other governments	2939	2822	2771	2611	2466	2610	2640	3284
Local government grants received	397	521	523	548	599	758	823	961
Local government capital outlays								
Total capital outlays	1174	1194	1330	1427	1538	1385	1641	1662
Total outlays	1924	2052	2331	2568	2871	3189	3724	4166
Outlays by purpose:								
Transport and communications	663	651	717	777	813	876	1010	1124
Total outlays as a % of GDP	**2.5**	**2.3**	**2.4**	**2.4**	**2.3**	**2.3**	**2.3**	**2.4**

Source: Compiled from Mathews and Grewal, 1997, Tables 6.3 (186), 6.9 (213) and 6.10 (214).

It is thus clear that the Whitlam Government broke from the past and recast the relationship between the Commonwealth and local government. Mathews and Grewal (1997, 212) observed that, by contrast, 'local government finances were relatively stable' over the entire period of the Fraser Government from 1975/76 to 1982/83. However, the Fraser administrations nevertheless maintained a funding regime to local government similar to that set down by the Whitlam administrations. The broad shape of these arrangements is outlined in Table 6.3.

Several points can be gleaned from Table 6.3. First, *prima facie* the value of Commonwealth Government outlays directed to local government fell from 1976/77 onwards. However, grants received by local government continued to increase, from $397 million in 1975/76 to $961 million in 1982/83. This putative contradiction is resolved when it is recalled that under the New Federalism Policy initiated by the first Fraser Government, significant monies were directed to local government '*through* state governments' (emphasis added), the total quantum of which increased significantly over the course of the Fraser Government, from $5415 million in 1975/76 to $13,195 million in 1982/83. Second, despite the Commonwealth severely curtailing direct grants to local government following 1975/76, this funding stream had nevertheless reached $25 million by 1982/83. Third, total capital outlays for local government only rose incrementally over the same period (from $1174 million to $1662 million). Moreover, as a proportion of total capital outlays, they fell significantly, from 61% in 1975/76 to 40% in 1982/83. Finally, the 'transport and communications' category of all local government outlays – a key indicator of infrastructure spending – almost doubled in the same period, from $663 million to $1124 million. Mathews and Grewal (1997, 212) could thus characterise local government finances as being 'relatively stable' during this period. While this is accurate, it does not emphasise sufficiently what clearly was a time of consolidation of intergovernmental transfers to local government in the post-Whitlam era, albeit with a significant proportion of the monies directed through the states.

Other significant changes can be discerned by examining Commonwealth Government payments to or for local government by type over the period of the Fraser Government, depicted in Table 6.4. Various trends can be observed in this table. In the first place, despite the legislative changes in funding arrangements and an initial decrease in direct payments for 1976/77 and 1977/78, local government continued to be the recipient of an increased quantum of direct payments in nominal terms. Second, with regard to payments made through the states for specific purposes, the categories of funding were significantly narrowed during the Fraser period, and there were significant changes to particular types of funding. For example, while aged care and community care services continued to receive increasing support from the Commonwealth, childcare did not; all employment grants monies delivered through the states ceased from 1976/77, alongside the Australia Assistance Plan. Third, funding for roads continued to increase, from $75.28 million in 1975/76 to $172.61 million in 1982/83. However, other avenues of infrastructure funding ceased, such as flood mitigation and monies previously allocated for the national sewerage plan. Finally, while Commonwealth payments to local government as a percentage of gross domestic product (GDP) ebbed to 0.31% in 1977/78 and 1979/80 and did not reach the 0.45% it had done under Whitlam, it had nevertheless stabilised at 0.39% in the last years of the Fraser Government.

In addition to these changes, three important adjustments to policy affected infrastructure funding at the local level. First, intergovernmental fiscal arrangements were altered with the introduction of the New Federalism Policy, under which a system of income tax sharing took the place of Financial Assistance Grants introduced by the Whitlam Government. Under the new tax-sharing arrangements, both the states and local government were given a specified quantum of personal income tax. Local government was allocated assistance based on (i) a weighted percentage of per capita grants and (ii) equalisation grants, both of which were paid through the Grants Commissions of the states (as opposed to the CGC). Over the course of the Fraser administrations, changes to the personal income tax allocated to local government yielded what Mathews and Grewal (1997, 263–4) described as 'very large increases in general assistance revenue for local government': 23.6% in 1979/80, 35.6% in 1980/81, 16.6% in 1981/82 and 21.0% in 1982/83.

Table 6.4. Commonwealth Payments to or for Local Governments 1975/76 to 1982/83 ($ million)

	1975/76	**1976/77**	**1977/78**	**1978/79**	**1979/80**	**1980/81**	**1981/82**	**1982/83**
General purpose assistance for local government	79.91	140.00	165.33	179.43	221.74	300.79	350.87	424.49
Direct payments (various purposes[a])	106.50	13.41	14.17	17.37	15.93	21.68	27.19	43.57
Total direct payments	**186.41**	**153.41**	**179.5**	**196.8**	**237.67**	**322.47**	**378.06**	**468.06**
Other payments through the States								
Aged care and community services	5.57	6.59	7.10	7.15	8.87	9.77	8.82	13.63
Preschool and child care	7.34	7.68	7.94	1.65	4.74	5.66	5.03	4.90
Employment grants	14.89	–	–	–	–	–	–	–
Urban services	53.68	20.26	5.47	2.36	1.58	0.77	0.30	0.41
Roads	**75.28**	**87.02**	**116.95**	**124.19**	**131.42**	**141.87**	**167.31**	**172.61**
Other	0.29	0.17	0.11	0.35	0.35	–	–	2.92
Total other payments	157.04	121.71	137.56	135.71	146.97	158.06	181.45	194.47
Australian Assistance Plan	0.29	–	–	–	–	–	–	–
Northern Territory	1.75	1.96	2.56	–	1.88	2.45	2.80	3.86
Total other payments	**345.48**	**277.08**	**319.63**	**332.51**	**386.52**	**482.98**	**562.31**	**666.39**
Total, all transfers	**531.89**	**430.49**	**499.13**	**529.31**	**624.19**	**805.45**	**940.37**	**1134.45**
% GDP	**0.45**	**0.32**	**0.34**	**0.31**	**0.31**	**0.34**	**0.35**	**0.39**

Source: Mathews and Grewal, 1997, Table 8.13 (303).

Note: (a) These direct payments comprised very small amounts spent on a variety of human services, such as child care, aged care, employment, homelessness and Aboriginal advancement. As such, they were aggregated for the purposes of this table.

Table 6.5. Economic Transactions of Commonwealth, State and Local Governments 1982/83 to 1994/95 ($ million; select data)

	1982/83	1983/84	1984/85	1985/86	1986/87	1987/88	1988/89	1989/90	1990/91	1991/92	1992/93	1993/94	1994/95
Commonwealth Government outlays:													
To state governments	13195	15135	16618	17867	15912	17020	17351	18624	19563	20456	21420	22309	23440
Onpassed through state governments	0	0	0	0	3426	2718	3860	4163	4535	5155	5439	5972	6751
To local governments	25	33	57	94	87	89	81	97	97	155	190	185	196
Total	**14120**	**15168**	**16675**	**17961**	**19425**	**19827**	**21292**	**23274**	**24195**	**25766**	**27049**	**28466**	**30387**
Capital grants and advancements to other governments	2226	2793	2166	3246	3300	3089	3093	3556	4357	3721	5290	3863	3188
Local government grants received	961	1240	1361	1360	1389	1531	1573	1652	1647	1742	2142	1930	1915
Local government capital outlays													
Total capital outlays	1662	1682	2015	2224	2383	2470	2661	3293	2098	2773	2897	2706	2715
Total outlays	4166	4490	5114	5624	6081	6482	7010	8225	8354	8257	8601	8169	8245
Outlays by purpose:													
Transport and communications	1124	1255	1414	1551	1639	1692	n.a.	1887	2078	2100	2273	2220	2112
Total outlays as a % of GDP	**2.4**	**2.3**	**2.4**	**2.3**	**2.3**	**2.2**	**2.1**	**2.2**	**2.2**	**2.1**	**2.1**	**1.9**	**1.8**

Source: Mathews and Grewal, 1997, Tables 10.3 (408), 10.13 (458) and 10.14 (459).

Table 6.6. Commonwealth Payments to or for Local Governments 1982/83 to 1993/94 ($ million)

	1982/ 83	**1983/ 84**	**1984/ 85**	**1985/ 86**	**1986/ 87**	**1987/ 88**	**1988/ 89**	**1989/ 90**	**1990/ 91**	**1991/ 92**	**1992/ 93**	**1993/ 94**	**1994/ 95**
General purpose assistance	424.5	461.5	488.9	538.5	585.6	641.5	668.8	689.5	711.4	726.1	748.3	751.1	745.6
Roads assistance	172.6	208.1	213.2	215.3	221.5	250.5	267.4	277.9	287.3	326.7	347.2	333.3	325.7
Aged/disabled and community services	27.4	12.9	25.0	56.5	51.9	57.0	54.5	73.7	82.5	87.1	106.8	29.2	32.5
Children's services	20.4	27.5	45.9	58.1	68.9	80.6	81.9	80.3	76.6	136.1	152.8	162.8	197.3
Housing grants	–	–	1.3	6.0	6.4	5.7	4.4	9.2	11.9	16.0	23.5	–	–
Local capital works	–	–	–	–	–	–	–	–	–	–	**297.2**	**50.4**	**0.1**
Community employment program	–	114,5	168.2	123.0	75.2	48.4	2.7	–	–	–	–	–	–
Aerodrome local ownership	14.3	16.5	15.5	14.6	9.3	10.3	29.6	9.5	12.6	24.2	22.9	2.0	–
Natural disaster/relief/ flood mitigation	–	3.7	3.1	5.0	3.4	3.6	8.4	15.5	103.7	421.0	331.7	–	–
Other	7.2	2.0	7.4	16.1	9.2	8.1	10.1	3.6	2.9	0.9	9.8	3.9	11.9
Total	**666.4**	**846.7**	**968.5**	**1033.2**	**1031.5**	**1105.6**	**1122.9**	**1159.3**	**1288.9**	**1738.1**	**2040.2**	**1332.6**	**1313.2**
% of GDP	**0.4**	**0.4**	**0.4**	**0.4**	**0.4**	**0.4**	**0.3**	**0.3**	**0.3**	**0.4**	**0.5**	**0.3**	**0.3**

Source: Mathews and Grewal, 1997, Table 12.10 (603).

Second, following long-running discontent on the part of the states that the Loans Council exercised too much control over infrastructure spending by limiting state extra borrowing on the domestic capital market, it was decided at the 1977 Premiers' Conference that overseas borrowing by semi-government authorities would be allowed for major infrastructure projects. The Loans Council still retained significant oversight of these financial arrangements. However, the policy shift did allow other avenues of credit to be sought. This was taken advantage of primarily by state-based electricity utilities. While this relative fiscal autonomy came as a relief to some government entities requiring capital for infrastructure spending, Mathews and Grewal (1997, 285–6) nevertheless forcefully argued that this policy shift had adverse systemic consequences for infrastructure funding *per se* and the Australian economy more generally:

> The combination of tight controls over ordinary borrowing programmes and free reign to electricity borrowing in the market sector guaranteed a misallocation of resources within the public sector, just as the combination of severe Loans Council restrictions on the level of public sector borrowing and free access to the capital market resulted in a misallocation of resources between the public and the private sectors...
>
> Thus it was that, after 1976/77, the Fraser Government started the Australian economy down the slippery slope of public sector capital depletion and financial deregulation, policies which were taken up with great enthusiasm, and with damaging results for both the public and the private sectors, by Treasurer and Prime Minister Keating in the succeeding Labor governments.

To place culpability for Australia's ensuing and systemic infrastructure funding problems in the hands of one policy adjustment by the Fraser Government in 1977 – which then set the tune for subsequent policy changes – seems odd. While it does not fall within our present purposes to fully investigate this claim by Mathews and Grewal, it is at least worth mentioning this perspective in our synoptic review of infrastructure funding in the post-WW2 era.

The third change to infrastructure financing arrangements which occurred during this period was that, rather than go "cap in hand" to the Loans Council or seek finance in the limited domestic market or oversees, the states developed alternative instruments to fund infrastructure spending. For example, the Queensland Government began requiring mining companies to lodge security deposits for the use of existing infrastructure. These security deposits were then used to fund infrastructure renewal and recouped by the Queensland Government through the fees paid by the mining companies to use the its railways (Mathews and Grewal, 1997, 287). Other funding arrangements implemented by the states included 'leveraged and financial leases, sale and leaseback arrangements, trade credit, deferred payments and repayable front-end capital contributions' (Mathews and Grewal, 1997, 287). It thus seems that "necessity was the mother of invention" when it came to the states seeking additional funding.

An interesting similarity in federal government funding of local governments can be found between the Curtin and Chifley Governments on the one hand and the Whitlam Government on the other. Both were centrally concerned with economic development and spatial redistribution in their attempted reconfigurations of Australia's federal relations, with the latter more successful than the former. Furthermore, consecutive Whitlam administrations deployed significant resources toward these broader policy goals, a situation which was not significantly rescinded during the course of the Fraser Government.

In contrast to this *largesse* lay the approach adopted under the Hawke and Keating administrations. Table 6.5 provides a portrait of intergovernmental financial relations for the 13-year Hawke-Keating period, while Table 6.6 provides a portrait of Commonwealth payments to local government for the same period.

Table 6.5 underlines the incremental nature of increases to both state and local government funding from the Commonwealth in nominal terms over the 13-year period. For example, all outlays to both lower tiers of government increased from $14,120 million in 1982/83 to $30,387 million in 1994/95. A similar nominal increase occurred in the amount of grants received by local government; from $961 million in 1982/93 to $1915 million in 1994/95. The only marked increase took place in the category of direct transfers from the Commonwealth to local government which occurred from 1991/92 onwards. Mathews and Grewal (1997, 426) suggested that, whereas much of this increase in funding was allocated for capital works, following the release of the *One Nation Statement* in February 1992 it was aimed at the 23 council regions which were experiencing high levels of unemployment. It was thus targeted at unemployment alleviation rather than infrastructure improvement as a discrete policy goal. Moreover, it is apparent from Table 6.5 that total local government outlays declined significantly as a proportion of GDP (from 2.4% to 1.8%). In addition, the ratio of local government capital outlays to total outlays declined from approximately 40% in 1982/83 to 33% in 1994/95, representing a clear de-prioritisation. Local government spending generally and, within this, spending on infrastructure had become a less significant element of Australian government outlays as a whole.

This portrait is reinforced by a consideration of all disaggregated Commonwealth payments to local government in the same period, represented in Table 6.6. The categories for direct payments were streamlined compared to those in both the Whitlam and Fraser governments (see Tables 6.2 and 6.4 respectively). Mathews and Grewal (1997, 457) observed that these grants fell relative to GDP (as did grants to the states). Furthermore, funding for roads and general purpose assistance only increased nominally over the 13-year period, with 'local capital works' benefitting only in the two years 1992/93 and 1993/94 as a result of monies announced in the *One Nation Statement*. Mathews and Grewal (1997, 589) concluded that funding for 'housing and community amenities, transport and industry assistance ... fell in real terms', while funding for child services increased from $20.4 million to $197.3 million (by 967%) over the same period.

Mathews and Grewal (1997) also offered some interesting observations on the general approach of the Hawke and Keating Governments towards relations with local government, as well as highlighting some specific policy settings that had a direct impact on the federal government's funding of local government infrastructure. First, they divided the approach of the consecutive Labor administrations into three phases. From 1982 for a period of approximately two years, the initial Hawke Government was in the main consultative about mooted reforms. Yet this mode of interaction with both local and state governments lacked sincerity. For example, commenting on attempts at tax reform during this period, Mathews and Grewal (1997, 522) argued that while 'taxation reform in a federation cannot be meaningfully considered if state and local taxes are totally excluded', they observed that 'this is precisely what happened' at the National Tax Summit held in 1995. From 1986 to 1999, they argue that (then) Treasurer Keating presided over a 'period of confrontation and domination of the states by the Commonwealth', where the states were 'stunned by the ruthlessness of the cutbacks' to both grants received and permitted borrowings, justified by the overarching goal of reducing public sector indebtedness. Mathews and Grewal (1997, 523) contend that from 1990 the Commonwealth 'softened its fiscal stance towards the states' due to the achievement of budget surplus 'in the three years leading to 1989–90'. However, this did not alter the fact that 'the burden of fiscal restraint' had been shifted to the states, which saw payments to them reduced from 9.6% of GDP in 1983/84 to just 7% in 1989/90. Furthermore, whereas some significant reforms requiring state cooperation were introduced during this latter phase, not the least of which were the initiation of the Council of Australian Governments (COAG) in May 1992 and the implementation of the National Competition Policy in 1995, Mathews and Grewal (1997, 525) noted that, dating from the beginnings of this period:

> Prime Minister Keating's actions soon indicated that he was more interested in maintaining and extending the Commonwealth's fiscal dominance than in reforming intergovernmental financial arrangements, and all progress towards cooperation … ended. From this point, Commonwealth participation in cooperative arrangements was only forthcoming if the Commonwealth was prevented by constitutional restraints from acting unilaterally and therefore needed agreement by the states to its policy proposals.

In addition to these shifts in its overall stance, Mathews and Grewal (1997) made several other observations concerning changes to federal and local government financial arrangements over this period. First, the Commonwealth introduced a 'global limits approach' to borrowings, where ceilings were set for all borrowings by all state and local governments. While initially proposed as negotiated limits on borrowing, to be introduced only for a trial period, from the 1985 meeting of the Loans Council the global limits approach was mandated as the new technique for oversight of borrowings, through which the Commonwealth effectively set limits on the amount of capital that could be raised by the states and local government. The Commonwealth went so far as to threaten to reduce Queensland's FAG payments if it did not agree to a global limit on its borrowings in 1988 (Mathews and Grewal, 1997, 595–6).

Second, the Loans Council changed its methodology for calculating the limits of global borrowing, from one which was based on population-based formulae to one where the quantum of loans was calculated *after* state and local governments had nominated their projected loan requirements. The *prima facie* justification for this was that it allowed the Commonwealth to better coordinate the allocation of capital and risk, particularly where sub-national authorities were engaged in public-private partnerships. In effect, it was yet another restriction on the availability of capital. Mathews and Grewal (1997, 599) pointedly observed that 'the whole approach [was] an exercise in fiscal restraint, with the major emphasis ... being placed on reduction in budget deficits and reduction in government outlays, rather than on the goals of reducing unemployment, fostering growth and *reversing the rundown of the public infrastructure*' (emphasis added).

Third, local government received some relief from these grant and borrowing regimes primarily through an indexing of both Financial Assistance Grants and roads grants as an element in the *Local Government (Financial Assistance) Act 1991* (Cth). In addition, changes following the recommendations of the National Inquiry into Local Government Finance, headed by Professor Peter Self, which presented its report in October 1985, witnessed moves toward greater fiscal equalisation between local governments (see, for example, Aulich, 1999). However, the 13-year trend of the reduction in grants to local government in real terms – particularly in relation to capital – alongside the restrictions on borrowing, "hollowed out" local government capacity for infrastructure renewal, requiring policy action by the ensuing Howard and Rudd governments.

6.3 Concluding remarks

This chapter has set the scene for Part C of the book, which concentrates on the analysis of different methods of funding the local government infrastructure backlog in Australian local government by examining the historical foundations for the genesis of the infrastructure shortfall. While discussion centred on the evolution of the financial relationship between the Commonwealth and local government under the federal administrations of Curtin, Chifley, Menzies, Whitlam, Fraser, Hawke and Keating, and the role of this relationship in the origins of the contemporary infrastructure crisis, it should be noted that other factors also contributed to the problem, not least the expansion of the ambit of local government service provision in the post-WW2 era.

Although emphasis in this chapter naturally fell on questions of Commonwealth policy towards local government and regional development, the contribution of the structure of Australian fiscal federalism should not be forgotten. Part A of the book considered this thorny problem in depth. Whereas Chapter 2 looked at the aggregate dimensions of Australian fiscal federalism and its attendant twin problems of vertical fiscal imbalance and horizontal fiscal imbalance, Chapter 3 provided a detailed investigation of local government expenditure, including outlays on infrastructure, local government revenue, Financial Assistance Grants, and the allocation and distribution of funds to local government. This analysis underlined the fact that, without additional sources of revenue, local government would inevitably experience financial hardship in the absence of transfers from higher tiers of government.

Formidable constitutional and political obstacles stand in the way of the reform of Australian fiscal federalism to better accommodate the expanding functional responsibilities confronting local government. This necessarily implies that, as a matter of pragmatic realism, in the short term other measures be instituted to help ameliorate the local infrastructure backlog. Part C of this book considers the most promising policy instruments for this purpose. Chapter 7 thus critically evaluates a federal government infrastructure fund, Chapter 8 assesses the establishment of an Australian municipal bond market and Chapter 9 tackles municipal banking as well as a Commonwealth bond bank.

It is concluded that a bond bank represents the best feasible method currently available for dealing with the local government infrastructure shortfall. This policy prescription requires qualification lest it be mistaken for a panacea. It is thus critical to add the caveat that whereas a bond bank will increase the availability of funds and lower the costs of borrowing for all local authorities, regardless of size and financial stature, it will not enhance the ability of local councils to repay loans. Only the addition of some new source of income to the revenue arsenal of local government will address its ultimate ability to pay.

Chapter 7
Commonwealth Government Infrastructure Fund

7.1 Introduction

This chapter considers the case for financing the Australian local government infrastructure backlog through a federal government infrastructure fund. A fund of this kind has recently been suggested as a possible approach to funding what the Finance Working Group of Infrastructure Australia (Infrastructure Australia, 2011a, 13–15) described as 'nationally significant' infrastructure. However, the Finance Working Group's examination of this policy option was cursory. Indeed, it even failed to distinguish between infrastructure funds and infrastructure banks. While we concern ourselves with municipal banking and municipal bond banks in Chapter 9, this chapter examines a federally financed local government infrastructure fund.

The chapter is divided into five main sections. Section 7.2 provides a synoptic description of the *Roads to Recovery* (R2R) program launched by the Howard Government as a recent example of direct Commonwealth funding of local government infrastructure. Section 7.3 sets out the case for a federally financed local government infrastructure fund, drawing primarily on the work of Dollery, Byrnes and Crase (2007). Section 7.3 also juxtaposes this model with the actual workings of Infrastructure Australia, a statutory body initiated by the Commonwealth in 2008, and argues that, in its current form, Infrastructure Australia is functionally distinct from a local government infrastructure fund since it has a largely advisory role concerning infrastructure designated as 'nationally significant' (Infrastructure Australia 2008, 12). Section 7.4 critically evaluates the case for a federally financed local government infrastructure fund. The chapter ends in section 7.5 with some brief concluding remarks.

7.2 Roads to Recovery and the nation building economic stimulus plan

7.2.1 The Roads to Recovery (R2R) program

In Chapter 6 we saw that, alongside the real reduction in Commonwealth funds to local government under the Hawke and Keating Governments, the same period had also witnessed a significant change to the mix of local government outlays, away from the traditional 'services to property' focus towards a more 'services to people' focus. In its *Review of the Operation of the Local Government (Financial Assistance) Act 1995*, the Commonwealth Grants Commission (CGC, 2001) found that, although expenditure on roads had remained the largest single item of expenditure across all Australian local governments, its comparative importance had nevertheless declined from approximately half of all expenditure in the 1960s to around one quarter in the 1990s. This change in infrastructure expenditure is illustrated in Figure 7.1.

In Figure 7.1, we observe that expenditure on 'Transport and Communications' had contracted significantly as a percentage of overall local government outlays in the last two years of the Keating Government. Furthermore, alongside a general decrease in Commonwealth spending over the first two budgets of the Howard Government for financial years 1996/97 and 1997/98, local government outlays in the category of 'transport and communications', inclusive of roads, continued to ebb at historically low levels.

In the face of this historically low funding regime, political pressure was brought to bear by the local government sector. For instance, the Australian Local Government Association (ALGA) commissioned two reports that presented a strategic case for Commonwealth funding of local roads, while the state local government associations argued that their member councils had taken steps to upgrade their asset management capabilities. These steps culminated in the inaugural National Roads Summit, held in Moree in March 2000 (DOTARS/ALGA, 2003). In response to the concerns raised at this conference, in November 2000 the

Figure 7.1. Australian Local Government Outlays by Purpose 1992/93 to 2005/06

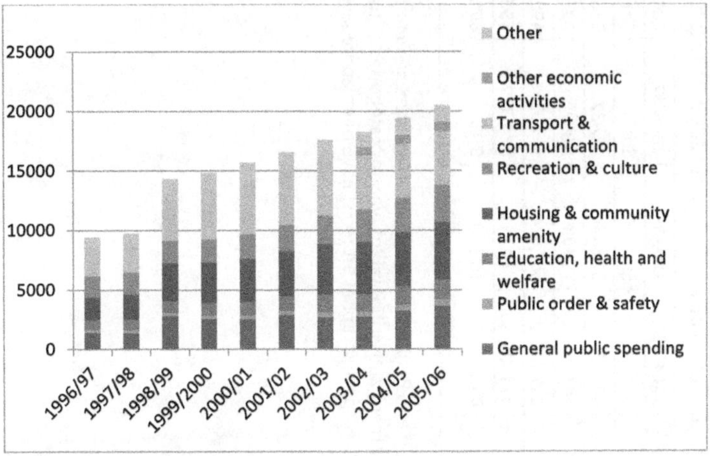

Source: Department of Transport and Regional Services, *Local Government National Report* (DOTARS, various years). Data for 2004/05 sourced from Australian Bureau of Statistics, *Government Finance Statistics* (ABS, 2012b), 32, 'General Government Expenditure by Purpose; Local'.

Howard Government announced a new road expenditure plan, known as *Roads to Recovery* (R2R), later rebadged 'Austlink'. The Commonwealth decided that the R2R Program should operate under simple administrative arrangements in order that councils minimise administrative costs and devote funding to road works. Moreover, it was argued that by allowing local decision-making, a flexible system was ensured with local councils prioritising projects according to their own circumstances (DOTARS, 2006). Although the Commonwealth had previously provided funding to local government, particularly through Financial Assistance Grants (FAGs), the R2R program was unique because the grants were provided directly to local authorities from the federal government, thereby bypassing state and territory governments (Dollery, Pape and Byrnes, 2008).

Table 7.1. Commonwealth Government direct payments to local governments (aggregated current and capital expenditures), R2R/Austlink payments and R2R/Austlink payments as per cent of all direct payments 2000/01 to 2007/08

Payment Type	**2000/01**	**2001/02**	**2002/03**	**2003/04**	**2004/05**	**2005/06**	**2006/07**	**2007/08**
SPPs	$m	$m	$m	$m	$m	$m	$m	$m
Current	70,545	79,728	2,000	56,030	60,916	87,884	68,432	52,284
Capital	7,223	6,522	2,018	11,942	444	15,108	2,867	8,150
R2R/Austlink	33,661	416,339	276,986	300,000	249,922	607,624	303,030	496,140
Total direct payments	**111,429**	**502,589**	**281,004**	**367,972**	**311,282**	**710,616**	**374,329**	**556,574**
R2R/Austlink total as % of total direct payments	30%	83%	99%	82%	80%	86%	81%	89%

Source: Figures for 2000/01 to 2007/08 were derived from Department of Transport and Regional Services, *Local Government National Reports* (DOTARS, various years), Specific Purpose Payments (SPPs) direct to local government authorities tables. Various categories of current and capital expenditure (for example, spending on aged care and childcare, as well as specific capital projects) have been aggregated for the purposes of Table 7.1.

The R2R program was set to run between 1 January 2001 and 30 June 2005, entailing a tranche of $1.2 billion, $850 million of which was to be spent in rural and regional Australia (DOTARS, 2002). Local councils were required to register with DOTARS. Initial funding was triggered by the submission of a schedule of works. For each financial quarter thereafter, councils were required to submit a report on work carried out, including details of all expenditure and an updated schedule of anticipated works. The difference between these two financial accounts was then credited to the particular council in question. In effect, the Commonwealth made advance payments to councils for road work yet to be carried out. To guard against the possibility of R2R funding being expended on outlays other than road construction and maintenance, as well as to measure the impact of the program, local authorities were required to report annually, in considerable detail, on how the funds were spent.

The first iteration of R2R was followed by several other tranches of funding from the Commonwealth, all directly to local governments. The quantum of these funds from 2007/08, their assignation as current or capital expenditures, and R2R/Austlink payments as a percentage of total direct payments to local government, are presented in Table 7.1.

Several points can be made with respect to Table 7.1. First, for financial years 2000/01 to 2005/06, R2R funding was categorised as a component of *current* direct grants to local government. Other current direct grants funding included, for example, childcare, aged care, disability services and specific Commonwealth-funded programs, such as the *Strengthening Tasmania* program. Second, as a proportion of both current and capital outlays to local government, R2R funding represented a significant sum for these years. Third, when R2R was subsumed under Austlink (which consisted of funds designated to programs other than R2R, but for which R2R comprised the vast majority of allocated funds), it was designated to the category of *capital* outlays, of which it formed an overwhelming share, as in fact it did of all direct Commonwealth funding to local government (81% over 2006/07 and 89% over 2007/08). Beyond the direct funding from the Commonwealth to local governments represented in Table 7.1, under the Rudd and Gillard Governments, a further $350 million annually was allocated for roads funding from 2009/10 through to 2013/14 (DITRDLG, 2012). The question thus arises: To what extent has R2R/Austlink assisted in ameliorating the funding backlog for roads?

In Chapter 4, we saw that a host of national inquiries estimated the magnitude of the infrastructure funding gap that Australian local government faces (see, for example, PWC Report, 2006). In their *Report on the Roads to Recovery Programme,* the Department of Transport and Regional Services (DOTARS) and the Australian Local Government Association (ALGA) produced an estimate of the funding gap in relation to roads (DOTARS/ALGA, 2003), reproduced in Table 7.2.

Table 7.2. Gap between Local Roads Renewal and Expenditure 2004–2009

State	Length of the national local road network (%)	Estimated annual local road renewal shortfall ($ m)
NSW	22.3	$156
VIC	20.0	$176
WA	19.0	$61
SA	11.6	$66
Total	**72.9**	**$459**
Australia (estimated)	**100**	**$630**

Source: Adapted from Department of Transport and Regional Services and the Australian Local Government Association, ***Report on the Roads to Recovery Programme,*** (DOTARS/ALGA, 2003, 7).

These estimates drew upon several state-specific studies, including the 2001/02 NSW Department of Local Government's council annual reports, the June 2002 Victorian Auditor General's Report *Management of Roads by Local Government,* the Victorian Office of Local Government Department of Infrastructure's *Facing the Renewal Challenge* report (1998), the Western Australian Local Government Association's *Assets and Expenditure* report (2000/01) and the South Australian Government's *A Wealth of Opportunities* report. DOTARS/ALGA (2003) then extrapolated this information to estimate a $630 million national shortfall in local government road funding. It also noted that beyond its five-year projections, work covering Victoria and South Australia had estimated that the gap in funding would increase due to rapidly ageing road stock (DOTARS/ALGA, 2003).

At first glance, the accumulative quantum of funds directly allocated to local government under R2R and subsequent programs (see Table 7.2) would appear to ameliorate the infrastructure funding gap with respect to local road stock, particularly if we assume that the DOTARS/ALGA (2003) estimate of the gap was sound. However, this conclusion over-simplifies the nature of the problem. The DOTARS/ALGA (2003) report is instructive in this regard. Council spending on roads can be decomposed into four categories: (i) maintenance (which is essentially an operating expense for the road asset), (ii) renewal (necessary expenditure brought about by the life-cycle of the asset), (iii) desirable improvement to existing road stock (in some instances required for safety reasons) and (iv) expenditure on new road assets. The 2003 review of R2R found that 'most of the … funding was spent on the existing asset with approximately half being allocated to renewal and the other half to upgrading the existing road to a higher standard' (DOTARS/ALGA, 2003, 9). In other words, while R2R has assisted in the achievement of one policy goal - the maintenance and renewal of the existing road network - and reducing the renewal cycle from 55 to 47 years (according to the DOTARS/ALGA Report), the other policy goal, which the DOTARS/ALGA Report defined as extending the 'existing sealed road network to meet to meet increased community expectations' (DOTARS/ALGA, 2003, 9) is still beyond the funding relief provided by R2R. In fact, only 5.9% of R2R funding up to 2003 was spent on new assets, while 46.3% was spent on 'reconstruction, rehabilitation and widening (on existing roads)', while the remainder of funds was spent on other activities (eg resealing, bicycle paths, drainage structures). Furthermore, in its examination of 343 instances of R2R funding, 'Economic Development' was offered as a reason for funding in only 30 cases, as against 'Safety' (113), 'Transport Efficiency' (86), 'Social/Equity' (59) and 'Asset Management' (DOTARS/ALGA, 2003, 16–17). Moreover, no comprehensive evaluation of funding under the Austlink program has yet been undertaken, nor of the R2R funding from 2009/10 onwards. However, taking into consideration the fact that the monies involved for each financial year are roughly equivalent to those in the first years of the program (see Table 7.2), it seems reasonable to suppose that these continued funds would still be directed principally at maintenance rather than on improving infrastructure, 'in line with community expectations'.

In this context the primary point is that even with the acts of financial largesse from the Commonwealth to local governments under the R2R and Austlink programs, local governments are still "chasing their tails" in terms of renewing their roads infrastructure and more particularly in attempting to provide new roads infrastructure for projected increases in population and as an element to continued economic prosperity. Importantly, the same can be said of other acts of financial largesse which have flowed from the Commonwealth to local governments under the Rudd and Gillard Labor administrations, for example those designed to curb the effects of the 2008 Global Financial Crisis (GFC). In his opening address to the 2010 annual meeting of the Australian Council of Local Governments, the then Minister for Infrastructure, Transport, Regional development and Local Government, Anthony Albanese, highlighted the accumulated additional $1.1 billion that had been directed toward local government since the 2008/09 federal budget (Albanese, 2010). However, again these monies were acts of largesse on the part of the Commonwealth and as such cannot be defined as an element of the sustainable financing of local government and local government infrastructure requirements. We will return to this point in the concluding remarks of this chapter.

7.3 The case for a Commonwealth asset fund

Against the reality of intermittent direct Commonwealth funding to local government detailed thus far in Chapter 6 and Chapter 7 of this book, Dollery, Byrnes and Crase (2007) mounted a case for what they labelled a 'Commonwealth Infrastructure Asset Fund', modelled partially on the experience of R2R. Their arguments comprised four main parts. First, they provided an account of the nature of Australian local government responsibilities in relation to infrastructure. Second, they briefly examined other proposed solutions to the problem and rejected these solutions. Third, they put forward a case for a Commonwealth-funded infrastructure fund. Finally, they sketched the institutional design for such a fund. We examine these components of their argument in turn.

7.3.1. Local government infrastructure

Dollery, Byrnes and Crase (2007) argued that any generic definition of local government infrastructure ought to recognise that it comprises varying asset types alongside a variety of roles for councils. Drawing from the *Local Government National Report 2004-05* (DOTARS, 2006) they observed that 'local government plans, develops and maintains key infrastructure for its communities', which includes 'local roads, bridges, footpaths, regional aerodromes, water and sewerage (in Queensland, regional New South Wales and Tasmania), stormwater drainage, waste disposal, public buildings, parks, recreational and cultural facilities' (Dollery, Byrnes and Crase, 2007, 5). Local government 'also has planning responsibilities that affect provision of infrastructure, whether by government or by business' that encompass 'town planning, land rezoning, subdivision approval, development assessment and building regulation' (Dollery, Byrnes and Crase, 2007, 5).

While it may seem trite to reiterate a basic definition of local government responsibilities for infrastructure, this definition stands in stark contrast to the way that infrastructure funding has been conceived under the various federally funded programs outlined in section 7.2 (ie, as a specific type of asset – for example, roads). Further, Dollery, Byrnes and Crase (2007) emphasised that every council has a differing combination of infrastructure requirements and, as a consequence, particular infrastructure financing requirements determined by various factors, including geography, demography and the extent to which local councils had absorbed the costs of functions previously undertaken by other tiers of government. Identification of the particular infrastructure responsibilities of each council is thus a complex task.

Second, Dollery, Byrnes and Crase (2007) argued that any attempt to determine the value of infrastructure would be intrinsically difficult. Similarly, while the *Local Government National Report 2004-05* had estimated the (then) value of local government infrastructure at approximately $170 billion, inclusive of $50 billion in land, $12 billion in buildings, $80 billion in local roads and $103 billion in what it termed 'other construction infrastructure', any estimate of the value of infrastructure had to take into account 'five distinct types of infrastructure expenditure' (Dollery, Byrnes and Crase, 2007, 6). These five types they classified as (i) entirely new assets, (ii) current assets requiring regular maintenance, (iii) backlog maintenance (such as that discussed with respect to the R2R program in section 7.2), (iv) asset renewal expenditure, which they defined as 'funds that aim to reinstate an asset to its original state or replace an asset when its economic life is exhausted, and (v) so-called 'asset enhancement', where 'an asset 'is boosted beyond its original intended service capacity' (6). Furthermore, they argued that, due to the complexity of different types of infrastructure spending, all local councils ought to have in place an asset management system 'capable of accommodating … the entire life of the asset, not least asset finance, asset acquisition, asset registration, asset accounting, asset operations, asset maintenance, asset renewal, asset enhancement, and asset disposal' (6).

Third, Dollery, Byrnes and Crase (2007) argued that the problem of measuring infrastructure requirements was further complicated by the fact that, at the time, different jurisdictions had different regulatory and monitoring structures dealing with assets. They cited the Allan Report's (2006) observations that local governments were not required to rigorously report on their infrastructure assets, that in many instances they did not allow for depreciation and, as a result, they significantly underestimated the size of the infrastructure renewal problem. In addition, Dollery, Byrnes and Crase (2007) noted (as we saw in Chapter 4 of this book) that other state-based inquiries, including the WALGA (2006) Report and the South Australian Financial Sustainability Review Board's *Rising to the Challenge* Report (FSRB, 2005), had identified similar problems to that of New South Wales in their respective jurisdictions.

Fourth, Dollery, Byrnes and Crase (2007, 8) argued that any account of the crisis facing Australian local government infrastructure ought to acknowledge that 'specific categories' of local governments were more acutely affected, especially 'small rural shires with large spatial jurisdictions' which operated with declining own-source revenue due to dwindling population bases. Against this background, they suggested that three overriding conclusions could be drawn: (i) most councils have an infrastructure backlog problem, but that the nature of the problem differs between councils; (ii) asset management and reporting is typically poor, to the extent that accurately measuring the scale of the problem might prove impossible, and (iii) small rural shires face the most significant infrastructure backlog problems.

7.3.2 Proposed solutions

Dollery, Byrnes and Crase (2007) briefly examined four proposed solutions to the problem which had been put forward by inquiries into local government sustainability from 2003. While the recommendations of these inquiries, along with those of several others, were described in depth in Chapter 4 of this book, in this context we consider the arguments of Dollery, Byrnes and Crase (2007). First, they noted that the Commonwealth House of Representatives Standing Committee on Economics, Finance and Public Administration report, *Rates and Taxes: A Fair Share for Responsible Local Government* (Hawker Report, 2003), contained two 'Recommendations' in this regard. Recommendation 9 proposed that 'local government bodies be required to audit the state of their infrastructure', employing 'a nationally accepted methodology' and 'provide status reports to the Commonwealth Grants Commission to be used as criterion for Financial Assistance Grants'. Recommendation 10 argued that Specific Purpose Payments (SPPs) to local government (which we have documented extensively in Chapter 2 of this book, as well as in section 7.2 above) be conditional on the states not reducing their effort at local government reform generally. Dollery, Byrnes and Crase (2007, 9) also observed that the Hawker Report (2003) suggested five methods of funding the infrastructure shortfall: (i) by increasing tied federal funding of local government infrastructure for a specific period; (ii) by increasing local government's own revenue-raising capacity; (iii) by increasing private sector involvement in the form of investment; (iv) by allocating 20% of fuel taxes to fund a continuing R2R program; and (v) by adopting a whole of government approach to infrastructure funding.

Placing to one side Dollery, Byrnes and Crase's (2007) assessment of the recommendations of the Hawker Report (2003), we consider their examination of the recommendations of the South Australian FSRB report, *Rising to the Challenge* (FSRB, 2005). Of these, Dollery Byrnes and Crase (2007, 9) argued that they were squarely focused on the issue of 'financial governance as the key to tackling both the infrastructure problems … as well as the larger issue of financial sustainability'. This was done by (i) amending the South Australian *Local Government Act (1999)* to include a standard definition of sustainability focused on long-term financial performance; (ii) introducing standard key financial indicators, inclusive of those measuring outlays on renewals and replacements of existing assets and net borrowings; (iii) providing a definition of capital expenditure sustainability which would serve as a qualitative benchmark for all infrastructure funding activities; (iv) stipulating that councils value their non-financial assets annually; (v) requiring that council annual reports distinguish between the renewal and replacement of existing assets and the acquisition of new assets in their annual reports, alongside an annual estimate of the infrastructure backlog; and (vi) requiring that all councils adopt a standard set of 'best practice' principles for financial reporting. Finally, the FSRB (2005) recommended that (vii) councils make 'prudent use' of borrowing to finance the infrastructure backlog.

Dollery, Byrnes and Crase (2007) examined the recommendations of the Independent Inquiry into the Financial Sustainability of NSW Local Government (Allan Report, 2006). They noted that four (from a total of 49) recommendations dealt with councils' approach to the infrastructure backlog: (i) Recommendation 6, which argued for the state government to provide 'strong incentives' for all councils to adopt total asset management systems within three years; (ii) Recommendation 7, that overall funding of councils should be increased by $900 million per annum, derived from a variety of sources (intergovernmental grants, cost savings by councils and higher rates, fees and charges); (iii) Recommendation 8, 'which called for each municipality "to fully cash-fund its depreciation within three to five years and dedicate such funds exclusively for asset renewals" '; and (iv) Recommendation 9, that the state government shoulder increased responsibility for regional and shire roads, particularly in instances where local authorities could not afford to maintain them.

Dollery, Byrnes and Crase (2007) considered the argument of Beresford-Wylie, Watts and Thurairaja (2006) that the private sector ought to be 'enlisted' to address the financing of the infrastructure backlog, principally with the implementation of various types of public-private partnerships (PPPs). Dollery, Byrnes and Crase (2007) immediately identified several problems with the arguments of Beresford-Wylie, Watts and Thurairaja and of PPPs more generally, including the legal implications of such arrangements (see also Dollery, Grant and Crase, 2010) and the lack of availability of suitable projects at the local level. Furthermore, they distilled the arguments of the Hawker (2003), FSRB (2005) and Allan (2006) reports and of Beresford-Wylie, Watts and Thurairaja (2006) into three observations. First, all four analyses were 'in complete agreement' that 'local infrastructure renewal, maintenance and investment are unsustainable on current trends and that decisive action is warranted' (Dollery, Byrnes and Crase, 2007, 11). Second, the Hawker (2003), FSRB (2005) and Allan (2006) reports had all emphasised that asset management had to be addressed. Third, both the Hawker (2003) and Allan (2006) reports had emphasised that other funds had to be found, and that these funds ought to come from multiple sources, including from local government itself.

It was precisely the need for more funding, and the requirement that it be garnered from a variety of sources, that Dollery, Byrnes and Crase (2007) highlighted in their assessment of all four studies. However, they also noted that while the Hawker (2003), FSRB (2005) and Allan (2006) reports had contended that local government borrowing ought to be viewed as part of the solution, paradoxically none of these three major inquiries had adequately explained how local government borrowings would alleviate - rather than worsen - the overall financial sustainability of local government. More pointedly, they observed that all four reports 'ignore[d] the fact that ... the Australian public is ill at ease with borrowing by local councils' (Dollery, Byrnes and

Crase, 2007, 12) – an instinct that proved correct in the wake of the 2008 GFC (see, in particular, Jones and Bowrey, 2010).

7.3.3 Case for a federal infrastructure fund

Dollery, Byrnes and Crase (2007) listed four reasons for a Commonwealth Government asset fund. First, state governments have proved both unwilling and unable to pass on substantial increases in Commonwealth funds to local government, despite enjoying a significant windfall in revenue through the flow of GST funds from 2000/01 onwards. Further, they argued that even if real increases in intergovernmental transfers could be observed in some jurisdictions (which in fact is very difficult to determine due to the lack of transparency surrounding allocations of funds from the various state government Grants Commissions), these real increases had to be seen in relation to the cost-shifting of functional responsibilities onto local government by both their state and federal counterparts – a fact that the Commonwealth Grants Commission (CGC, 2001) had documented extensively and which the Hawker Report (2003) had also considered in detail.

Second, Dollery, Byrnes and Crase (2007) argued that, while state governments had consistently returned large budget deficits, by contrast the Commonwealth had managed to achieve operating surpluses over several financial years, thereby demonstrating its fiscal capacity to prudently allocate funds for the purposes of addressing the local government infrastructure backlog.

Third, directly funding local councils would introduce the possibility that monies could be allocated according to uniform national guidelines and thus more thorough accounting practices should be introduced, especially in infrastructure management, such as those stipulated by the International Infrastructure Management Manual (IIMM). This in turn would produce nationally consistent data on local government infrastructure more generally, a positive externality of the federally-based fund which would reap benefits in other areas of decision-making and institutional design.

Fourth, Dollery, Byrnes and Crase (2007) observed that the theory of fiscal federalism offered a sound defence of such an allocation of funds on the grounds of both equity and efficiency. In terms of equity, it is naturally desirable that all local government areas enjoy adequate infrastructure (or at least do not suffer under a burgeoning infrastructure backlog). In terms of efficiency, an obvious consequence of having improved infrastructure for all local government areas is that allocative efficiency is improved within those areas and to adjacent jurisdictions.

In addition, Dollery, Byrnes and Crase (2007) specified *a priori* observations concerning the design of such a fund. For example, the Hawker (2003), FSRB (2005) and Allan (2006) reports had all concurred that the most heavily burdened councils in terms of an infrastructure backlog were rural councils with small populations but large infrastructure responsibilities. However, the assumption that this type of council ought to receive a greater portion of infrastructure funding might be misplaced, since the management of infrastructure financing in these councils could be poor; caution would be necessary with respect to the design of such a fund and the selection of the specific type of grant that would be used to distribute funds (Dollery, Pape and Byrnes, 2008). Moreover, drawing on the work of Dollery, Crase and Johnson (2006, 81), Dollery, Byrnes and Crase (2007) offered six criteria for the determination of needs-based grant system design: (i) that the need in question must be common to all jurisdictions, (ii) that the needs must be capable of being accurately measured, (iii) that the relationship between any one particular indicator of need and the need being met by the expenditure must be verifiable, (iv) that indicators must not be manipulable by either the recipients (local governments) or the grant allocating body, (v) that any chosen indicator ought not be prone to large fluctuations and (vi) that limited covariance, or dependability, should exist between indicators. While Dollery, Byrnes and Crase (2007) added that these stipulations for the criteria of needs-based grant systems were difficult to achieve in total, they nevertheless formed useful guidelines for the implementation of such a system.

7.3.4 Operational aspects of a federal infrastructure fund

Finally, Dollery, Byrnes and Crase (2007) turned their attention to the operational elements of a federal infrastructure asset fund. While they suggested that part of the appeal of such a fund was founded on the success of the R2R program, they noted that R2R had relied upon an extensive pre-existing database of national road stock, upon which funding allocations could be based. As we have seen, such a database in the case of local government infrastructure is sorely lacking. Dollery, Byrnes and Crase (2007, 16) also noted that a similar funding scheme – the Australian Government Water Fund (AGWF) – had operated in the absence of comprehensive information on national water resources. The National Water Commission, the administering body of the AGWF, had issued a 'call for proposals' for funding from the community at large. The proposals were subsequently collated, ranked and assessed by the Commission, and funding was awarded.

Dollery, Byrnes and Crase (2007, 17) observed that this scheme was not without its disadvantages – such as funding applications being costly for applicants – although they also noted several advantages. In 'making a case' for funding, councils would produce evidence-based reasons, a process which would, they argued, serve to 'crystallize' the specific allocation of funds sought. Further, they argued that this approach would diminish the moral hazard inherent in grants from higher to lower levels of government. Finally, they argued that a federally-financed local government fund ought to be administered by the (then) Department of Transport and Regional Services, which – conveniently – housed the National Office of Local Government, and they concluded that while 'more detailed work is required, particularly on the mechanics of the fund and the selection of beneficiary councils, we submit that the case for such a fund remains strong' (Dollery, Byrnes and Crase, 2007, 18).

As we have seen in Chapter 2, in 2008 the Commonwealth Government initiated a statutory corporation within the [then] Department of Infrastructure, Transport, Regional Development and Local Government (the present Department of Infrastructure and Transport) under Minister Anthony Albanese. This statutory corporation is known as Infrastructure Australia. However, as the discussion in Chapter 2 also noted, Infrastructure Australia is not an infrastructure fund. We turn now to clarify its operations in more detail.

7.3.5 Infrastructure Australia

At first sight, Infrastructure Australia looks remarkably like an infrastructure fund of the kind proposed by Dollery, Byrnes and Crase (2007). For example, it receives submissions from both state and local government bodies (Infrastructure Australia, 2011c). In addition, it has produced several reports, including the *Infrastructure Finance Reform: Issues Paper* (Infrastructure Australia, 2011a) which considered methods of financing infrastructure, such as infrastructure bonds and infrastructure funds, although unfortunately in very limited detail.

However, looks can be deceptive. In fact, section 5(1) of the relatively concise *Infrastructure Australia Act 2008* (Australian Government, 2008) lists the body's 'primary function' as 'providing advice'. More specifically:

> (1) Infrastructure Australia has the primary function of providing advice to the minister, Commonwealth, state, territory and local governments, investors in infrastructure and owners of infrastructure on matters relating to infrastructure, including in relation to the following:
>
> (a) Australia's current and future needs and priorities relating to *nationally significant infrastructure;*
> (b) policy, pricing and regulatory issues that may impact on the utilisation of infrastructure;
> (c) impediments to the efficient utilisation of national infrastructure networks;
> (d) options and reforms, including regulatory reforms, to make the utilisation of national infrastructure networks more efficient;
> (e) the needs of users of infrastructure;
> (f) mechanisms for financing investment in infrastructure (Australian Government, 2008, 3; emphasis added).

Section 5(2) of the *Act* describes what it refers to as Infrastructure Australia's 'additional functions':

(2) Infrastructure Australia has the following additional functions:

(a) to conduct audits to determine the adequacy, capacity and condition of nationally significant infrastructure, taking into account forecast growth;
(b) to develop lists (to be known as Infrastructure Priority Lists) that prioritise Australia's infrastructure needs;
(c) to review and provide advice on proposals to facilitate the harmonisation of policies, and laws, relating to development of, and investment in, infrastructure;
(d) to evaluate proposals for investment in, or enhancements to, *nationally significant infrastructure;*
(e) to identify any impediments to investment in *nationally significant infrastructure* and identify strategies to remove any impediments identified;
(f) to promote investment in infrastructure;
(g) to provide advice on infrastructure policy issues arising from climate change;
(h) to review Commonwealth infrastructure funding programs to ensure they align with any Infrastructure Priority Lists;
(i) to undertake or commission research relating to Infrastructure Australia's other functions;
(j) any functions that the minister, by writing, directs Infrastructure Australia to perform;
(k) any other functions conferred on Infrastructure Australia by this Act or any other law (Australian Government, 2008, 3; emphasis added).

Examining both these sections of the *Infrastructure Australia Act 2008* highlights several noteworthy points. First, the statutory body is specifically directed to concern itself with 'nationally significant infrastructure' (sections 5(1)(a), 5(2)(d) and 5(2)(e) above). As such, it is by definition proscribed from any lengthy considerations of infrastructure that is principally local in function – the very topic under consideration in our discussion here. Second, the advisory role emphasised in section 5(1) is augmented with a research, or information-gathering and disseminating role specified in section 5(2). Third, the overall shape of these research and advisory roles can be described as both profiling infrastructure at a strategic level within state and federal governments, and more specifically *between* the Commonwealth, state and local governments. This is reflected by the fact that it reports not only to the Minister, but also to the Council of Australian Governments (COAG), principally in the form of written reports (Infrastructure Australia, 2008, 2011b). For example, the 2008 Report identified seven 'themes' designed to 'steer a course for solutions to meet the gaps, deficiencies and bottlenecks and gaps in our nation's infrastructure', including 'a national broadband network', the 'creation of a national energy market', 'competitive international gateways', 'a national rail freight network', 'adaptable and secure water supplies', a 'transforming our cities' priority and 'providing essential indigenous services' (Infrastructure Australia, 2008, 7).

In sum, while Infrastructure Australia receives submissions from some local governments suggesting priorities for infrastructure spending (see, for example, Infrastructure Australia, 2011b), it is in essence a 12-member board and ancillary staff (including an executive officer somewhat misleadingly titled the 'Infrastructure Coordinator' – see Australian Government, 2008, section 27) which acts both as an observer of, and advocate for, nationally significant infrastructure. It is thus not of direct concern for our discussion here. Nevertheless, if we examine sections 5(2)(j) and 5(2)(k) of the *Infrastructure Australia Act 2008*, we can observe that the option is available for either the Minister or the parliament to significantly alter the functions of the statutory body. Accordingly, it is conceivable that Infrastructure Australia could form the institutional basis of a local government infrastructure fund of the type advocated by Dollery, Byrnes and Crase (2007).

7.4 Evaluation

In evaluating the case for a federally-funded local government infrastructure fund, it is instructive to recall the four reasons put forward by Dollery, Byrnes and Crase (2007) in support of the idea: (i) it bypasses the state governments who have historically been both unwilling and unable to increase funding to local government; (ii) the Commonwealth has the fiscal capacity to undertake such a task; (iii) undertaking such a program would require the introduction of uniform standards of infrastructure management which, in itself, would generate significant positive externalities; and (iv) the theoretical reasons for undertaking such a funding program – for example, those grounded in arguments pointing to increased allocative efficiency and increased equity between local government areas – would be borne out in the context of Australia's federal system. How do these reasons stand up in light of the R2R and Nation Building programs, the commencement of Infrastructure Australia, as well as other reforms and developments?

Certainly, the lack of both financial capacity and political will on the part of the state governments has not altered since Dollery, Byrnes and Crase (2007) put forward their arguments. Furthermore, the possibility of state governments making increased contributions to local government funding appears significantly less likely given the fall in state government GST revenues. Similarly, the argument that the Commonwealth ought to undertake such a program of funding because it alone has the fiscal capacity has also been reinforced since Dollery, Byrnes and Crase (2007) set forth their arguments. Both the Rudd and Gillard Governments have deployed this fiscal capacity to counter the effects of a potential decrease in demand following the 2008 GFC. As we have seen, some of this money has been allocated to local government for spending on infrastructure. Finally, the arguments that Dollery, Byrnes and Crase (2007) found in the theory of fiscal federalism for a federally-funded local government infrastructure fund, as well as the positive externalities they reasoned would flow from the introduction of uniform asset management principles, all remain cogent.

However, there are several substantive reasons against pursuing the policy option of a federally-funded local government infrastructure fund. First, as we saw in Chapter 6, the Commonwealth can choose to treat local governments – and, due to the increased centralisation of fiscal authority that has characterised Australian federalism since federation, to a large extent, the states – almost whimsically. For example, Chapter 6 demonstrated that funding for infrastructure increased in real terms under the Whitlam Government and, to a lesser extent, during the Fraser administrations. Yet as Mathews and Grewal (1997) have pointed out, it declined significantly in real terms under the Hawke and Keating administrations – the genesis of the infrastructure backlog under which Australia currently labours, and which the subsequent Howard, Rudd and Gillard Governments have gone some way to address.

The very unpredictability of this financial history contrasts starkly with the definition of financial, non-financial and holistic sustainability arrived at in Chapter 3 and Chapter 4 of this book. It may be tempting to argue that institutionalising a federally-funded local government infrastructure fund – such as by extending the functions that currently fall under the ambit of Infrastructure Australia to include the allocation of funds alongside its current advisory role – would provide some measure of protection from the actions of a capricious federal government. However, statutory corporations of the Commonwealth are created by federal parliament and as such can equally be abolished by federal parliament. The history of the deregulation of Australia's agricultural industries abounds with examples of statutory corporations ceasing to exist with the stroke of a pen (see, for example, Gow and Grant, 2010). A more recent example is the Howard Government's abolition of the Aboriginal and Torres Strait Islander Commission in 2004 (see, for example, Morrissey, 2006). Placing the threat of abolition of such a body to one side, a more likely scenario would see funding of local government infrastructure through an instrument of this kind subject to downward adjustments when fiscal austerity is required by the Commonwealth. It can easily be argued that the maintenance and improvement of local road stock is a far less urgent national priority than, for instance, funding for health, education, defence or a host of other Commonwealth responsibilities.

Second, Dollery, Byrnes and Crase (2007) argued that the theory of fiscal federalism contains within it sound reasons to suggest an allocation of funds by higher tiers of government to functions like infrastructure maintenance and renewal, on the grounds of improved equity and enhanced allocative efficiency.

Theoretical considerations aside, the most robust reason for not instituting a federally-funded local government infrastructure fund is that direct payments from the Commonwealth to local government rest on very shaky legal grounds. Commenting upon the R2R program, Dollery, Pape and Byrnes (2008) provided an account of why this is the case. They cited *inter alia* Chief

Justice Gleeson's remarks in *Austin v Commonwealth* concerning the nature of the Australian federation:

> It involves the co-existence of national and state or provincial governments, with an established division of governmental powers: legislative, executive and judicial. *As in the United States, the national government was given limited, specific powers.* An approach to constitutional interpretation which stressed a reservation of state powers, flourished for a time after federation, but was reversed by the Engineer's case in 1920. Even so as in the United States, the federal nature of the Commonwealth has been held to limit the capacity of the Federal Parliament to legislate in a manner not inconsistent with the constitutional role of the States (Gleeson, cited by Dollery, Pape and Byrnes, 2008, 39, emphasis added).

The two important points to be gleaned from this extract are that in the Australian Constitution residual powers fall to the states, while the authority of the Commonwealth is specified. Further, Dollery, Pape and Byrnes (2008, 38) argued that 'under Section 51 of the Constitution, there are a number of topics assigned to the Commonwealth Parliament upon which it can legislate. Construction and upkeep of local roads is not one of them'. In the case of R2R, the Commonwealth had relied upon a broad interpretation of Section 81, the appropriations power, to authorise payments. However, Dollery, Pape and Byrnes (2008, 40) argued that 'Section 81 specifies that "all revenues or monies raised or received by Executive Government of the Commonwealth shall form one consolidated revenue fund, to be appropriated for the purposes of the Commonwealth in the manner and subject to the charges and liabilities imposed by the Commonwealth" '. In other words, the Commonwealth was acting unconstitutionally in directly funding local government in the R2R program and all previous programs, including those undertaken by the Whitlam Government.

In 2008 this was a moot point of interest only to those persons – such as the legal scholar Bryan Pape – who had consistently decried the increasing centralisation of authority in Australia at the expense of states' rights. Moreover, as Dollery, Pape and Byrnes (2008) also pointed out, it was only the state governments themselves which had standing as *bona fide* complainants in the jurisdiction of the High Court against the Commonwealth directly allocating monies to local governments. As Pape (2005, 8) had earlier pointed out, the states had regarded these monies as 'windfall gains' and had consistently reacted by 'putting the Nelsonian telescope to the blind eye': there was nothing an individual citizen could do as they had no standing in the High Court.

However, this situation changed radically when Pape challenged the validity of the *Tax Bonus for Working Australians Act (No 2) 2009*. Pape successfully gained standing in the jurisdiction of the High Court because *he himself* had received a payment from the Commonwealth as part of the stimulus package designed to counter the effects of the GFC. On 3 April 2009, a majority of the High Court (4:3) ruled that the Act was lawful. However, in its full decision, published 7 July 2009, the High Court warned that in acting as it did, the Commonwealth was acting unconstitutionally and that further challenges to the Commonwealth overstepping its role as defined by sections 51 and 81 of the Constitution would, in all probability, lead to a very different result. In his summing up, Chief Justice French expressed the point as follows:

> Future questions about the application of the executive power to the control or regulation of conduct or activities under coercive laws, absent authority supplied by a statute made under some head of power other than s 51(xxxix) alone, are likely to be answered conservatively (High Court of Australia, 2009, 10).

Thus, while historically no individual state or any number of states joined together had challenged the constitutional validity of direct payments from the Commonwealth to local governments, following *Pape v Commissioner of Taxation* (High Court of Australia, 2009) an entirely different scenario had become – and to this day remains – a possibility. In a recorded interview with Bligh Grant and Brian Dollery, Pape described this scenario vividly:

> Now that the High Court has conclusively held that s 81 does not authorise such spending, it is permissible for a citizen to commence prosecution proceedings in accordance with s 13 of the *Crimes Act 1914* (Cth) that a minister was 'misapplying' or 'improperly using' public money within the meaning of s 14 of the *Financial Management and Accountability Act 1997* (Cth). A conviction carries a term of imprisonment for 7

> years. Of course it would be preferable for the Australian Federal Police to investigate. If an offence was considered to have been committed then to refer the matter to the Commonwealth Director of Public Prosecutions to decide whether to prosecute.

The plausibility of an individual citizen initiating criminal proceedings against a Commonwealth Minister for improperly using public money in, for example, continuing to fund a program, such as R2R, may seem peculiar. However, we would do well to remember that it was Pape himself who very nearly successfully managed to charge the Commonwealth with acting unconstitutionally for granting him a sum in accordance with the *Tax Bonus for Working Australians Act (No 2) 2009*. It is thus by no means beyond the realms of possibility.

The point of our excursion into the eccentricities of one particular High Court case is clear. A federally-funded local government infrastructure fund may well prove to be unconstitutional. This hardly forms a sound basis for its operational sustainability.

7.5 Concluding remarks

This chapter has examined the case for a federally-financed local government infrastructure fund. After noting that this particular policy issue has received scant attention despite the existence since 2008 of Infrastructure Australia, section 7.2 documented recent Commonwealth attempts to overcome the infrastructure backlog, in particular several iterations of the R2R program and the Nation Building program following the GFC. We argued that, while well intentioned, both these programs, alongside other tranches of funding paid directly to local government, were acts of largesse on the part of the Commonwealth and, while going a substantial way to ameliorating some of the local government infrastructure backlog, they did not accord with the definitions of sustainability reached in Chapter 3 of this book.

Section 7.3 then examined the case for a federally-financed local government infrastructure fund as advanced by Dollery, Byrnes and Crase (2007). In particular, we examined the reasons underlying the case for such a fund: (i) the states appear both unwilling and unable to increase funding - for any purpose - to local government; (ii) the Commonwealth has the demonstrated fiscal capacity to finance such a fund; (iii) in bypassing state governments, payments to individual local governments would foster the gradual introduction of national standards of infrastructure management, generating significant long-term positive externalities for the sector and the Australian economy generally; and (iv) there are sound theoretical reasons for the implementation of such a fund, grounded in the principles of allocative efficiency and equity.

By way of clarification, we also briefly set out the present role of Infrastructure Australia, noting that while the *Infrastructure Australia Act (2008)* leaves open the option of significantly altering the functioning of the statutory body, at present it is concerned with undertaking an advisory role with respect to 'nationally significant' infrastructure and, as such, is presently proscribed from considering local government infrastructure.

Section 7.4 critically reflected upon the proposal for a federally-financed infrastructure fund, as advanced by Dollery, Byrnes and Crase (2007), in light of the synoptic history of intergovernmental fiscal relations and the account of the R2R program and other subsequent policies that have channelled funding directly from the Commonwealth to local governments. We argued that the proposed fund suffered from weaknesses. First, as a statutory corporation of the Commonwealth, any funding directed to local government through this vehicle would be (justifiably) subject to any reductions in funding a particular government would see fit to implement. Second, we argued that, following the decision of the High Court in *Pape v Commissioner of Taxation* (High Court of Australia, 2009), any such fund could be challenged as being unconstitutional on the basis of its relying upon a wide interpretation of the appropriations power of the Australian Constitution (section 81) - an interpretation about which the High Court has explicitly expressed its misgivings.

We therefore continue our investigation into a sustainable basis for local government infrastructure funding in Chapter 8, which addresses local government infrastructure being funded through an Australian municipal bond market.

Chapter 8
Municipal Bond Markets

8.1 Introduction

The question of attacking the local government infrastructure backlog through intergovernmental transfers was considered in detail in Chapter 7. It was concluded for several reasons that transfers of this kind did not provide a feasible solution to the problem, not least because of pecuniary constraints on the Commonwealth fiscus. Alternative methods of tackling the backlog must thus be pursued. In this chapter, we examine municipal bond markets as a potentially fruitful approach to the problem.

In many developed and developing countries, local government infrastructure finance has traditionally been provided through grants or loans from national or provincial government agencies. However, recent decades have witnessed the steady decentralisation of fiscal and other responsibilities to sub-national governments, including local government systems. This has created difficulties in many countries, including Australia, since local government typically faces severe fiscal constraints derived from narrow tax bases and restrictions on revenue raising (Shah, 2005, 2006). This has obliged local government to seek funding from other sources, such as debt markets, which offer access to the long-term capital necessary for local infrastructure development. However, the transition from intergovernmental transfers to well-functioning securities markets is fraught with difficulties. As Martell and Guess (2006, 89) have argued, it is not a simple matter 'to encourage a balanced evolution of the municipal credit system that does not jeopardise sovereign ratings, rewards municipalities for fiscal responsibility, and still shelters disadvantaged municipalities that are building market discipline'.

The evolution of the US municipal securities market is instructive. From the late 1970s onwards, local government in the United States was confronted by a harsh financial environment - not altogether dissimilar from contemporary Australian local government - which included less federal aid, as well as various tax and expenditure limitations. Noting that 'crises tend to spawn innovation', Hildreth and Zorn (2005, 132–3) have described the development of a vigorous capital market with a steady trend towards 'customising' borrowing instruments to 'a specific financing need rather than relying solely on a long-term, fixed coupon general obligation (GO) bond'. As a consequence, revenue bonds rather than general obligation bonds came to predominate. Moreover, new methods have proliferated, such as Certificates of Participation, tax increment financing, bond banks and revolving loan funds. Given these developments, in this chapter we consider whether municipal bonds and municipal bond markets could represent a possible solution to the Australian local infrastructure backlog.

The Infrastructure Finance Working Group, which was established by the Commonwealth agency Infrastructure Australia to investigate the problem of securing adequate infrastructure funding at all levels of government, in its *Infrastructure Finance Reform* (Infrastructure Australia, 2011a, 9) briefly considered 'infrastructure bonds', including 'revenue bonds' and 'covered bonds', in which it defined an infrastructure bond as a 'debt instrument issued by governments or private companies to raise funds for infrastructure projects'. It pointed out that both the principal and coupon repayment of infrastructure bonds are generally funded by income derived from the infrastructure project in question, such as water tariffs charged by local council water utilities. This kind of bond is often described as a revenue bond and should be distinguished from traditional general obligation bonds financed by general government income and secured against all assets of the issuing entity.

Infrastructure Finance Reform (Infrastructure Australia, 2011a, 10–11) attributes various advantages to revenue bonds. These include 'providing an objective market test for the viability of the project', 'promoting full cost pricing of the service', 'facilitating shared financing' through public–private partnerships and the transfer of the 'economic risks of operation to investors without loss of ownership and control'. Revenue bonds have been attacked on several counts. For instance, critics have pointed to the US municipal bond market, which has seen the proliferation of two million separate bonds covering around $2.4 trillion. The comparatively small size of individual issues has tended to exclude large institutional funds, such as superannuation funds, which wish to invest substantially larger sums than most individual municipal finance debt issues allow.

Covered bonds represent an alternative to revenue bonds and general obligation bonds. In essence, covered bonds represent debt securities secured by 'cash flows from public sector loans or private sector mortgages' (Infrastructure Australia, 2011a, 11). By contrast with other types of pooled securities, the 'underlying obligations remain on the bond issuer's consolidated balance sheet' and investors have recourse to a 'pool of assets that secures or "covers" the bond if the originator (usually a bank or other financial institution) becomes insolvent'. At the same time, 'the issuer of a covered bond gains the benefits of pooling its individual (smaller) obligations'.

In the public sector, covered bonds generally pool loans to central, state and local governments, which are either 'guaranteed by the relevant governments or by the cash flows from commercial infrastructure projects' (Infrastructure Australia, 2011a, 11–12). For example, a given infrastructure project which may be too small on its own to attract sufficient investor interest could be combined with other small projects to form a revenue stream sufficiently large to justify the issuance of a single covered bond issue. From the perspective of investors, 'the appeal of covered bonds for investors is that they represent a large, liquid, and high quality asset class', whereas for banks they constitute a type of borrowing which is typically low cost and long term since 'they are backed by low risk collateral and are government guaranteed'. In addition, covered bonds are an efficacious method efficient of securing funding not otherwise available 'due to inadequate size and liquidity'.

Infrastructure bonds are a complex and multi-faceted question with numerous institutional manifestations. In order to reduce these complexities to manageable proportions, in this chapter we follow Byrnes, Dollery, Crase and Simmons (2008) and focus on the development of an Australian market for municipal revenue bonds, rather than on generic local government infrastructure bonds. In Chapter 9 we consider a specific kind of covered bond markets in the form of municipal bond banks.

This chapter is divided into five main sections. Section 8.2 describes the infrastructure renewal problem currently facing local government in New South Wales, with particular attention paid to the water and wastewater sector, by way of a concrete example of the kind of problem which municipal revenue bonds could tackle. Section 8.3 provides a synoptic account of municipal bond finance in the United States which could be adopted in Australian local government. Section 8.4 outlines the main principles embodied in the Byrnes, Dollery, Crase and Simmons (2008) approach relating to the cost of capital and the structure of asset-backed securities. Against the background example of local water utilities in New South Wales, section 8.5 considers the long-term debt which could be raised by local authorities through asset-backed securities. The chapter ends in section 8.6 with some brief concluding remarks.

8.2 Local infrastructure renewal in New South Wales

Byrnes, Dollery, Crase and Simmons (2008) use the NSW local government infrastructure backlog as a representative example of how a municipal bond market might work in the Australian institutional milieu. In its deliberations, the Allan Report (2006) sketched a sombre picture of infrastructure maintenance and renewal in NSW local government. The Allan Report (2006, 13) noted that 'studies commissioned by the Inquiry estimate that overall under-spending on infrastructure renewal has been of the order of $400 to $600 million per annum', which implied that 'it would cost over $6.3 billion to restore these assets to a satisfactory condition'. In addition, a further $14.6 billion would be required to restore existing infrastructure over the period to 2020, which does not include the new infrastructure required to accommodate population growth.

A complicating factor not illustrated in these aggregate data was that the infrastructure problem was not uniformly distributed across New South Wales, with 7% of rural councils and 25% of urban councils 'renewing less than 30 per cent of the infrastructure that should be replaced each year' (Allan Report, 2006, 13). Moreover, while only 20% of councils managed infrastructure risk through asset management plans and risk management plans, only a further 'five to 37 per cent of any asset class within councils is subject to asset management planning'. The net result is that the risk of exposure faced by local authorities is rising as assets deteriorate.

The Allan Report argued that the problem required urgent attention. It recommended *inter alia* local councils borrow $3.8 billion to finance the local infrastructure backlog. This did not include water and sewerage infrastructure, which could be independently funded through fees and charges. Local government should also seek an additional $900 million per annum in income to both 'close the renewals gap ($500 million) and meet the new debt charges ($400 million)'. Furthermore, local authorities should raise an extra $900 million in revenue through $200 million in increased grants ($100 million from the Commonwealth as well as $100 million from the NSW Government), $200 million through 'council expenditure savings' and $500 million from higher fees, charges and rates (Allan Report, 2006, 28). Unfortunately, in the period since the Allan Report, neither increased intergovernmental grants nor the elimination of rate-capping have come to fruition.

Following research undertaken by Roorda and Associates (2006, 25) for the Allan Report, the water and wastewater component of NSW local government (known as Local Water Utilities (LWUs)) have an accumulated infrastructure backlog of around $955 million. However, a detailed breakdown of this backlog is not available. For instance, Roorda and Associates (2006) did not denote the proportion of this funding required for pipeline replacement, treatment plant repair and the like. Moreover, the methodology employed to calculate the value of the infrastructure backlog has been questioned by Maxwell (2006). Despite these misgivings, Byrnes, Dollery, Crase and Simmons (2008, x) accepted the Roorda and Associates (2006) estimate as the 'best currently available'.

Given these circumstances, Byrnes, Dollery, Crase and Simmons (2008, 118–9) argued that 'local infrastructure renewal cannot be completed over a relatively short time horizon; careful planning and adequate cost/benefit analysis are required to determine the net benefit of renewing local infrastructure to the local community in question before any program can be implemented'. Furthermore, 'undertaking any major construction project over a relatively short period of time is likely to result in higher construction costs and thus impose an even greater long-run financial impost on the local community that must eventually pay for the infrastructure'.

In its response to the Allan Report (2006) findings on LWUs, the (then) Department of Energy, Utilities and Sustainability (DEUS) observed that the infrastructure backlog was in fact fully funded because LWUs had reserves of about $1.1 billion which could be used to finance infrastructure renewal (DEUS, 2006). DEUS also argued that most LWUs had set average residential tariffs bills which could fund capital and operating expenses over the next three decades (Allan Report, 2006, 120). Byrnes, Dollery, Crase and Simmons (2008, 119) argued that 'if this argument was accepted at face value, then one might be tempted to conclude that there is no need to remedy the situation through direct borrowing, a federal government infrastructure renewal fund, capital raised in the bond market, or any other proposed approach'. However, they observed that 'the relatively low default risk on a bond issued by local government is likely to result in a cost of capital relatively less than the risk adjusted returns that could be earned by local government through the investment of funds set aside for infrastructure renewal in a balanced portfolio'. As a result, 'it may be rational for LWUs to raise funds through a bonds issue despite the fact that they already have investments and cash in excess of the identified expenditure requirement'.

Byrnes, Dollery, Crase and Simmons (2008, 119) pointed out that intergenerational equity is an additional critical consideration. They argued that intergenerational equity principles (Auerbach and Lee, 2001) 'will be violated if the current generation of water and wastewater service consumers in New South Wales were to entirely fund infrastructure renewal through higher charges, when subsequent generations will benefit from this asset renewal process'. In addition, apportioning the 'infrastructure renewal expense across those generations that are likely to benefit from the renewal, it seems more equitable to fund this investment through borrowings to be repaid over the life of the renewed assets'.

8.3 US municipal infrastructure finance

Byrnes, Dollery, Crase and Simmons (2008, 120–1) observe that US state and municipal governments have extensive experience in employing debt instruments to fund both general obligations and specific infrastructure projects. Municipal bonds of this kind are referred to as 'municipal securities'. Tax-exempt status granted to accrued interest payments represents a distinctive characteristic of municipal securities in the United States and it has made this form of investment comparatively advantageous for investors. However, over time, successive US federal and state governments have gradually eliminated tax exemption in order to increase tax revenues (Hildreth, 1993).

US municipal securities can be classified into two main categories. In the first place, there is tax-backed debt consisting of bonds issued by municipalities which are secured by future tax income. In the context of the Byrnes, Dollery, Crase and Simmons (2008) analysis, a special type of instrument in this class known as a 'double-barrelled in security' is especially significant. In this case, the revenue stream backing the asset comprises general tax revenue and income generated by a particular class of tax or charge (Fabozzi, 2000).

Revenue bonds constitute the second category of US municipal bond. As we have seen in section 8.1, revenue bonds are secured by the income generated by a given project. Revenue bonds of this kind are classified according to the type of revenue stream used to finance the bond, such 'utility revenue bonds', 'seaport revenue bonds' and 'transportation revenue bonds' (see, for instance, Fabozzi, 2000).

As a general rule, the municipal securities issuance process in the United States involves several participants. First, as the ultimate issuer, it is customary for local authorities to sell a debt instrument to an underwriter, which is typically an investment bank. The underwriter then resells the security on the market to investors. As a result, the investor receives coupon payments, usually in six-monthly instalments. While it is the issuer which ultimately pays the coupon, the method by which the coupon is delivered differs considerably. For instance, in some cases trustee arrangements are established into which revenues from local government are transferred to service coupon payments. It is also imperative that sound legal advice is sought to make sure that the debt instrument satisfies all regulatory requirements (Hildreth, 1993; Fabozzi, 2000). Since each of the participants in the process extracts fees, as a consequence the funds raised per bond are less than the face value of the bond. It follows that fee minimisation is an important consideration in the capital raising process.

Capital raising in the United States using municipal security markets has experienced some difficulties. Feldstein and Fabozzi (1987) have noted that many municipal securities have 'rate covenants' linked to how user charges can be determined in regulated environments, which has increased the difficulty of credit analysis by market participants. In an analogous vein, 'priority of revenue' covenants often also tend to induce a 'hierarchy' of claims on local government revenue under which third parties can sometimes legally secure funds from municipal revenue before bondholders (Beers and Cavanaugh, 1997).

The 2008 Global Financial Crisis (GFC) has seen a significant deterioration of the US municipal bond 'muni' market. Prior to 2008, investors seeking the potential muni benefits of tax-free income and diversification could secure muni exposure relatively easily without much credit expertise. Moreover, within the 'high-grade' market, most muni bonds were insured by bond insurers and generally carried AAA credit ratings from the three major credit rating agencies. As a consequence, it was widely assumed that few, if any, credit risks existed for these securities, since bond insurers guaranteed the timely repayment of principal and interest in the event of a default. However, following the GFC, as credit markets deteriorated, the credit ratings of the bond insurers fell, largely because most insurers had expanded coverage to include bonds backed by subprime mortgage debt. The collapse of the subprime mortgage market and the resulting massive liabilities crippled bond insurers' ability to insure newly-issued munis. As a consequence, currently only about 5% of newly-issued muni bonds offer insurance protection, which is in any event no longer rated AAA. Without bond insurance, muni investors have been obliged to evaluate the underlying credit quality of all munis under consideration as investments. At the same time, the GFC also contributed to a rapid deterioration in US public sector revenue. State and local governments faced severe budget shortfalls as tax revenues plunged, which has, in turn, led to further market uncertainties.

Writing immediately prior to the GFC, Byrnes, Dollery, Crase and Simmons (2008, 121) were optimistic that Australia should follow the US example:

> It is thus clear that whereas local government in Australia has not traditionally accessed the capital market directly for funding, comparable levels of government in the United States have been following this practice for years. This demonstrates that our proposal for Australian local councils to seek funds in capital markets to finance the infrastructure backlog is feasible. Adequate funds for New South Wales LWU infrastructure restoration and investment could be raised by means of the issuance of debt instruments since this is not only already accepted practice in the United States, but it also generates sufficient levels of funding.

However, Byrnes, Dollery, Crase and Simmons (2008, 121) were at some pains to qualify their proposal. They stressed that 'the sources of finance differ between Australian local government systems and its American counterparts', especially in the sense that 'many American local government jurisdictions can employ local income taxes and local sales taxes, which represent "growth taxes" in circumstances of a growing economy, a fact recognised by the investment community'. In sharp contrast, Australian local government possesses no analogous growth tax. This implied that the 'absolute magnitude of borrowing' would be smaller than that available in the United States.

8.4 Rationale for asset-backed securities

In their paper, Byrnes, Dollery, Crase and Simmons (2008, 121–4) set out some salient conceptual considerations which would guide the development of an Australian municipal bond market. A critical factor in local government debt finance revolves around the cost of capital, and the different approaches to raising funding, including municipal bond markets, have different implications for the cost of capital. In essence, the cost of debt to a borrowing local government entity amounts to offering the required rate of return necessary to attract the magnitude of funds sought. One gauge of the cost of debt is the debt margin which a firm must offer to persuade investors to acquire a risky debt instrument on sale. A debt margin is usually expressed as the spread between the risk-free rate offered on government securities and the rate on the risky bond. Byrnes, Dollery, Crase and Simmons (2008, 121–4) noted that recent regulatory decisions regarding pricing by the Victorian water sector applied a debt margin of 1.1%, which corresponded to assigning a credit rating of BBB+ to the water utilities in question (Essential Services Commission (ESC) 2004).

An alternative method of computing the cost of capital approach is to approximate the cost of debt by the means equation (8.1) developed by Gitman, Juchau and Flanagan (2002). Under this approach an appropriate interest rate (i) necessary to attract investors must still be taken into account:

$$k_d = \frac{I + \frac{PV - N_d}{n}}{\frac{N_d + PV}{2}} \tag{8.1}$$

where:

k_d = before-tax cost of debt
I = annual interest in dollars
PV = par value of bond
N_d = net proceeds from the sale of debt (bond)
n = number of years to the bond's maturity

The Gitman, Juchau and Flanagan (2002) methodology sets the cost to the issuer of raising debt in terms of the interest payment to be made each year relative to the magnitude of funding raised by the bond issue. The advantage of this approach is that it enables transactions costs to be incorporated into the reckoning.

Byrnes, Dollery, Crase and Simmons (2008, 122–3) have argued that asset-backed securities have a number of unique features which can affect their marketability and make them suited to Australian local government, and they outline the more important of these characteristics. Asset-backed securities were initially issued by US mortgage banks, but were later successfully employed in corporate debt finance. In essence, an asset-backed security creates a bond aimed at raising capital which is secured by a claim on a specific asset held by the borrowing entity, rather than on all the assets owned by the entity. For instance, a bank can create a bond that is backed by claims to a defined loan portfolio instead of the entire asset base of the bank (Fabozzi, 2000). In order to guarantee that this claim is directed exclusively against a particular asset, the asset is typically sold to an entity – known as a special purpose vehicle (SPV) – separate from the issuing organisation. The net result is that the asset-backed security is held by the SPV, not by the bank. The main advantage of this approach has been that the asset has been detached from the balance sheet, which has allowed banks to reduce their regulatory capital holdings accordingly (Choudhry, Joannas and Pienaar, 2005). A second advantage flowing from the creation of an SPV resides in the fact that the credit rating associated with the bond float is entirely related to the SPV rather than to the issuing entity. For example, a borrowing organisation which might be allocated a BBB credit rating when issuing debt in the bond market can raise the capital through an SPV that has a AAA credit rating, which has obvious implications for perceived risk and the required rate of return. It should be added that the higher credit rating can be attained through credit enhancement characteristics, such as bond insurance (Fabozzi, 2000).

The process of securitisation is conceptually similar to that followed by municipalities when issuing revenue bonds, as outlined in section 8.3. In general, there is normally an originating entity which sells the asset to the SPV, and the SPV in turn issues bonds backed by the asset held by the SPV. For mortgage-backed securities, the asset transferred to the SPV includes interest payments on the mortgage. However, in the case of other kinds of assets, such as water utilities, revenue streams which service coupon payments are also transferred to the SPV (Choudhry, Joannas and Pienaar, 2005).

Byrnes, Dollery, Crase and Simmons (2008, 123) argued that, for New South Wales LWUs, SPVs would typically not be required:

> [I]t is unlikely that LWUs would need to make use of an SPV in order to generate a lower credit rating on the bond. The fact that the bond would most likely be issued by the New South Wales Treasury Corporation, combined with the nature of the revenue flows from LWUs, would ensure a relatively high credit rating would be secured. However, the ability of an SPV to package income streams from a diverse spread of LWUs, with differing credit qualities, makes the use of an SPV especially attractive. In particular, the Treasury Corporation could construct an SPV into which the reserve for asset maintenance currently held by LWUs could be sold. The SPV would then establish a revenue fund into which an agreed quantum of income from LWU's turnover could be deposited per annum. Coupons on the bonds issued by the SPV would be paid out of this fund. Thus, the SPV would act as a conduit through which a varied mix of LWUs could raise capital at a uniform yield, and presumably at a lower yield on average than would otherwise be the case had individual LWUs sought to access the capital market directly on an individual basis. Furthermore, since advice is only required on the bond issuance from the SPV managed by the Treasury Corporation, management expenses could be held to a minimum.

8.5 Asset-backed securities by local water utilities

Byrnes, Dollery, Crase and Simmons (2008, 124–8) applied these considerations to calculate the approximate cost of long-term debt to LWUs making use of equation (8.1) on the assumption that a $955 million infrastructure backlog existed in NSW local government infrastructure funding. In effect, they sought to determine the cost of raising $955 million, with transactions costs presumed to equate to 2% of the face value of the bond issue. In order to simplify the computation process, they further assumed a par value of $1,000 for each bond, thus requiring that 955,000 bonds be issued in total.

While Byrnes, Dollery, Crase and Simmons (2008, 124) did not estimate 'a specific estimate of the debt margin pertaining to this particular security', they did assume that an asset backed by cash flows from utilities owned by local government and issued via the relevant state government debt office would not require a substantially higher rate of return than a risk-free asset. The calculations were made as follows.

Given a spread on 10-year NSW Treasury Corporation bonds over Commonwealth Government Securities (with a current yield of 6%) of equal maturity equal to 54 basis points (Reserve Bank of Australia (RBA) 2007), it seems reasonable to suggest a yield of 7% would prove sufficient compensation to investors. This results in an annual coupon payment of $70. Finally, the bond will be issued with a maturity of 10 years and, for the sake of simplicity, we assume the bond devoid of any put or call options. Table 8.1 summarises the parameters used for this calculation.

Table 8.1. Parameters for Cost of Capital Approximation

Capital to raise	$955,000,000
Par Value (*PV*) of bond	$1,000
Interest cost in dollars (*I*)	$70
Net proceeds from bond (N_d)	$980
Coupon periods (n)	10

Note: *I* implies a coupon of 7% on a bond with a *PV* of $1,000

Substituting the values from Table 8.1 into equation (8.1), we arrive at a cost of debt, k_d, equal to 7.27 %:

$$k_d = \frac{70 + \frac{\$1{,}000 - \$980}{10}}{\frac{\$980 + \$1{,}000}{2}} \qquad k_d = 0.0727 \text{ or } 7.27\%$$

Byrnes, Dollery, Crase and Simmons (2008, 124) then argued that 'LWUs would be able to use this as a comparative rate when investigating the viability of alternative funding arrangements', like securing finance from a commercial bank. Moreover, 'individual LWUs could approach financial institutions to determine the relative cost of capital from individual borrowing, rather than the collective approach outlined here', and it seems probable that 'some LWUs may be able to enter a conventional loan arrangement with a bank at a relatively lower cost of capital, while others would be faced with the opposite outcome'. Byrnes, Dollery, Crase and Simmons (2008, 124) stressed that 'of crucial importance to the success or otherwise of the debt issuance is the ability of the LWUs to service both the annual coupon payments and repayment of the principal upon maturity'. Each of these factors is now considered separately.

In the first place, the coupon funding requirement is equal to the number of bonds issued multiplied by the coupon paid on each bond. In the present example, if it is assumed that the bond issue was fully subscribed, then the annual aggregate interest outlay would equal $66.85 million, expressed in nominal rather than real terms. Following DEUS (2006), the aggregate turnover of LWUs for the 2004/05 fiscal year was $850 million, net of capital works grants. In addition, DEUS recorded that the 'average operating, maintenance and administration (OMA) expense per property for all LWU's was $530'. Taken together with 'connected properties totalling 790,000 for the sector in 2004/05, this equates to an aggregate OMA expense of $418.7 million'. Accordingly, 'subtracting OMA expenses from aggregate turnover of LWUs leaves $431.3 million per annum to fund coupon payments'. Although Byrnes, Dollery, Crase and Simmons (2008, 124) conceded that this is 'a crude approximation of "surplus" revenue available to meet annual coupon expenses', they contended that it 'may actually overstate the true OMA since maintenance expenses are likely to decline following infrastructure renewal'.

As we have seen in section 8.2, DEUS (2006) estimated that total financial assets held by NSW LWUs for asset renewal were $1.1 billion. On this basis, Byrnes, Dollery, Crase and Simmons (2008, 124) argued that 'if an SPV was to be used as the conduit by which bonds were issued, this fund would be transferred to the SPV in order to retire the debt at maturity' and therefore 'principal repayment at maturity is more than adequately covered by the assets to be held by the SPV', ignoring taxation factors. However, if it is assumed that the SPV trustee invested the funds in 'an optimum portfolio of risky and risk-free assets' with an average annual return of 10%, and interest income is retained at that rate, then the market value of the portfolio after 10 years would be $2.85 billion. Following the repayment of bonds in question on maturity, the net increase in portfolio value would equal $1.89 billion. If it is presumed that the fund was invested at the 2007 risk-free rate on a 10-year bond (ie, 6%), then the market value of the fund at maturity would be $1.97 billion, which would see a net increase in the market value of the fund equal to $1.01 billion. If this is compared to the aggregate fixed coupon payments of the debt issuance of $668.5 million, then it is clear that LWUs have benefited financially through the funding of infrastructure renewal by means of long-term debt rather than retained equity.

Byrnes, Dollery, Crase and Simmons (2008, 126) conceded that their approach is 'deliberately simple for the sake of expositional clarity'. Moreover, they contended that 'it is most likely that LWUs would not raise the entire $955 million from a single market issue for two reasons'. In the first place, it would be 'very difficult to undertake the renewal task in one year, given the considerable logistical hurdles of such an exercise'. Second, interest expense would be 'unnecessarily inflated by borrowing funds before they are required to fund expenses'. This suggests two alternative strategies: (i) a 'revolving facility' through which bonds are periodically issued to match expenditure needs; or (ii) bonds being issued to the value of $955 million but with differing terms to maturity.

Byrnes, Dollery, Crase and Simmons (2008, 126) observed that 'marketability' is a critical element in a financial instrument. While many investors may be attracted to the relatively risk-free nature of the municipal bonds, they contend that portfolio managers of managed funds may find this kind of bond especially appealing. Arguing in the pre-GFC period, they noted there had been substantial growth in the number of managed funds providing either 'partial or full exposure to the global water industry sector'. For instance, in April 2007 the Macquarie Bank launched the *Macquarie Global Water Index* (Macquarie Bank, 2007) and the Australian MFS Group issued the *MFS Water Fund*. The latter was aimed at providing investors with coverage of 'a broad and diverse range of water and water-related businesses including utilities, infrastructure and technology companies and the owners of water assets and water rights' (MFS Group, 2007, x). These funds appear to consist mostly of equity holdings in water-related entities. Thus in 2007 the *Macquarie Global Water Index* had 13 publicly listed companies with a (then) combined market capitalisation of US$60 billion.

Noting that a central principle of modern portfolio theory resides in the reduction of systemic risk through diversification, particularly through the addition of securities that are not correlated with the broader market, Byrnes, Dollery, Crase and Simmons (2008, 126) argued that 'it may well be the case that an existing market, formed by the growing number of managed funds seeking exposure to the water sector, is in place for the private placement of the [asset-backed securities]'. Moreover, they stressed that, although the major risk to this asset is a change in the cash flows emanating from the water and wastewater businesses operated by local councils, this risk is probably not correlated with the returns on a portfolio of risky financial assets, since demand for the services of LWUs is relatively income inelastic, citing the empirical work of Hoffmann, Worthington and Higgs (2006) on water demand in Brisbane.

However, they conceded that 'at least' two risks remain present. In the first place, notwithstanding the income inelasticity of the revenue stream underlying these water bonds, investors may still 'hold reservations regarding the probability of LWUs failing to transfer the revenue stream into the SPV'. Although the probability of this eventuating is low, investors may nevertheless demand a higher return. By way of a remedy, Byrnes, Dollery, Crase and Simmons (2008, 127) pointed to examples of underwriting or guaranteeing municipal bonds in the United States. For example, the Virginia bond guarantee program allows the Virginian Governor to withhold grants to local authorities which default on debt obligations. The grant revenue in question is diverted to pay interest or principal to affected bond holders

(Fabozzi, 2000). Byrnes, Dollery, Crase and Simmons (2008, 127) then considered whether a similar arrangement would be feasible for Australian federal and/or state governments. They argued that the Commonwealth could hypothecate Financial Assistance Grants to be paid to fund the coupon obligations of defaulting LWUs. An alternative could be a credit enhancement, such as a line of credit, arranged by the trustee of the SPV with a private sector financial institution.

Second, Byrnes, Dollery, Crase and Simmons (2008, 127) noted that 'a vigorous policy debate continues in Australia as to the most appropriate pricing regime for urban water and wastewater services', citing work by Watson (2007) and Dwyer (2006). One consequence of the debate is that 'a degree of uncertainty regarding the future trajectory of water charges remains' and 'in the eyes of financial markets, uncertainty equates to risk, and the higher the risk associated with the returns of a financial asset, the higher the required return'. It follows that it would be reasonable to assume that 'current policy uncertainty regarding the principles by which water prices should be set may contribute to relatively higher costs of capital for regulated utilities'.

In concluding their case for the adoption of asset-backed securities in Australian local government, Byrnes, Dollery, Crase and Simmons (2008, 128) suggested that 'our scheme would generate a relatively bountiful and cheap source for the LWU entities owned by councils and thereby effectively address the current local infrastructure renewal crisis in that sector'. They added a caveat regarding the generalisation of their arguments to general obligation or 'tax-backed' bonds:

> [W]hile this article has demonstrated that it is feasible to make use of a revenue bond in the context of Australian local government, a similar argument in support of a 'tax-backed' bond has not been advanced. This was a deliberate omission since recent inquiries into the financial status of local government in Australia have noted that local councils are reliant upon a relatively 'slow growth' tax to fund general expense obligations ... In order to successfully market a tax backed bond, local government finance would most likely need significant reform, perhaps in the form of access to a growth tax such as the Goods and Services Tax.

8.6 Concluding remarks

Seen against the background of the sheer size of the Australian local government infrastructure backlog, the transparent inability of most local councils in the local government sector to finance this backlog from 'own-source' revenue, and the implausibility of Commonwealth and state governments providing sufficient funding, the Byrnes, Dollery, Crase and Simmons (2008) municipal bond market model has much to commend it as a practicable policy option. However, Dollery, Kortt and Grant (2011) have argued that this municipal bond market model ignores several important institutional characteristics of Australian local government. In particular, the model has overlooked the inability of most small local councils to participate effectively in a municipal bond market. This is especially problematic in the Australian milieu for two main reasons.

First, a comparatively high proportion of Australian municipalities are small, as measured by total population size. This has a significant spatial dimension since most small Australian local councils and shires are found in regional, rural and remote areas. Table 8.2 illustrates this fact by decomposing Australian local government entities by total population size and area.

Table 8.2. Population of Local Government Areas in 2007[a]

Council Population	Rural Areas	Urban Areas	Total
Up to 10,000	373[b]	16	389
10,001–30,000	69	67	136
30,001–70,000		82	82
70,001–12,000		42	42
120,001–200,000		40	40
More than 200,000		6	6
Total Number of Entities	**442**	**253**	**695**

Source: Adapted from Australian Centre for Excellence in Local Government (ACELG, 2011, 14, Table 2.2).
Notes: (a) Pre-dates recent amalgamations in Queensland and Northern Territory and includes some non-elected bodies; (b) Includes 30 small indigenous councils in Queensland officially classified as 'urban'.

Table 8.2 shows that, in 2007, 56% (or 389) of local authorities, mostly in rural and remote areas, had total populations of fewer than 10,000 people, with only 6.6% (or 46) of councils with populations in excess of 120,000 residents.

Second, a body of empirical research has explored local government fiscal capacity as it relates to organisational size, largely in the US institutional milieu (see, for example, Berne and Schramm, 1986; Clark, 1994; Honadle and Lloyd-Jones, 1998; Higgins, 1986; Simonsen, Robins and Helgerson, 2001). This literature has found that small rural jurisdictions are especially afflicted by administrative and technical incapacity, particularly in terms of financial management, which incorporates budgeting, accounting, performance measurement, auditing, asset management, capital-facilities planning, cash management and debt administration. For instance, Lehan (1991) found that small local governments typically have fewer staff with less finance training and fewer finance capabilities than larger municipalities. In a similar vein, Sokolow and Honadle (1984) established that rural local governments often use comparatively untrained administrative clerks as budget and finance officers. Simonsen, Robins and Helgerson (2001, 710) found that small local authorities seldom employ finance specialists and almost never have adequate debt-management capacity. They concluded that while 'it is clear from the literature that economies of scale exist for financial-management capacity', small municipalities 'typically do not have the same level of financial-management capacity, in terms of skilled staff and resources, as larger communities'.

Simonsen, Robins and Helgerson (2001, 710–11) argued further that 'the implications of this difference in capacity are likely to be more pronounced in debt administration', especially since 'small communities sell bonds infrequently and therefore managers are less likely to have extensive bond-sale experience'. Moreover, dealing in municipal bond markets is a 'complex and obscure process that involves multiple private-sector firms'. This indicates that 'it is harder for small communities to navigate their way through the complicated municipal market because of their limited internal-management capacity'. Not only are municipal bond markets complicated, but it is not even a single market; rather, numerous different markets with 'municipal bonds are traded by multiple independent firms, making each firm in effect a market of its own'. As a consequence, 'only the market prices of the most widely traded bonds are clear', which creates an 'information asymmetry between the underwriter, who has direct access to traders and investors, and the issuer, who does not'. The authors also pointed out that municipality size is a 'relevant factor in determining the investment quality of a bond issue and is a predictor of the appeal of a particular security'. One direct implication of this is that the segmentation of the US municipal bond market into local, regional and national markets corresponds with the bond sale amount, which in turn seems to be related to municipal population size. As a result of this kind of market segmentation, smaller municipalities face 'higher borrowing costs and interest premiums'. Finally, they contended that 'there are economies of scale related to the administrative and preparation costs' attached to a given bond issue since 'some of the cost of issuance is fixed'.

Since financial expertise generally correlates with council size, it can be argued that a majority of Australian local authorities would have been unable to use a municipal bond market economically if one had been established. Furthermore, most of the public inquiries into local government, including the PWC Report (2006), found that the local infrastructure backlog was most acute in small regional, rural and remote local government areas, where population densities were low. In other words, those local authorities most afflicted by an infrastructure backlog would have benefited least by the introduction of a municipal bond market.

A viable solution to the Australian local government infrastructure thus requires at least two conditions be met. In the first place, a reliable source of cheap private long-term capital to fund local infrastructure investment is essential. Second, financial expertise and capacity-building assistance for small councils without the requisite skills is vital. By itself, the Byrnes, Dollery, Crase and Simmons (2008) model meets only the first of these two conditions. We thus need to explore alternative institutional avenues which can meet both conditions. Chapter 9 considers two promising options: municipal banking and bond banks.

Chapter 9
An Australian Local Government Bond Bank

9.1 Introduction

In Part C of this book, we have thus far examined two main methods of tackling the crippling local infrastructure backlog in Australian local government: a Commonwealth local infrastructure asset fund and an Australian municipal bond market. In this chapter, we consider two final policy instruments which could be used: municipal banking and a national local government bond bank. We argue that the latter approach represents the best possible option given the characteristics of contemporary Australian local government.

For some years, researchers working under the auspices of the Centre for Local Government at the University of New England have advocated the establishment of an Australian national local government bond bank in both a series of scholarly papers (see, for instance, Dollery, Kortt and Grant, 2011, 2012) as well as at various local government conferences. This work at last appears to be paying off, with the question of an Australian national local government finance authority at last receiving serious attention from public policy makers. For example, in November 2011 the Commonwealth Department of Regional Australia, Local Government, the Arts and Sport (DRALGAS) engaged commercial consultants Ernst and Young to 'review the prioritisation and financing of local infrastructure' in Australia. On 18 June 2012, a report entitled *Strong Foundations for Sustainable Local Infrastructure: Connecting Communities, Projects, Finance and Funds* (Ernst and Young, 2012) was published on the DRALGAS website. In this report, Ernst and Young (2012, 3) recommended that the Commonwealth investigate the establishment of a 'national financing authority for local government' which 'would have a mandate to invest directly in local government programs by providing competitive and low-risk finance, and to facilitate inward investment'. Furthermore, 'the authority would have the ability to bundle approved council borrowings into a limited number of bond issues, which could be underwritten by the Australian Government'.

In the present context, three key points can be derived from the recommendations of the Ernst and Young (2012) report. In the first place, many of the principal findings of the Report echo the analysis offered in this book. For example, the 'Findings' of Chapter 2 in Ernst and Young (2012) concerning the funding sources for local government and its limitations reflect the analysis in Chapter 2 of this book, as well as the conclusions in Byrnes, Dollery, Crase and Simmons (2008). Similarly, discussion in *Strong Foundations for Sustainable Local Infrastructure: Connecting Communities, Projects, Finance and Funds* has already been exhaustively explored by Dollery, Kortt and Grant (2012).

Second, a number of the 'Recommendations' offered by the Ernst and Young (2012) report have previously been examined in depth. For example, 'Recommendation 8' – that the 'Australian Government should work with the states and territories to establish a national body to provide skills and oversight of local government infrastructure' – was initially proposed by Dollery, Byrnes and Crase (2007) and canvassed in Chapter 7 in this book. In fact, in Chapter 7 of our present discussion we stressed that the role proposed by Ernst and Young (2012) in this regard has been largely fulfilled by Infrastructure Australia since 2008. Similarly, 'Recommendation 7', which argues for a re-examination of the roles and responsibilities of local government as an element to the Australian federation, has been extensively explored (see, for example, Dollery, Wallis and Allan, 2006).

Finally, the chief recommendation in Ernst and Young's (2012) report proposed that 'the Australian Government should work with the states and territories to investigate the feasibility of establishing a national financing authority to aggregate local government borrowing and facilitate the creation of debt products for private investors'. However, a most unfortunate aspect of the Ernst and Young (2012) report resides in the absence of a comprehensive analysis focused on the nature and characteristics of the recommended bond. In this chapter we attempt to address this neglect.

This chapter is divided into four main sections. Section 9.2 canvasses municipal banking as a putative solution to the Australian local government infrastructure shortfall. Section 9.3 sets out the case for a national bond bank. Section 9.4 considers three 'case studies' of existing municipal bond banks: the Local Government Finance Authority of South Australia (LGFA), the New Zealand Local Government Funding Agency (NZLGFA) and the Municipal Finance Authority of British Columbia (MFABC). The chapter ends with some brief concluding remarks in section 9.5.

9.2 Municipal banking

In historical terms, municipal banking has been seen as an alternative approach to municipal bond finance as a method of mobilising private capital for local government infrastructural investment. In contrast to the North American approach, with its strong focus on private funds secured through competitive municipal bond markets, municipal banking was the principal means of financing infrastructure in many European local government systems for much of the 20th century (Chandavarkar, 1994; De Fiore and Uhlig, 2005). A number of European nations created specialist municipal banks in order to supply capital and associated financial services to local government, such as the Credit Local de France and the Municipal Bank of the Netherlands. Dollery, Kortt and Grant (2012) have argued that, as a general rule, municipal banks acquired not only monopoly status in dealing with local authorities, forcing municipalities to keep accounts and deposits with them, but also exclusive access to cheap, long-term savings allowing them to provide low-cost, long-term loans to local government entities.

George Peterson (2002) has argued that European municipal banking had three main components: 'relationship banking', 'delegated monitoring' and 'bundled services and bundled pricing'. With respect to relationship banking, European banks established ongoing relationships with local councils through which banks assisted municipalities to 'prepare and structure their budgets, design investment projects, and conduct financial analysis of cost recovery strategies', and often managed council 'financial accounts and maintained the municipality's deposits', as well as long-term loans to fund investment projects. In addition, in some instances, municipal banks 'served as the designated intermediary between the central government and municipalities by handling tax-sharing arrangements or administering local government grant allocations on behalf of the central government' (Peterson, 2002, 5).

The monopoly privileges bestowed on municipal banks were justified on the basis that local councils had weak administrative and technical capacities and thus required far-reaching support for prolonged periods in order to operate effectively as financial entities. It was also argued that municipal banks could afford to 'nurture communities through the learning process only if the bank is subsidised by central government policy or enjoys partial protection from competition so that it can create a long-term client'. Accordingly, as the financial and managerial capacities of local government improved, 'relationship banking' would become steadily less important.

'Delegated monitoring' refers to the fact that municipal banks operate as financial intermediaries between borrowers and lenders in place of individual councils performing this function on their own. Delegated monitoring is upheld on grounds that 'it is inefficient for each saver to try to monitor financial conditions and all other factors affecting loan payment' and that a single municipal bank can more successfully collect 'savings from numerous sources, assemble specialized professionals capable of loan appraisal and loan oversight, allocate capital, and then monitor loans and borrowers' (Peterson, 2002, 5–6). In the event of difficulties, 'a well-functioning municipal bank will initiate loan-restructuring discussions with a borrower when the client encounters serious financial difficulty' because 'loan restructuring is preferable to accumulating nonperforming loans'.

Under 'bundled services and bundled pricing' municipal banks effectively charge all local authorities the same prices, despite individual differences. Peterson (2002) has contended that prices charged for services and loans by municipal banks do not accurately reflect marginal costs or the underlying risks involved. For instance, 'the bundled services that municipal banks offer rarely are broken out or priced to correspond with incremental costs for a particular service'. Moreover, price discrimination to mirror the creditworthiness of borrowing councils is atypical since 'municipal banks lend to all municipal clients at the same interest rate'. As financial markets have become less regulated and the supply of 'below cost' funds from public sector agencies has diminished, the 'one price' system adopted by municipal banks has become unsustainable. As a consequence, in many countries municipal banks have lost preferential access to cheap long-term savings, which has obliged them to compete in money markets for loan finance.

Given the daunting problems confronting local infrastructure finance in Australian local government, at first sight municipal banks appear to have much to offer. After all, a majority of Australian local authorities are not only small, but also frequently lack sufficient financial proficiency. Relational banking is thus a desirable policy option since –in contrast to their counterparts in the commercial banking sector – municipal banks adopt a proprietary view of client councils and offer general advice, expertise and monitoring. Furthermore, from the perspective of Commonwealth and state governments, and agencies such as the Commonwealth Grants Commission, which partially finance local government, a national municipal bank with a strong oversight role has many benefits, including acting as a safeguard for the prudent disbursement of public monies. An Australian municipal bank could play a key part in the process to enhance asset management through financial capacity development in local government.

Notwithstanding these apparent advantages, Dollery, Kortt and Grant (2012) have argued that municipal banking has several weaknesses. For example, the infrastructure backlog in Australian local government has occurred in part because Commonwealth and state government remittances to local government have not adequately kept pace with the demands placed on local government. One consequence is that private capital has become indispensable for ameliorating the infrastructure shortfall. Because municipal banks could compete effectively with the commercial banking sector for capital, this would undermine their comparative advantage, since they would lose preferential access to cheap long-term finance. Dollery, Kortt and Grant (2012) have contended that, since a limited pool of Commonwealth funds exists for local government infrastructure investment, a national municipal bank is unlikely to be able to expand this pool.

9.3 Municipal bond banks

9.3.1 Characteristics of local government bond banks

As we saw in Chapter 8, the argument advanced by Byrnes, Dollery, Crase and Simmons (2008) for the establishment of an Australia municipal bond market to assist local government borrowing was based in part on the US municipal bond market. The US market has given individual local authorities direct access to funding, private credit ratings and insurance institutions. The vitality of the US market derives chiefly from the fact that municipal bonds are traded actively, allowing even short- and medium-term investors to purchase long-term bonds which can be traded in secondary markets. However, despite the efficiency of this market, and in stark contrast to their counterparts, small US councils cannot readily participate due to high fixed costs covering disclosure documentation, bond insurance, securing credit ratings and the like. In order to overcome this problem, numerous US states have established bond banks to reap economies of scale in bond issuance. State governments have also conferred default security guarantee measures to boost creditworthiness (American Council of Infrastructure Financing Authorities (CIFA), 1997).

National and state-based local government finance entities or bond banks have been established in numerous advanced economies, including several Nordic countries, many US states, some Canadian provinces, New Zealand and South Australia. These institutions exhibit a high degree of heterogeneity. No single definition thus adequately covers all of these institutions. However, the CIFA (1997, 2) has presented a broad depiction which encompasses most of these entities: a bond bank is 'an entity that sells its own securities and relends bond proceeds to local governmental entities'. This generic definition can include private for-profit firms, non-profit organisations and public institutions, 'many of which only issue debt for a single purpose'. The CIFA (1997) has also offered a more precise description of a bond bank as 'a state-sponsored entity that makes local infrastructure projects feasible by providing access to the municipal bond market and by providing direct and indirect financial subsidies to localities primarily through debt issuance'. It noted that 'in distinguishing between these two definitions, the concept of state sponsorship and assistance is important in distinguishing those borrowing entities that enjoy an element of state "legitimacy" and support, as opposed to those entities that are purely free-standing and unassisted'. In addition, the main aim of most bond banks is to provide local government with cheap infrastructure funding by means of debt issuance, characteristically with government support.

Dollery, Kortt and Grant (2011) have observed that, in terms of organisational structure, most US bond banks were established by state government legislation, which seldom embraced taxation powers. While bond banks typically exist as autonomous authorities, with independent governing boards and an administrative arm with considerable financial expertise, some bond banks operate within state government administrative hierarchies. Most US bond banks are financially sovereign insofar as they do not depend on state governments to supply them with operating funds. As a general rule, bond banks rely on a variety of types of revenue. The most common funding method levies fees and charges on borrowing municipalities, including lump-sum fees at the close of an issue, an annual fee based on outstanding loans and mark-up interest rates.

Although great variation occurs in the operation of different bond banks, a common pattern seems applicable to most municipal finance corporations (CIFA, 1997; Gilbert and Pike, 1995; Kidwell and Rogoski, 1983; Martell and Guess, 2006; Peng and Brucato, 2003; Robbins and Kim, 2003; Solano, 2005; Yusuf and Lui, 2008). Dollery, Kortt and Grant (2011) have argued that, while bond banks offer different kinds of financing programs to the local government sector, these can be broadly divided into three main categories: (i) long-term bond pools, such as the refinance of existing debt; (ii) cash flow financing, intended to align income and expenditure streams over the financial year; and (iii) equipment lease financing, used to acquire costly facilities and machinery. Since we are considering local infrastructure funding, we are primarily concerned with long-term bonds as in category (i). In general, Dollery, Kortt and Grant (2011) have contended that two approaches have been followed, often by the same institution. In the first place, bond banks pool together the smaller issues of multiple local governments into a single large bond sale. Second, bond banks issue bonds for single, normally large, local authorities.

Against the background of the comparatively small size of most Australian local councils, Dollery, Kortt and Grant (2011) have argued that an Australian national bond bank would deal largely with long-term bond pooling. The technicalities of long-term bond pooling are relatively straightforward. A bond bank usually issues bonds under its own legal identity and uses the resultant revenue to acquire debt obligations from a large number of small councils, which have sought finance from the bond bank. These banks typically apply credit requirements which borrowing councils must meet to qualify for loans. Preconditions may take the form of a general obligation by local borrowers or minimum requirements for debt service coverage. These credit requirements obviously have major implications for the credit ratings of bond banks.

Dollery, Kortt and Grant (2011) have argued that numerous benefits flow from this approach. First, purchasers of bonds are secured by loan repayments from the pool of many local council borrowers instead of a single municipality. In addition, if the operations of the bond bank are guaranteed by a central government or a state government, then borrowers receive further security through this 'credit enhancement'. National and state governments provide credit enhancement or financial support of different types to bond banks, but they all serve to diminish the costs of borrowing (Gilbert and Pike, 1995). In turn, this lowers interest rates on bond bank debt since state credit ratings are usually higher than local government ratings for the same debt instruments. The most common form of credit enhancement provided to US bond banks comprises state government moral obligation pledges to secure debt service reserve (DSR) funds. Bond bank debt issues are often accompanied by a DSR fund which equals the maximum annual debt service that could be assumed if default on debt service payments occurred. In case of a default, under these arrangements the bond bank will seek state financial intervention to reinstate the DSR fund to its required level. Investors still face the risk that state legislatures will decline to replenish a DSR fund. However, credit rating agencies normally recognise a state moral obligation pledge with a rating one category lower than that state's general obligation rating. In fewer cases, state governments pledge their full credit support to a pooled issue sold by the bond bank. Finally, in numerous US state jurisdictions, bond banks have acquired statutory authority to seize state aid to local authorities, if these councils fail to pay on their obligations to the bond bank. 'Intercepts' of this type can have a major impact on credit ratings in those local government jurisdictions in which local authorities receive a sizeable proportion of their income from state governments. In some US states, bond banks benefit simultaneously from several types of credit enhancement.

A second critical factor from the perspective of the cost of funds resides in the diversification offered in the bond pool. In general, it means that investors need lower interest rates than they would accept if they were purchasing a single obligation from a single local authority, especially a small, little-known municipality. Third, bond pooling can yield operational scale economies since it spreads the fixed costs associated with issuance – rating fees, legal fees and so forth – over a larger number of lenders and borrowers. Furthermore, economies of scale in purchasing originate from the capacity to negotiate lower fees for bond insurance, advertising and the like than would otherwise prevail in more limited single issues. Fourth, in addition to these savings, the local government sector as a whole, and particularly smaller local councils with limited managerial and financial capacity, which constitute the preponderance of Australian local authorities, can acquire significant other benefits from bond banks. More specifically, access to skilled staff, with specialised knowledge of financial markets, can secure sound financial advice to small local authorities seeking to borrow. In practice, bond banks typically simplify complicated debt issuance processes, which usually require participating councils to complete a few uncomplicated forms. Moreover, bond banks often structure customised repayment schedules especially for small municipalities with monthly rather than semi-annual payment deadlines.

Despite the fact that bond banks have substantial benefits for local government, principally smaller municipal entities, Dollery, Kortt and Grant (2011) have pointed to various disadvantages which have been acknowledged in the literature (CIFA, 1997). For example, in some instances the terms at which borrowing takes place can be inflexible because these terms have been designed to meet national and state statutory obligations on bond banks. In an analogous vein, councils which hold both the skills and credit ratings required by the market can often secure lower total interest costs than a bond bank by simply issuing on their own debt, since they do not have to implicitly cross-subsidise smaller councils with less creditworthiness (Robbins and Kim, 2003). As a result, bond banks characteristically offer more to smaller councils with limited capacity and weaker ratings than to their larger, wealthier counterparts.

The advantages of bond banks for different-sized municipalities have been described by Robbins and Kim (2003, 92–3) as follows:

> [Smaller local authorities] may receive lower prices (and bear higher interest rates) for their bonds than their larger counterparts because of the small amount of the issue, high per bond marketing costs, smaller secondary markets, limited information for bond dealers and buyers, difficulty in affording quality legal and financial advisers, or because their issues are unrated. Larger governments are also more frequent issuers, and experience itself has been demonstrated to reduce certain borrowing costs. Larger governments may also possess resident expertise and debt management capacity that smaller governments lack. Finally, larger governments may benefit from relationships established with market actors over the course of many issues.

Dollery, Kortt and Grant (2011) have contended that, given the size composition of Australian local government, with its numerical preponderance of small local councils, these disadvantages are not significant from a public policy perspective.

9.3.2 A national bond bank model for Australian local government

As discussed in more detail in section 9.4.2, an Act of Parliament passed in 2011 in the New Zealand Parliament established the New Zealand Local Government Funding Agency (NZLGFA), which was designed as a national New Zealand bond bank. The NZLGFA was intended to borrow on a large scale and re-lend to local authorities looking for funding for any purpose, not only infrastructure finance. It is jointly owned by local and central government in proportion to their respective capital contributions. No council is obliged to borrow from the NZLGFA, and local governments can thus seek other sources of funds. A guarantee has been stipulated for all establishment shareholders, as well as borrowers above $20 million, in order to ensure the NZLGFA solicits a high credit rating. The guarantee has been spread across all contributors on a pro rata basis in proportion to the ratepayer base of participating entities. Since no New Zealand local council has ever defaulted, the likelihood of the guarantee being called is minimal.

Dollery, Kortt and Grant (2011) have argued that the local government systems of Australia and New Zealand have numerous close similarities: a comparatively narrow range of services, a common political structure of local councils, limited 'own-source' forms of revenue available to local authorities, substantial prescribed expenditure, tightly stipulated local infrastructure requirements (Marshall, 2008; Reid, 2008) and a substantial local infrastructure backlog (Dollery and Mounter, 2010). Dollery, Kortt and Grant (2011, 125) have argued further that this suggests 'possible elements which the design of an Australian national bond bank could take into account from the structure of the New Zealand LGFA'. However, they caution that 'apart from the question of the scale of operations of an Australian bond bank, which would have to be much larger than its New Zealand counterpart, several other thorny problems would have to be overcome'.

In the first place, Dollery, Kortt and Grant (2011) have observed that, while New Zealand has a single national local government system with uniform standards with respect to local infrastructure, different Australian state and territory local government systems employ different reporting standards, collect different data, use different criteria for assessing financial sustainability, have different asset planning and management frameworks, and use different financial planning and reporting standards. The consequence is 'a mosaic of local government infrastructure systems with little in common' (p.x), except the size of the backlog. These complications compound the difficulties facing an Australian national bond bank seeking to apply consistent prudential standards to borrowing councils. However, Dollery, Kortt and Grant (2011) have noted that the Australian Local Government and Planning Ministers Council has recently adopted a nationally consistent framework on financial sustainability covering three broad areas: assessing financial sustainability, an asset planning and management framework, and a financial planning and reporting framework. In addition, the Institute of Public Works Engineering Australia (IPWEA) (2011) has published *Australian Infrastructure Financial Management Guidelines*, for the first time providing nationally applicable standards. Although they have yet to be put into practice at the level of the individual local councils, the foundation exists which can be used by a future bond bank.

Second, Dollery, Kortt and Grant (2011, 126) have contended that a 'significant complicating factor in the design of an Australian bond bank, which distinguishes sharply between the Australian and New Zealand local government systems, resides in the inescapable fact that under the Australian constitution local government falls under state and not national government jurisdiction'. They have noted that this means state legislation controls local government and state local government oversight mechanisms are not uniform across Australia (Dollery, O'Keefe and Crase, 2009). For instance, 'each state imposes its own regulatory authority on local government borrowing and, as a general rule, all council borrowing in all jurisdictions must be approved by respective state Ministers for Local Government'. However, in the past this has not proved a major impediment to council borrowing, nor has council default been a problem (Dollery, Crase and Johnson, 2006). Dollery, Kortt and Grant (2011) stressed that, from the perspective of prudent conduct by a bond bank, and the credit requirements it would want to apply to borrowing municipalities, this mélange of state regulation need pose 'no real problem'. In particular, given the lack of council loan default in Australian local government history, the bond bank could allow the state Minister for Local Government to decide whether or not a specific local authority can borrow.

Third, Dollery, Kortt and Grant (2011, 126) have pointed to complications arising from the nature of activities for which funds are furnished. Whereas the NZLGFA permits local authorities to borrow for any purpose, they contend that 'borrowing through an Australian bond bank should be specifically limited to local government infrastructure investment, maintenance and improvement'. The basis for this restriction is twofold: the '*raison d'être* of the bond bank revolves around ameliorating the local infrastructure crisis rather than simply acting as a general source of funding, and it would thus be unwise to permit scarce funds from being used for other ends' and the 'political imperative involved in securing Commonwealth Government support means that the bond bank should focus exclusively on infrastructure finance'.

However, Dollery, Kortt and Grant (2011, 126) have contended that 'apart from these complexities, the structure of the bond bank and its operations should be comparatively straightforward'. In particular, the Commonwealth Government should contribute about 'half of the initial funds', with state Local Government Associations (LGAs) 'combining in some agreed proportion', using population size, total rate base or some other measure, with the rest of the initial capital sum required. A board of directors would constitute the governing body structure, with half of all board positions drawn from the federal government and the remainder appointed by state LGAs. The bond bank would be managed by an executive director and comprise a secretariat containing infrastructure finance experts, as well as an administrative arm.

In operational terms, Dollery, Kortt and Grant (2011, 127) argued that the Commonwealth would 'fully guarantee all debt issued by the bond bank' which would result in a credit rating 'comparable to standard Commonwealth debt issues'. Debt issued by the bond bank would be pooled and issued on a regular basis. This would serve to reap 'operational scale economies' and pool perceived risk. Local councils which had been granted borrowing permission by their state government could apply for funding for 'defined types of infrastructure', which would be 'secured by obligations made out by individual councils and protected by state government guarantee'. The bond bank would make available 'extensive financial advice' to local authorities on a user pays basis. This would provide small councils with 'negligible financial expertise' with affordable and disinterested expert advice. Dollery, Kortt and Grant (2011, 127) stressed that this would 'perform a vital function' for small councils which suffered not only 'acute financial distress', but also 'chronic technical incapacity'. Furthermore, in addition to infrastructure funding, the bond bank could provide advice on asset management to borrowing councils.

9.4 Case studies

9.4.1 Local Government Finance Authority of South Australia

The Local Government Finance Authority of South Australia (LGFA) came into being with the assent of the *Local Government Finance Authority Act* (SA) on 22 December 1983. Since then the legislation has undergone some minor alterations (Government of South Australia 1999, 14).[1] However, the details of the original

1 Of note is the fact that amendments under the *Local Government Finance Authority Regulations 2005* expanded the definition of ***prescribed local government body*** to include a variety of other types of organisations alongside local government bodies. These included eight hospitals and other health facilities and several other statutory corporations and professional bodies, including the Australian Institute of Building Surveyors, Local Government Managers Australia, South Australian Division, the Murray Darling Association, Incorporated and The Council Purchasing Authority Pty Ltd (see *Local Government Finance Authority Regulations 2005*, 1–2), thereby extending lines of finance to these bodies.

Act – and therefore the operation of the LGFA – have remained largely intact. The Authority is a statutory corporation of the South Australian Government, operating under the *Public Corporations Act 1993* (SA), and all 68 local councils in South Australia are *de jure* members. The Authority is overseen by a seven-member Board of Trustees, each of whom serves for two years. Two members of the Board are elected; two members are appointed at an annual general meeting of all members of Authority after nomination by the South Australian Local Government Association (SALGA); one member is appointed by the Minister for State-Local Government Relations; one is appointed by the Treasurer; and the seventh member is the Secretary of the Local Government Association. All Board members must be either council members or council officers, and all Board members can be reappointed. The Board has both a Presiding Member and a Deputy Presiding Member (Government of South Australia, 1999, 3–5). The Board is thus a representative structure of all South Australian local government as well as being intertwined with the core executive of the South Australian government.

Part 3 section 21(1) of the *Local Government Finance Authority Act 1983* (Government of South Australia, 1999, 8) specifies the functions of the LGFA broadly:

(a) to develop and implement borrowing and investment programmes for the benefit of councils and prescribed local government bodies; and
(b) to engage in such other financial activities as are determined by the minister, after consultation with the LGA, to be in the interests of local government.

In order that these functions are undertaken, the Act (section 22(2)) holds that the LGFA may:

(a) borrow money within or outside Australia; or
(b) accept money on deposit or loan from a council or prescribed local government body; or
(c) lend or invest money held by the Authority; or
(d) issue, sell, purchase, pay-off, repurchase, redeem, convert or otherwise deal in or with securities or shares; or
(e) open and maintain accounts with an ADI [Australian Depositor Institution] or any other financial institution within or outside Australia; or

(f) appoint an ADI or other person to act as underwriter, manager, trustee, attorney or agent in connection with any transaction within or outside Australia; or
(g) enter into contracts of guarantee or indemnity; or
(h) acquire, hold, deal with and dispose of real and personal property; or
(i) enter into partnerships and joint ventures and form companies; or
(j) enter into any agreement or arrangement of a kind not previously mentioned in this subsection or acquire or incur any other rights or liabilities; or
(k) exercise any other powers that are necessary or expedient for the performance of its functions. (Government of South Australia 1999, 8–9)

It is noteworthy that after specifying several types of activity, such as the capacity to borrow overseas, the Act also provides for the LGFA to exercise 'any other powers that are necessary or expedient for the performance of its functions' (section 21(k)). Under Part 3 section 21(3) of the Act, the LGFA can act as a financial adviser to individual local governments. The only caveat to the exercising of all these types of authority is that it must do so 'with the approval of the Treasurer' (Government of South Australia, 1999, 10).

Sections 22–24 of the Act further prescribe the operations of the LGFA. Section 22 specifies that the LGFA must operate 'with a view to avoiding a loss' and that 'any surplus of funds remaining' may be 'retained and invested by the Authority', 'distributed amongst the councils and prescribed local government bodies', or 'applied for the benefit of any council or prescribed local government body' (Government of South Australia, 1999, 9). Section 23 empowers the Treasurer to provide funds for the LGFA 'on such terms and conditions as may be agreed between the Treasurer and the Authority', including an initial sum of $10 million. Section 24 specifies that liabilities incurred by the LGFA will be guaranteed by the South Australian Government. Section 31 of the Act specifies that the LGFA may – or may not – charge fees for its services while section 31A specifies that the Treasurer may – or may not – require the LGFA to pay tax. Section 32 of the Act specifies that the Treasurer can exempt the LGFA from all taxes (Government of South Australia, 1999, 9). Under section 33, the

LGFA is subject to fiduciary reporting requirements, including selective auditing by the Auditor General.

An illustrative account of the LGFA's current activities can be derived from the 2011 Annual Report (LGFA, 2011). In essence, the LGFA operates as a bank, the exclusive clients of which are South Australian local authorities as well as prescribed local government bodies. The LGFA offers several types of secure investments: 'at call deposits', 'short term deposits' ranging from 30 to 180 days, and 'long term deposits', which vary from 1 to 5 years (LGFA, 2012).

The LGFA offers two broad types of loans: fixed-rate and floating-rate. At the end of 2010/11 total loans outstanding were $564.6 million, comprising $416.9 million in fixed rate loans and $147.7 million in variable rate loans (LGFA, 2011, 5). Furthermore, all borrowings are free of any fees and lenders may receive an annual bonus based upon the overall annual performance of the Authority (LGFA, 2012). The LGFA (2012) distinguished between four types of borrowings:

- Credit fancier style loans: fixed interest rate loans that are repaid with equal instalments of principal and interest for the term of the loan;
- Interest only borrowings: where instalments for interest are taken and repayment of the principal occurs at the end of the loan;
- Specially structured loans: 'tailored to meet the individual borrower's needs', and
- Cash advance suite of products: where funds are accessible either on a 24-hour floating rate basis or variable rate for terms of 30 to 180 days. Alternatively, they may be available for a fixed rate for periods of 1 to 5 years within a single long term funding facility.

The LGFA offers funds to its member councils and other prescribed local government bodies on extremely flexible terms. furthermore, the range of projects for which funds are loaned is broad. For example, in its 2011 Annual Report, the LGFA (2012, 3) noted that the City of Marion borrowed $3.5 million from the LGFA, which formed a contribution to the $120 million South Australian Aquatic and Leisure Centre and GP Plus Health

Care Centre. Even small loans are entertained. For instance, the District Council of Streaky Bay financed the construction of a new home for its CEO with a $215,000 loan from the LGFA.

Table 9.1. LGFA Financial Indicators 2010 and 2011

	2010 $'000	2011 $'000
Statement of Comprehensive Income		
Income		
Interest on Investments	3,096	3,314
Interest on Loans and Advances	43,896	51,877
Other Income	675	515
Total Income	**47,667**	**55,706**
Expenses		
Interest on Deposits from Councils and Local Government Bodies	14,597	18,442
Interest on Borrowings	25,685	29,810
Fees for the Guarantee of the Treasurer of S.A. on Liabilities	962	1,022
Administration Expenses	1,651	1,749
Total Expenses	**42,895**	**51,023**
Profit Before Income Tax Equivalents	4,772	4,683
Income Tax Equivalent Expense	1,432	1,405
Profit After Income Tax Equivalents	3,340	3,278
Total Comprehensive Result	**3,340**	**3,278**
Statement of Financial Position		
Total Assets (cash, net loans and advances, property, plant, etc.)	595,696	629,943
Total Liabilities (deposits, interest payable, borrowings, etc.)	542,653	575,362
Net Assets	53,043	54,581
Total Equity (attributable to owners)	**53,043**	**54,581**

Source: Adapted from the 'Annual Report 2011' of the Local Government Finance Authority of South Australia (LGFA, 2011, 10–11).

The overall financial position of the South Australian LGFA is shown in Table 9.1, which demonstrates that the LGFA is a comparatively modest financial institution. For example, the Bank of Queensland's (BOQ) normalised operating profit for 2011 was $176.6 million, with total equity amounting to $2,573.6 million (BOQ, 2011). In 2012 the Commonwealth Bank of Australia (CBA) reported a net operating profit of $3,624 million (CBA, 2012) for the previous financial year. By contrast, the 'total comprehensive result' for the LGFA for 2010/11 averaged $3,309,000. However, profitability is not the central concern of the LGFA. On the contrary, as we have seen, the LGFA's primary role is to provide funds to its member bodies, which are the sole owners of equity in the Authority. In this sense, the LGFA conforms to a shared service as defined by Dollery, Grant and Kortt (2012). More precisely, the LGFA can be defined as a 'vertical shared service', as defined by Dollery, Grant and Kortt (2012), since management of the LGFA rests with a Board that includes two members appointed by the state government, and it is both overseen as well as underwritten by the state Treasury. Its operations thus differ from a for-profit entity, a point that Dollery, Grant and Kortt (2012) took some lengths to emphasise. The non-profit nature of the LGFA is further reinforced when we recall that it distributes surpluses to its member contributing councils and that it has not incurred any bad debts since the commencement of operations in 1984 (LGFA, 2011, 14). While the operations of the LGFA are straightforward, it nonetheless represents a potential model for a municipal infrastructure fund – in the form of a bank – which might be replicated at a national level.

9.4.2 New Zealand Local Government Funding Agency

The New Zealand Local Government Funding Agency Ltd (NZLGFA) came into being under the *Local Government Borrowing Act 2011* (NZ). It was incorporated on 1 December 2011 and registered under the *Companies Act 1993* (New Zealand Government, 2011, 2). In common with the South Australian LGFA, the NZLGFA is owned by 30 Local Authority Councils and the Crown, with the national government providing NZ$5 million investment and securing a 20 per cent shareholding, and local government contributing the remaining NZ$20 million. It describes itself as a 'Council Controlled Organisation (CCO) operating under the Local Government Act 2002' (NZLGFA, 2011, x). It thus also conforms to the Dollery, Grant and Kortt (2012) definition of a vertical shared service in much the same way as the South

Australian LGFA. However, the *Local Government Borrowing Act 2011* did have to accommodate some of the institutional aspects of local government in New Zealand to enable the NZLGFA to operate effectively.[2] The NZLGFA has been designed to 'provide more efficient funding costs and diversified funding sources (including foreign currency) for NZ local authorities'. Additionally, 'it will provide investors with a new source of securities rated at AA+ (domestic long term) by international credit ratings agencies' (NZLGFA, 2011). A guarantee has been stipulated for all establishment shareholders, as well as borrowers above $20 million, in order to ensure the NZLGFA solicits a high credit rating. The guarantee has been spread across all contributors on a pro rata basis in proportion to the ratepayer base of participating entities. Since no New Zealand local council has ever defaulted, the prospects of the guarantee being called are minimal.

According to the NZLGFA (2011), its 'primary purpose' is to 'provide more efficient funding costs and diversified funding sources (including foreign currency) for NZ local authorities' by providing investors 'with a new source of securities [bonds] rated at AA+ (domestic long term) by international credit ratings agencies'. While the NZLGFA shares some common characteristics with the South Australian LGFA (for example, local authorities are not obliged to borrow from it) it is nevertheless fundamentally different in a number of respects. For instance, the South Australian LGFA provides a range of financial services

2 Section 9 of the *Local Government Borrowing Act 2011* lists several exemptions from the *Local Government Act 2002* such that the NZLGFA can operate. In particular, section 9(3) states:

> Despite section 63 of the Local Government Act 2002, a local authority may lend money, or provide any other financial accommodation, to the Funding Agency on terms and conditions that are more favourable to the Funding Agency than those that would apply if the local authority were (without charging any rate or rate revenue as security) borrowing the money or obtaining the financial accommodation (New Zealand Government, 2011, 4).

In this sense individual councils can enter into various types of financial arrangements with the NZLGFA. Under section 11 of the *Local Government Borrowing Act 2011*, the NZLGFA is also exempt from a prohibition on borrowing in foreign currency (New Zealand Government, 2011, 5).

exclusively to member councils, the deposits of which then form the basis of funding from the LGFA to member councils. By contrast, the NZLGFA issues bonds on the open market which are secured by the capital value of New Zealand local government and from which member councils can then draw upon for funding purposes. In other words, the NZLGFA provides access to a potentially far larger source of funds, provided that investors find the bonds attractive in terms of both security and rate of return.

In its 2011/12 'Statement of Intent', the NZLGFA (2011/12, 3) developed a 'business case' for its financial forecasts for the three years to 30 June 2014 (Table 9.2).

Table 9.2. Business Case for the NZ Local Government Funding Agency

Period to June 30 ($m)	**2012**	**2013**	**2014**
Local government interest income	9.9	31.2	50.9
LGFA interest expense	8.4	27.2	46.4
Net liquidity income	0.0	0.1	0.1
Total net income	**1.5**	**3.9**	**4.4**
Overheads	1.4	2.7	2.8
Pre establishment costs	4.6	--	--
Net profit	**4.4**	**1.2**	**1.6**
Borrower notes interest	0.1	0.5	0.8
Principal shares dividend	0.0	0.7	0.7
Retained surplus / (deficit)	4.6	0.0	0.0
Total assets	**621.5**	**1,099.5**	**1,605.8**
Total local government assets	**565.0**	**999.5**	**1,459.8**
Total liabilities	**592.1**	**1,063.1**	**1,562.0**
Total equity	29.5	36.4	43.8
Shareholder funds / total assets	4.7	3.3	2.7

Source: NZLGFA 'Statement of Intent', 2011/12, 3.

Table 9.2 demonstrates the NZLGFA is not a profit-maximising entity in its own right. Total net income is projected to rise only from $1.5 to $4.4 million from 2012 to 2014, while net profit is expected to *decrease* from $4.4 million to $1.6 million over the same period. This conforms to the NZLGFA's 'primary objective' of 'optimising the debt funding terms and conditions for participating local authorities', including 'providing debt to participating local authorities at the lowest possible interest rates commensurate with the relevant maturity' (NZLGFA, 2011/02, 2), which 'will be no more than 0.40 %' (NZLGFA, 2011/12, 3). This is reflected in the projected growth of both the NZLGFA's assets over the three-year period and the assets of participating local government authorities over the same time period: \$621.5–\$1,605.8 million and \$565.0–\$1,459.8 million, respectively. The 'Statement of Intent' (NZLGFA, 2011/12, 4) also projected that total lending to participating councils would increase from 'at least' \$500 million at 30 June 2012 to 'at least' \$1,400 million at 30 June 2014, with 'over 30' local authorities participating.

With respect to governance, the 2011/12 'Statement of Intent' (NZLGFA, 2011/12, 4) specifies that a Board of Directors will 'comprise between four and seven directors with a majority of independent directors', which will be responsible for the 'strategic direction and control of the [NZ]LGFA's activities ... in accordance with the *Local Government Act 2002*, the *Local Government Borrowing Act 2011*, the Company's Constitution, the Shareholder's Agreement for [NZ]LGFA and this SOI [Statement of Intent]'. Further, the Board must comply with a 'General Charter' which is 'developed and agreed with Shareholders'. Moreover, the SOI stipulates that the Board will meet 'no less than 11 times per year'. This high degree of activity is reflected in the fact that the NZLGFA is obliged to produce annual, half-yearly and quarterly reports, and that an annual general meeting be held between 30 September and 30 November in order 'to present an annual report to all shareholders'. In addition, a 'Shareholders Council' is also appointed, comprising nine individuals drawn from member councils and one 'from the Crown'. The Shareholders Council undertakes four functions: (i) 'to review the performance of the [NZ]LGFA and the Board, and report to Shareholders'; (ii) to 'make recommendations to Shareholders as to the appointment, removal, replacement and remuneration of directors'; (iii) to make recommendations to the Shareholders with respect to policy changes; and (iv) to 'ensure Shareholders are fully informed on [NZ]LGFA matters and to coordinate Shareholders on governance decisions' (NZLGFA, 2011/12, 5).

Table 9.3. NZLGFA Bonds Tender Results History, Data at 21 March 2012

Tender Date	Maturity Date	Tender No.	Volume Offered (Millions)	Volume Bid (Millions)	Volume Accepted (Millions)	Over/ Under Allocation (Millions)	Wtd. Avg. Successful Yield %	Range of Accepted Bids %	Wtd. Avg. Unsuccessful Yield %	Range of Unsuccessful Bids %
21 March 2012	15 December 2017	2	$180	$765	$180	$0	4.910	4.890–4.930	4.984	4.930–5.050
21 March 2012	15 April 2015	2	$85	$194	$85	$0	4.008	3.960–4.050	4.100	4.050–4.150
15 February 2012	15 December 2017	1	$250	$1,104	$250	$0	4.607	4.330–4.660	4.797	4.670–5.090
15 February 2012	15 April 2015	1	$50	$216	$50	$0	3.670	3.650–3.690	3.922	3.740–4.130

Source: 'LGFA Bonds' (NZLGFA, 2012).

At the time of writing the NZLGFA had been operating for only 15 months. However, it provided useful information on its first two bond issues, shown in Table 9.3.

Table 9.3 provides a most interesting 'snapshot'. It demonstrates that, despite its tender years, the NZLGFA has found a ready market with all its debt issues thus far fully subscribed. Indeed, in every case investors sought many more bonds than the offered volume. This bodes well for future bond issues.

9.4.3 Municipal Finance Authority of British Columbia

The third case study deals with the Municipal Finance Authority of British Columbia (MFABC). The MFABC is a municipal financial institution which takes considerable pride in its own history (see, for example, MFABC, 2012). As part of its 2010 Annual Report, Ray T Bryant, the original and still the serving lawyer for the Authority, provided a concise portrait of the genesis and 40-year operation of the organisation. Bryant (2011, 1) noted that the MFABC presently constitutes a capital borrowing program for British Columbia's 161 municipalities and holds a triple-A credit rating on 'all national and international bond markets'. He contrasted the present favourable situation with that before the establishment of the Authority, observing that prior to 1960 'each municipality was on its own for its capital borrowing and all were at the mercy of the bond market with varying interest rates being charged, depending on the size of the municipality' (Bryant, 2011, 1).

In response to this unsatisfactory state of affairs, during the mid-1960s the (then) Provincial Minister for Municipal Affairs, Dan Campbell, and the (then) Premier of British Columbia, W.A.C. Bennett, developed legislation to create regional districts accounting for all municipalities and Crown land in the Province. These regional districts, legislatively recognised in 1868, provided a tax base upon which 'a pooled funding agency as borrower' could then be constructed. In its own account of this history, the MFABC (2012a, x) observed that 'proponents of the MFA Bill [enacted in April 1970] emphasised the administrative and monetary economies of scale that collective borrowing would enable ... garner[ing] improved market acceptance and confidence'; and that 'the MFA model took this further by making all borrowing "joint and several", in effect guaranteeing that all debt undertaken would have the full backing of every unit of local government in the province'. Moreover, according to Bryant (2011, 2), a 'Debt Reserve Fund' was created alongside the Authority which to this day is financed by the payment of 1% of all principal borrowed by regional districts. While initially this fund was created as a form of insurance in the event of any defaults by borrowing municipalities, the Debt Reserve Fund has reinforced the MFABC bond credit rating because no defaults have ever occurred.

The implementation of the MFABC was politically contested at the time. Opponents argued that borrowings of individual municipalities should be underwritten by the Province of British Columbia.[3] Despite this opposition, the Authority has continued its operations and – like the South Australian LGFA – has extended borrowing privileges to other government services, including water and sewage services, emergency services and the Greater Vancouver Transit Authority. In addition, MFABC introduced a Pooled Investment Fund (PIF) financial instrument in 1989 which is used for the capital financing of schools, universities and the requirements of First Nation people (MFABC, 2012a).

With respect to governance, the operations of the MFABC are directed by two entities. The larger of these – the MFABC Authority – originally comprised the Chair of each regional board, alongside extra members for the significantly more populous Greater Vancouver Regional District (GVRD) (Bryant, 2011, 3). At present, members of the Authority are elected officials who are then appointed by their regional districts based

3 Noteworthy is the reasoning behind the opposition to the establishment of the Authority. The MFABC (2012a) described it thus:

> Opponents believed the provincial government was offloading responsibilities onto municipalities, then characterized paternalistically as it's "creatures" or "children". They asserted that municipalities should be supported instead by a provincial debt guarantee and were not convinced of the viability of this proposed and previously unheard of structure. At this time, provincial or state debt guarantees were practically universal and larger municipalities would go it alone in the debt financing markets to meet their long-term borrowing needs'.

on the population size of each regional district. The Authority currently comprises 28 members for each regional district, with an additional 11 members from the demographically larger regional districts, of which GVRD is the largest, with 10 elected representatives on the Authority (MFABC 2012b).

The second of these governing entities is the Board of Trustees, which forms an executive of the MFABC. Originally it comprised the Chair of the Authority (who was then President of the Union of British Columbia Municipalities (UBCM) and six other members of the Authority, of which two came from GVRD, one from the Capital Regional District (CRD) and four members were drawn at large from the other regional divisions. At present, the Board of Trustees has 10 members, one from the CRD who also fulfils the role as Chair, four from GVRD and five from other regional districts (Bryant, 2011, 3).

While in this context it is not possible to provide a comprehensive account of the MFABC's operational history, in common with the South Australian LGFA it is possible to provide a 'snapshot' of operations from the years 2010 and 2011. Table 9.4 contains some financial indicators.

The data in Table 9.4 resemble that presented in Table 9.1 (representing the South Australian LGFA). For example, the average profit over both reporting periods was a modest $65,348. This indicates that profit maximisation is not the central concern of the MFABC. Rather, the original objective of the Authority – to 'provide "financing of water, sewer, and pollution control abatement facilities for Regional Districts and their member municipalities" ' (cited by Bryant, 2011, 3) and its extended remit to include broad financial sustainability for the municipalities of British Columbia – appears to be the Authority's strategic and operational objective.

In addition to the information in Table 9.4, the Authority's '2011 Annual Report' (MFABC, 2011) provides a useful operational detail on the MFABC. Long-term financial needs are met through 'the placements of bullet debentures in capital markets', with the bond issuances being syndicated through six Canadian chartered banks and two other financial institutions (MFABC, 2011, 10). In 2011, the Authority issued three debentures which can be summarised as follows:

Table 9.4. MFABC Financial Indicators 2010 and 2011

	2010 $'000	2011 $'000
Consolidated Statement of Comprehensive Income		
Revenue		
Interest from loans to clients	327,740	317,850
Investment income	75,196	82,560
Financial service fees	1.802	1,903
Recoveries from new issues	32	50
Operating levy	211	220
Total Revenue	**404,981**	**402,583**
Expense		
Interest on long term debt	286,316	286,993
Interest on bank and short term indebtedness	2,621	4,918
Amortisation of [premium] discount and issue costs on long-term debt	(985)	409
Administration	3,225	2,945
Accrual of investment income due to clients	2,678	7,955
Debt managing and marketing	140	148
Loss from change in fair value of derivative contracts	27,689	51,817
Total Expenses	**42,895**	**51,023**
Profit for the year	**83,297**	**47,398**
Other comprehensive income		
Net change in fair value of available for-sale financial assets	51,678	96,610
Net change in fair value of available for-sale financial assets transferred to profit and loss	(21,950)	26,249
Other comprehensive income for the year	29,728	122,859
Total comprehensive income for the year	**113,025**	**170,257**
Statement of Financial Position	December 31 2010	December 31, 2011
Total Assets (cash, net loans and advances, property, plant, etc.)	6,803,634	7,210,385
Total Liabilities (deposits, interest payable, borrowings, etc.)	6,601,210	6,954,433
Equity		
Accumulated other comparative income	95,348	218,207
Retained earnings	107,076	37,745
Total Equity	202,424	255,952
Total Liabilities and Equity	**6,803,634**	**7,210,385**

Source: Adapted from the '2011 Annual Report' of the Municipal Finance Authority of British Columbia (MFABC, 2011, 16–17).

- A $225 million 10-year debenture with a return of 4.176% dated June 1, 2021. At the time of this issue, the Government of Canada 10-year bond was yielding 3.371%, while comparable issuers were returning a yield in the range 4.24–4.33% (issued 28 March);
- A $515 million five-year debenture with a return of 3.029%. At the time of this issue, the Government of Canada five-year bond was yielding 2.549%, while other municipal issuers were returning a yield in the range 3.12–3.27% (issued on 13 May); and
- An additional $105 million of the 1 June 2011 debenture with a return of 3.175%. At the time of this issue, the Government of Canada 10-year bond was yielding 2.005%, while other municipal issuers were returning a yield in the range 3.40–3.60% (issued 4 October) (MFABC, 2011, 12).

Commenting upon these bond issuances, the (then) Chair of the Board of Trustees, Frank Lennard, observed that the triple-A credit rating of the Authority allowed it to borrow funds at very low interest which, in turn, has allowed it to lend to constituent councils at consistently low rates, regardless of the size of individual local authorities (MFABC, 2011). Alongside these bond issuances, the actuarial detail of several of the other services already discussed were available for 2011. The Pooled Investment Program (PIP), whereby municipalities can invest surplus funds for short, intermediate and long terms, averaged $1.8 billion over the reporting period and peaked at $2.2 billion during the year (MFABC, 2011). The Authority accommodated the requirement for short-term cash by issuing over $1.5 billion through the Commercial Paper Program, usually for a term of 35 days, the rates for which were benchmarked against Government of Canada Treasury Bills (MFABC, 2011). In addition, the Debt Reserve Fund sat at an average of $113 million over the year (MFABC, 2011). The '2011 Annual Report' also reiterated that the MFABC had never defaulted on any debt obligation and had thus never made a claim on the Debt Reserve Fund (MFABC, 2011).

Describing the accumulated operating position of the Authority at the end of 2011, the Chief Administrative Officer (CAO), Rodin Stringer, observed that total assets under management were in excess of $7.2 billion, that the balance of long-term loans to 28 regional districts and three other entities at the end of the reporting period was $4.8 billion, that short-term loans and leasing agreements equalled $175 million, and that 'included in our assets [ie: monies owing] are investments of $2.1 billion that we manage as sinking funds [namely] payments collected from our clients, invested, and used to retire the client debt obligation to the MFA'. The CAO also noted that the Authority's long-term debt at the end of 2011 was $6.2 billion (MFABC, 2011, 4).

With respect to the overall operations of the MFABC, it can be observed that it is broadly the same type of financial entity as both the South Australian LGFA and the NZLGFA. However, in common with the NZLGFA, and unlike the South Australian LGFA, it issues bonds on the open market, and thus has access to a far greater quantum of funds. Moreover, in line with the NZLGFA, and unlike the South Australian LGFA, the transactions of the MFABC are not guaranteed by government. Yet it is nevertheless a 'vertical shared service', as defined by Dollery, Grant and Kortt (2012), due to the equity for the MFABC residing in the taxing power of British Columbia's Regional Districts (created in 1968) and not in the local authorities themselves. Nevertheless its status as a shared service has the effect that its *modus operandi* is grounded in operations other than profit maximisation, especially in providing a source of credit to local government authorities and other entities. In addition, the secure nature of the MFABC, grounded in the taxation capacity of the regional district system, sees it enjoying the highest possible credit rating. As a consequence, it is able to borrow at extremely low rates, offer low yields on deposits, and in turn offer loans to its constituent members at extremely competitive rates. We have also seen that, besides bond issuances, the MFABC has developed a range of financial instruments, including pooled investment funds and so-called 'sinking funds', the former providing a vehicle for local authorities to invest excess funds which are lent to a variety of local entities (such as schools and universities), the latter constituting a mechanism whereby paid down debt of individual borrowing authorities is reinvested, the proceeds of which are then also set against the MFABC's debt.

9.5 Concluding remarks

Against the background of the various feasible models for tackling the crushing local infrastructure backlog in Australian local government considered in Part C of this book, such as a Commonwealth local infrastructure asset fund in Chapter 7, an Australian municipal bond market in Chapter 8 and municipal banking in section 9.2 of Chapter 9, the main thrust of this chapter has been to argue the case for the establishment of a national local government bond bank. Perhaps the most persuasive aspect of this argument resides in the fact that existing and successful municipal bond banks already operate in a number of countries, including those nations which share much in common with Australia, such as Canada and New Zealand. In particular, this chapter examined three 'case studies' in some detail: the Local Government Finance Authority of South Australia (LGFA), the New Zealand Local Government Funding Agency (NZLGFA), and the Municipal Finance Authority of British Columbia (MFABC).

While a key theme in this book has been the prosecution of a national bond bank as the best available method of ameliorating the infrastructure shortfall in Australian local government, it is evident from the discussion on Australian fiscal federalism in Part A of the book that, by itself, a national bond bank cannot represent a complete solution to the problem. The reasons for this caveat are self-evident. While a bond bank will provide local councils with the requisite capital finance for infrastructure investment, maintenance and renewal in the most cost-effective manner possible, it cannot provide local authorities in general, and especially financially stricken small rural shires in particular, with the revenue necessary to fund capital borrowings. A full resolution of the problem of financial unsustainability in local government would require some kind of re-assignment of expenditure and taxation powers in the Australian federation, a matter which extends beyond the ambit of this book.

References

Aarts, K, 1995. 'Intermediate Organizations and Interest Representation', in *Citizens and the State*, eds HD Klingeman and D Fuchs. Oxford: Oxford University Press: 227–57.

Abelson, P, 2003. *Public Economics: Principles and Practice*. Sydney: Applied Economics.

ABS [Australian Bureau of Statistics], 2005. *Australian System of Government Finance Statistics, Concepts, Sources, and Methods* (Cat. No. 5514.0). Canberra: ABS.

ABS [Australian Bureau of Statistics], 2012a. *Australian Demographic Statistics* (Cat. No. 3101.0). Canberra: ABS.

ABS [Australian Bureau of Statistics], 2012b. *Government Finance Statistics* (Cat. No. 5512.0). Canberra: ABS.

ABS [Australian Bureau of Statistics], 2012c. *Taxation Revenue Australia* (Cat. No. 5506.0). Canberra: ABS.

ABS [Australian Bureau of Statistics], nd. *Classifications Manual for Government Finance Statistics, Australia* (Cat. No. 1217.0). Canberra: ABS.

Access Economics, 2006a. *Local Government Finances in NSW: An Assessment*, Research Report for the Independent Inquiry into the Financial Sustainability of NSW Local Government. Sydney: Access Economics.

Access Economics, 2006b. *Local Government Finances in Western Australia*, Research Report for the Western Australian Local Government Association. Perth: Access Economics.

ACELG [Australian Centre for Excellence in Local Government], 2011.), *Unfinished Business? A Decade of Inquiries into Australian Local Government*. Sydney: ACELG.

ACIR [Advisory Commission on Intergovernmental Relations (US)], 1973. *City Financial Emergencies: The Intergovernmental Dimension*. Washington: Government Printing Office.

Adger, WN, and Jordan, A, eds, 2009. *Governing Sustainability*. London: Cambridge University Press.

Albanese, A, (Rt. Hon.), 2010. 'Australian Council of Local Government 17–18 June', Media Release. URL: <http://www.ministers.infrastructure.gov.au/aa/releases/2010/June/AA398_2010. htm>. Consulted 25 October 2011.

Allan Report [NSW Independent Inquiry into Local Government], 2006. *Are Councils Sustainable? Final Report: Findings and Recommendations*, Sydney: NSW Local Government and Shires Association.

Auditor-General, 2006. *Roads to Recovery*. Canberra: Australian National Audit Office.

REFERENCES

Auerbach, A, and Lee, R, eds, 2001. *Demographic Change and Fiscal Policy*. New York: Cambridge University Press.

Aulich, C, 1999. 'From Convergence to Divergence: Reforming Australian Local Government', *Australian Journal of Public Administration* 58(2): 12–23.

Aulich, C, 2005. 'Australia: Still a Tale of Cinderella', in *Comparing Local Governance: Trends and Developments*, eds B Denters and LE Rose. Basingstoke: Palgrave MacMillan.

AURDR [Australian Urban and Regional Development Review], 1994. *Financing Local Government: A Review of the Local Government (Financial Assistance) Act 1986*, Discussion Paper No. 1. Melbourne: AURDR.

AURDR [Australian Urban and Regional Development Review], 1994b. *Local Government Funding Methodologies,* Discussion Paper No. 2. Canberra: Australian Government Printing Services.

Australian Bureau of Statistics *see* ABS.

Australian Centre for Excellence in Local Government *see* ACELG.

Australian Government, 2008. *Infrastructure Australia Act 2008. An Act to Establish Infrastructure Australia and Infrastructure Coordinator, and for Related Purposes,* URL: <http://www.austlii.edu.au/au/legis/cth/num_act/iaa2008293/>. Consulted 2 May 2012.

Australian Government, 2012a. *Australia's Federal Relations, 2011–12,* Budget Paper No. 3. Canberra: CanPrint Communications.

Australian Government, 2012b. 'Budget 2012-13', URL: <http://www.budget.gov.au/>. Consulted 4 June 2012.

Australian Urban and Regional Development Review *see* AURDR.

Bahl, R, and Linn, J, 1994, 'Fiscal Decentralization and Intergovernmental Transfers in Less Developed Countries', *Publius*, 27(1): 1–20.

Bailey, SJ, 1999. *Local Government Economics*. Basingstoke: Macmillan.

Bank of Queensland *see* BOQ.

Beers, DT, and Cavanaugh, M, 1997. 'Sovereign Ratings: A Primer', in *Handbook of Emerging Fixed Income and Currency Markets*, eds FJ Fabrozzi and A Franco. New York: Frank J Fabozzi Associates.

Beresford-Wylie, A, Watts, G, and Thurairaja, V, 2006. 'Financing Local Government Infrastructure: The Australian Experience', *Sustaining Regions* 5(2): 5–15.

Berne, R, and Schramm, R, 1986. *Financial Analysis of Governments*. Englewood Cliffs, NJ: Prentice-Hall.

Berry, FS, 1994. 'Innovation in Public Management: The Adoption of Strategic Planning', *Public Administration Review* 5(2), 322–30.

BOQ [Bank of Queensland], 2011. 'Shareholder Review 2011', URL: <http://www.boq.com.au/uploadedFiles/Shareholder/BOQ_Shareholder%20Review%20 2011_medium%20res.pdf>. Consulted 15 June 2012.

Boyne, GA, 1998. *Public Choice Theory and Local Government*. Basingstoke: Macmillan.

Breton, A, 1995. *Competitive Governments*. Cambridge: Cambridge University Press.

Brooks, J, 2006. *New South Wales Local Government Expenditure and Revenue Analysis,* Research Report to the Independent Inquiry into Local Government Inquiry. Sydney: Proteus Management Group.

Brown, CV, and Jackson, PM, 1990. *Public Sector Economics*, 4th edition. Oxford: Basil Blackwell.

Brown, KW, 1993. 'The 10-Point Test of Financial Condition: Toward an Easy-to-Use Assessment Tool for Smaller Cities', *Government Finance Review* 9(6): 21–6.

Brown, KW, 1996. 'Trends in Key Ratios Using the GFOA Financial Indicators Database 1989-1993', *Government Finance Review* 12(6): 30–4.

Brundtland Commission [World Commission on Environment and Development], 1987. *Report of the World Commission on Environment and Development*. New York: United Nations.

Bryant, RT, 2011. '40 Years of History. Municipal Finance Authority of British Columbia', extracted from the MFABC's *2010 Annual Report*, URL: <http://mfa.bc.ca/pdfs/MFA201>. Consulted 20 June 2012.

Buchanan, JM, 1950. 'Federalism and Fiscal Equity', *The American Economic Review* 40(4): 583–599.

Buchanan, JM, 1952. 'Federal Grants and Resource Allocation', *Journal of Political Economy* 60(3): 208–17.

Burgess, M, 2006. *Comparative Federalism: Theory and Practice*. New York: Routledge.

Byrnes, J, and Dollery, BE, 2002. 'Local Government Failure in Australia: An Empirical Analysis of New South Wales', *Australian Journal of Public Administration* 61(3): 54–64.

Byrnes, J, Dollery, BE, Crase, L, and Simmons, P, 2008. 'Resolving the Infrastructure Crisis in Local Government: A Bond Market Issue Approach Based on Local Council Income', *Australasian Journal of Regional Studies* 14(2): 115–31.

CBA [Commonwealth Bank of Australia], 2012. 'Shareletter April 2012', URL: <http://www.commbank.com.au/about-us/shareholders/pdfs/shareholder-information/2012_Commonwealth_Bank_Shareletter.pdf>. Consulted 15 June 2012.

CGC [Commonwealth Grants Commission], 1995. *Equality in Diversity. History of the Commonwealth Grants Commission* (2nd ed), Canberra: Australian Government Printing Services.

CGC [Commonwealth Grants Commission], 2001. *Review of the Operation of Local Government (Financial Assistance) Act 1995*, Canberra: Australian Government.

CGC [Commonwealth Grants Commission], 2012. *Report on GST Revenue Sharing Relativities – 2011 Update*, Canberra.

Chandavarkar, A, 1994. *Infrastructure Finance: Issues, Institutions, and Policies*, Washington: World Bank,

Choudhry, M, Joannas, RP and Pienaar, R, 2005. *Capital Market Instruments: Analysis and Valuation* (2nd ed), London: Palgrave Macmillan.

CIFA [Council for Infrastructure Financing Authorities]. 1997. *An Analysis of State Bond Banks*, CIFA Monograph No. 9, Washington: CIFA.

Clark, TN 1994. 'Municipal Fiscal Strain: Indicators and Causes', *Government Finance Review*, 10(3): 27-29.

Coleman, JS 1990. *Foundations of Social Theory*, Cambridge: Harvard University Press.

Commonwealth Bank of Australia *see* CBA.

Commonwealth Grants Commission *see* CGC.

De Fiore, F, and Uhlig, H, 2005. 'Bank Finance Versus Bond Finance: What Explains the Differences Between US and Europe?', *Working Paper Series* No. 547. European Central Bank, Frankfurt.

Denters, B, and Rose, LE, 2005a. 'Local Governance in the Third Millennium: A Brave New World?' in *Comparing Local Governance: Trends and Developments*, eds B Denters and LE Rose. Basingstoke: Palgrave Macmillan. 1–11.

Denters, B, and Rose, LE, eds, 2005b. *Comparing Local Governance: Trends and Developments.* Basingstoke: Palgrave Macmillan.

Department of Energy, Utilities and Sustainability (NSW) *see* DEUS.

Department of Infrastructure, Transport, Regional Development and Local Government (Cth) *see* DITRDLG.

Department of Post-War Reconstruction (Cth) *see* DPWR.

Department of Regional Australia, Local Government, Arts and Sport (Cth) *see* DRALGRS.

Department of Transport and Regional Services (Cth) *see* DOTARS.

DEUS [Department of Energy, Utilities and Sustainability (NSW)], 2006. *Water Supply and Sewerage NSW Performance Monitoring Report.* Sydney: DEUS.

Dillinger, W, and Fay, M, 1999. 'From Centralized to Decentralized Governance', *Finance and Development* 36(4): 19–21.

DITRDLG [Department of Infrastructure, Transport, Regional Development], 2009. *2007-08 Local Government National Report,* URL: <http://www.regional.gov.au/local/publications/pdf/LGNR_2007-08.pdf>. Consulted 4 June 2012.

DITRDLG [Department of Infrastructure, Transport, Regional Development and Local Government], 2010. *2007-08 Local Government National Report.* Canberra: Commonwealth of Australia.

DITRDLG [Department of Infrastructure, Transport, Regional Development and Local Government], 2012. *2008-09 Local Government National Report.* Canberra: Commonwealth of Australia.

Dollery, BE, 2002. 'A Century of Vertical Fiscal Imbalance in Australian Federalism', *History of Economics Review* 36: 26–43.

Dollery, BE, 2010. 'Are There Tensions between Democracy and Efficiency in Local Government?', *Urban Policy and Research* 28(1): 117–23.

Dollery, BE and Crase, L 2004. 'Is Bigger Local Government Better? An Evaluation of the Case for Australian Municipal Amalgamation Programs', *Urban Policy and Research,* 22(3): 265-276.

Dollery, BE, and Crase, L, 2006. 'A Comparative Perspective on Financial Sustainability in Australian Local Government', *Working Paper 01-2006.* Armidale: UNE Centre for Local Government.

Dollery, BE, and Grant, B, 2011. 'Financial Sustainability and Financial Viability in Australian Local Government', *Public Finance and Management* 11(1): 28–47.

Dollery, BE, and Hovey, M, 2010. 'Australian Federal Government Failure: The Rise and fall of the Home Insulation Program', *Economic Papers* 29(3): 342–52.

Dollery, BE, and Marshall, NA, eds, 1997. *Australian Local Government: Reform and Renewal.* Melbourne: Macmillan Education.

Dollery, BE, and Mounter, S, 2010. 'Local Infrastructure Investment, Maintenance, and Renewal: A Comparative Analysis of Contemporary Australian and New Zealand Local Government', *Australasian Journal of Regional Studies* 16(2): 217–32.

Dollery, BE, and Wallis, JL, 1997. 'Market Failure, Government Failure, Leadership and Public Policy', *Journal of Interdisciplinary Economics* 8(2): 113–26.

Dollery, BE, and Wallis, JL, 2001. *The Political Economy of Local Government: Market Failure, Reform and Leadership.* Cheltenham: Edward Elgar.

Dollery, BE, and Wijeweera, A, 2010. 'Time for Change? An Assessment of Rate-Pegging in New South Wales Local Government', *Commonwealth Journal of Local Governance* 6: 56–76.

Dollery, BE, and Worthington, AC, 1996. 'A Note on Political Factors in Federal Fiscal Arrangements in Australia', *Economic Papers* 15(4): 81–7.

Dollery, BE, Byrnes, J, and Allan, P, 2007. 'Optimal Structural Reform in Australian Local Government: An Empirical Analysis of Economies of Scale by Council Function in New South Wales', *Urban Policy and Research* 25(4): 473–86.

Dollery, BE, Byrnes, J, and Crase, L, 2007. 'The Infrastructure Crisis in Australian Local Government: A Proposed Federal Asset Fund Solution', *Australasian Journal of Regional Studies* 13(1): 3–19.

Dollery, BE, Byrnes, JD, and Crase, L, 2008a. 'A Note on Structural Reform in Australian Local Government', *Australian Journal of Political Science* 43(2): 333–9.

Dollery, BE, Byrnes, J, and Crase, L, 2008b. 'The Mirage of Municipal Self-Sufficiency: A Taxonomic Approach to Local Government Sustainability in Australia', *Public Policy* 3(1): 51–66.

Dollery, BE, Crase, L, and Byrnes, J, 2006a. 'Local Government Failure: Why Does Australian Local Government Experience Permanent Financial Austerity?' *Australian Journal of Political Science* 41(3): 395–409.

Dollery, BE, Crase, L, and Byrnes, J, 2006b. 'Overall Local Council Sustainability in Australian Local Government', *Working Paper 02-2006*. Armidale: UNE Centre for Local Government.

Dollery, BE, Crase, L, and Grant, B, 2011. 'The Local Capacity, Local Community and Local Governance Dimensions of Sustainability in Australian Local Government', *Commonwealth Journal of Local Governance* 8/9, May/November: 162–83.

Dollery, BE, Crase, L, and Johnson, A, 2006. *Australian Local Government Economics*, Sydney: University of New South Wales Press.

Dollery, BE, Fletcher, M, and Rao, DSP, 1998. 'Funding Local Government in Australia: The Evolution of Commonwealth Financial Assistance', *Journal of Public Budgeting, Accounting and Financial Management* 10(4): 481–98.

Dollery, BE, Garcea, J, and LeSage, E, eds, 2008. *Local Government Reform: A Comparative Analysis of Advanced Anglo-American Countries*. Cheltenham, Edward Elgar.

Dollery, BE, Grant, B and Crase, L, 2010. 'Not What They Seem: An Analysis of Strategic Service Delivery Partnerships in Local Government', *Australasian Canadian Studies* 28(2): 59–74.

Dollery, BE, Grant, B, and Kortt, M, 2012. *Councils in Cooperation: Shared Services and Australian Local Government*. Sydney: Federation Press.

Dollery, BE, Ho, CM, and Alin, J, 2008. 'No Lessons Learned: A Critical Analysis of the Queensland Local Government Reform Commission's Final Report', *Agenda* 15(1): 67–84.

Dollery, BE, Johnson, A, and Byrnes, J, 2008. 'Cost Shifting in Australian Local Government: An Analysis of the Spatial Impact of Pensioner Rate Concession Rebates in New South Wales', *Australian Geographer* 39(4): 467–78.

Dollery, BE, Kortt, MA and Grant, B, 2011. 'Tackling the Australian Local Government Infrastructure Backlog: The Case for a National Bond Bank', in *A Global Economy*, ed P van den Hoek. Amsterdam: Forum for Economists International. 116–30.

Dollery, BE, Kortt, M, and Grant, B, 2012. 'Harnessing Private Funds to Alleviate the Australian Local Government Infrastructure Backlog', *Economic Papers* 31(1): 114–22.

Dollery, BE, Marshall, NA, and Worthington, AC, 2003. *Reshaping Australian Local Government: Finance, Governance and Reform*. Sydney: University of New South Wales Press.

Dollery, BE, Marshall, NA, Sancton, A, and Witherby, A, 2004. 'Regional Capacity Building: How Effective is REROC?' Wagga Wagga: Riverina Eastern Regional Organisation of Councils.

Dollery, BE, O'Keefe, S, and Crase, L, 2010. 'State Oversight Models for Australian Local Government', *Economic Papers* 28(4): 279–90.

Dollery, BE, Pape, B, and Byrnes, J, 2008. 'Constitutional and Federalist Perspectives on the Australian Commonwealth Government Roads to Recovery Programme', *ICFAI University of Governance and Public Policy* 3(4): 34–51.

Dollery, BE, Stewart, M, and Worthington, A, 2000. 'Australian Fiscal Federalism: An Empirical Note on Long-term Trends in State and Local Government Finance, 1969/70 to 1994/95', *Economic Papers* 19(3): 16–27.

Dollery, BE, Wallis, J, and Akimov, A, 2010. 'One Size Does Not Fit All: The Special Case of Remote Small Local Councils in Outback Queensland', *Local Government Studies* 36(1): 36–42.

Dollery, BE, Wallis, JL, and Allan, P, 2006. 'The Debate that Had to Happen but Never Did: The Changing Role of Australian Local Government', *Australian Journal of Political Science* 41(4): 553–67.

DOTARS [Department of Transport and Regional Services], 1996. *1995-1996 Local Government National Report*. Canberra: Australian Government Printing Services.

DOTARS [Department of Transport and Regional Services], 1997. *1997-1998 Local Government National Report*. Canberra: Australian Government Printing Services.

DOTARS [Department of Transport and Regional Services], 1998. *1998-1999 Local Government National Report*. Canberra: Australian Government Printing Services.

DOTARS [Department of Transport and Regional Services], 1999. *1998-1999 Local Government National Report*. Canberra: Australian Government Printing Services.

DOTARS [Department of Transport and Regional Services], 2000. *1999-2000 Local Government National Report*. Canberra: Australian Government Printing Services.

DOTARS [Department of Transport and Regional Services], 2001. *2000-01 Local Government National Report*. URL: <http://www.regional.gov.au/local/publications/reports/2000_2001/pdf/LGR2000-01.pdf>. Consulted 4 June 2012.

DOTARS [Department of Transport and Regional Services], 2002. *2001-02 Local Government National Report*, URL: <http://www.regional.gov.au/local/publications/reports/2001_2002/pdf/LGR2001-02.pdf>. Consulted 4 June 2012. [AQ 6]

DOTARS [Department of Transport and Regional Services], 2003. *2002-03 Local Government National Report*, URL: <http://www.regional.gov.au/local/publications/reports/2002_2003/pdf/LGR2002-03.pdf>. Consulted 4 June 2012.

DOTARS [Department of Transport and Regional Services], 2005. *2003-04 Local Government National Report*, URL: <http://www.regional.gov.au/local/publications/reports/2003_2004/pdf/Local_report.pdf>. Consulted 4 June 2012.

DOTARS [Department of Transport and Regional Services], 2006. *2004-05 Local Government National Report*, URL: <http://www.regional.gov.au/local/publications/reports/2004_2005/pdf/Local_report.pdf>. Consulted 4 June 2012.

DOTARS [Department of Transport and Regional Services], 2007. *2005-06 Local Government National Report*, URL: <http://www.regional.gov.au/local/publications/reports/2005_2006/pdf/LGNR_2005-06.pdf>. Consulted 4 June 2012.

DOTARS [Department of Transport and Regional Services], 2008. *2006-07 Local Government National Report*, URL: <http://www.regional.gov.au/local/publications/pdf/Local_Governement_National_Report_06-07.pdf>. Consulted 4 June 2012.

DOTARS/ALGA [Department of Transport and Regional Services/Australian Local Government Association], 2003. 'Report on the Roads to Recovery Programme', URL: <http://www.infrastructure.gov.au/transport/publications/files/RoadstoRecoveryreport.pdf>. Consulted 4 June 2012.

DPWR [Department of Post-War Reconstruction (Cth), in conjunction with State Departments responsible for Regional Planning in each State], 1949. *Regional Planning in Australia. A History of Progress and Review of Regional Planning Activities through the Commonwealth.* Canberra (no publisher listed).

DRALGAS [Department of Regional Australia, Local Government, Arts and Sport], 2012. *2008-09 Local Government National Report*, URL: <http://www.regional.gov.au/local/publications/reports/2008_2009/LGNR_2008-09.pdf>. Consulted 4 June 2012.

Dwyer, T, 2006. 'Urban Water Policy: In Need of Economics', *Agenda* 13(1): 3–16.

Ernst and Young, 2012. 'Strong Foundations for Sustainable Local Infrastructure: Connecting Communities, Projects, Finance and Funds', Report produced in accordance with the instructions of the Department of Regional Australia, Local Government, Arts and Sport. URL: <http://www.regional.gov.au/local/lgifr/index.aspx>. Consulted 21 June 2012.

ESC [Essential Services Commission], 2004. *Estimating a Return on Capital Investment: Workshop Discussion Paper – Economic Regulation of the Victorian Water Sector*, Melbourne: ESC.

Essential Services Commission *see* ESC.

Fabozzi, FJ, 2000. *Fixed Income Analysis for the Chartered Financial Analyst Program.* New York: Frank J Fabozzi Associates.

Feldstein, SG, and Fabozzi, FJ, 1987. *The Dow Jones-Irwin Guide to Municipal Bonds.* Homewood: Dow Jones-Irwin.

South Australian Financial Sustainability Review Board *see* FSRB.

Fiscal Star Services, 2007. *Ratings Assessment Methodology*, Technical Paper No. 1, URL: <www.fiscalstar.com.au>. Consulted 7 August 2012.

FSRB [(SA) Financial Sustainability Review Board], 2005. *Rising to the Challenge.* Adelaide: South Australian Local Government Association.

Giblin, L, 1949. 'Financial Aspects of the Constitution', in *Federalism in Australia*, ed G Sawer. Melbourne: Cheshire.

Gilbert, M, and Pike, R, 1995. 'Credit Enhancement of Municipal Debt', *Canadian Public Administration* 38(2): 195–203.

Gitman, L, Juchau, R, and Flanagan, J, 2002. *Principles of Managerial Finance*, 3rd ed. Melbourne: Addison Wesley.

Goodin, R, ed, 1996. *The Theory of Institutional Design.* Cambridge: Cambridge University Press.

Government of South Australia, 1999. *Local Government Finance Authority Act 1983 – 1.7.1999.* URL: <http://www.legislation.sa.gov.au/LZ/C/A/LOCAL%20GOVERNMENT%20FINANCE%20AUTHORITY%20ACT%201983/CURRENT/1983.106.UN.PDF>. Consulted 11 June 2012.

Government of South Australia, 2005. *Local Government Finance Authority Regulations 2005.* URL: <http://www.legislation.sa.gov.au/LZ/C/R/LOCAL%20GOVERNMENT%20FINANCE%20AUTHORITY%20REGULATIONS%202005/2006.02.12_(2005.12.01)/2005.247.UN.PDF>. Consulted 11 June 2012.

Government of South Australia, 2012. Department of Premier and Cabinet, 'Home', URL: <http://www.premcab.sa.gov.au/>. Consulted 11 June 2012.

Gow, J, and Grant, B, 2010. 'Grape Grubbers: The Case against Wine Industry Reregulation', *Policy* 26(3): 26–31.

Grant, B, and Dollery, BE, 2010. 'Constitutionalism, Federalism and Reform: *Pape versus the Commissioner of Taxation and Anor*: A Conversation with Bryan Pape', *Public Policy* 5(1): 53–63.

Grant, B, and Dollery, BE, 2011. 'Political Geography as Public Policy? "Place-shaping" as a Mode of Local Government Reform', *Ethics, Policy and Environment* 14(2): 1–17.

Groenewegen, P, Patience, A, and Head, B, 1979. *From Whitlam to Fraser*. Melbourne: Oxford University Press.

Groenewegen, PD, 1990. *Public Finance in Australia: Theory and Practice*, 3rd ed. Sydney: Prentice Hall.

Hancock, J, and Smith, J, 2001. *Financing the Federation*. Adelaide: South Australian Centre for Economic Studies, Adelaide and Flinders Universities.

Hawker Report [House of Representatives Standing Committee on Economics, Finance and Public Administration], 2003. *Rates and Taxes: A Fair Share for Responsible Local Government*. Canberra: Commonwealth of Australia.

Helm, DR, and Smith, R, 1987. 'The Assessment: Decentralization and the Economics of Local Government', *Oxford Review of Economic Policy* 3(2): i–xxi.

Higgins, RG, 1986. 'Developing Financial Management Capacity: Integration at the Local Government Level', in *Perspectives on Management Capacity Building*, eds BW Honadle and AM Howitt. Albany, NY: SUNY Press. 182–206.

High Court of Australia, 2009. *Pape v Commissioner of Taxation* [2009] HCA 23 (7 July 2009), URL: <http://www.austlii.edu.au/au/cases/cth/HCA/2009/23.html>. Consulted 18 September 2009.

Hildreth, WB, 1993. 'State and Local Governments as Borrowers: Strategic Choices and the Capital Market', *Public Administration Review* 53(1): 41–9.

Hildreth, WB, and Zorn, CK, 2005. 'The Evolution of the State and Local Government Municipal Debt Market over the Past Quarter Century', *Public Budgeting and Finance* 25(4): 127–53.

Hoffmann, M, Worthington, A, and Higgs, H, 2006. 'Urban Water Demand with Fixed Volumetric Charging in a Large Municipality: The Case of Brisbane, Australia', *Australian Journal of Agricultural and Resource Economics* 50(3): 347–59.

Honadle, BW, and Lloyd-Jones, M, 1998. 'Analyzing Rural Local Governments' Financial Condition: An Exploratory Application of Three Tools', *Public Budgeting and Finance* 18(2): 69–86.

Honadle, BW, Costa, J, and Cigler, BA, 2004. *Fiscal Health for Local Governments*. New York: Elsevier.

Independent Pricing and Regulatory Tribunal (NSW) *see* IPART.

Infrastructure Australia, 2008. 'A Report to the Council of Australian Governments', URL: <http://www.infrastructureaustralia.gov.au/publications/files/A_Report_to_the_Council_of_Australian_Governments.pdf>. Consulted 3 June 2012.

Infrastructure Australia, 2011a. 'Infrastructure Finance Reform. Issues Paper. Infrastructure Finance Working Group. <http://www.infrastructureaustralia.gov.au/reform_investment/files/Infrastructure_Finance_Reform_July_2011.pdf>. Consulted 3 June 2012.

Infrastructure Australia, 2011b. 'Communicating the Imperative for Action: A Report to the Council of Australian Governments, June 2011', URL: <http://www.infrastructureaustralia.gov.au/2011_coag/files/2011_Report_to_COAG.pdf>. Consulted 2 May 2012.

Infrastructure Australia, 2011c. '2010/11 Submissions', URL: <http://www.infrastructureaustralia.gov.au/2011_coag/submissions.aspx>. Consulted 2 May 2012.

Institute of Public Works Engineering Australia *see* IPWEA.

IPART [Independent Pricing and Regulatory Tribunal (NSW)], 2009a. *Revenue Framework for Local Government: Draft Review*. Sydney: IPART.

IPART [Independent Pricing and Regulatory Tribunal (NSW)], 2009b. *Revenue Framework for Local Government: Final Report*. Sydney: IPART.

IPWEA [Institute of Public Works Engineering Australia], 2011. *Australian Infrastructure Financial Management Guidelines*. Sydney: IPWEA.

Johnson, A, 2003. 'Financing Local Government in Australia', in *Reshaping Australian Local Government: Finance, Governance and Reform*, eds BE Dollery, NA Marshall and AC Worthington. Sydney: University of New South Wales Press.

Johnson, FA, and Roswick, D, 1991. 'Local Fiscal Capacity', in *Local Government Finance: Concepts and Practices*, eds JE Peterson and DR Strachota. Chicago: Government Finance Officers Association.

Jones, G, and Bowrey, G, 2010. 'Local Government Investing: A Form of Gambling?', *Australasian Journal of Regional Studies* 16(1): 37–50.

Kelly, A, Dollery, BE, and Grant, B, 2009. 'Regional Development and Local Government: Three Generations of Federal Intervention', *Australasian Journal of Regional Studies* 15(2): 171–93.

Keohane, R, and Nye, J, 2000. *Governance in a Globalized World*. Washington: Brookings Institute.

Kersting, N, and Vetter, A, eds, 2003. *Reforming Local Government in Europe: Closing the Gap between Democracy and Efficiency*. Opladen: Leske and Budrich.

Kidwell, DS, and Rogowski, RJ, 1983. 'Bond Banks: A State Assistance Program that Helps Reduce New Issue Borrowing Costs', *Public Administration Review* 43(2): 108–13.

Kimber, M, Dollery, BE, Marshall, N, Mellor, R, Payne, G, Sproats, K, and Witherby, A, 1999. 'Australian Local Government: An Annotated Bibliography, 1988-1998'. Penrith: University of Western Sydney.

King, D, 1984. *Fiscal Tiers: The Economics of Multi-Level Government*, London: George Allen & Unwin.

King, D, 1992. 'Current Issues in Theory of Fiscal Federalism', in *Local Government Economics in Theory and Practice*, ed D King. London: Routledge. 23–42.

Kloha, P, Weissert, CS, and Kleine, R, 2005. 'Developing and Testing a Composite Model to Predict Local Fiscal Distress', *Public Administration Review* 65(3): 313–23.

Knack, S, and Keefer, P, 1997. 'Does Social Capital have an Economic Payoff? A Cross-country Investigation', *Quarterly Journal of Economics* 72(4): 1250–81.

Kortt, M, and Dollery, BE, 2012. 'The Home Insulation Program: An Example of Australian Government Failure', *Australian Journal of Public Administration* 71(1): 65–75.

Lehan, EA, 1991. 'Organisation of Finance Function', in *Local Government Finance: Concepts and Practices*, eds JE Peterson and DR Strachota. Chicago: Government Finance Officers Association.

Leigh, A, 2006. 'Trust, Inequality and Ethnic Heterogeneity', *Economic Record* 82: 268–80.

Leuenberger, DZ, and Bartle, JR, 2009. *Sustainable Development for Public Administration*. New York: ME Sharpe.

LGAQ [Local Government Association of Queensland], 2005. *Size, Shape and Sustainability of Queensland Local Government: Discussion Paper*. Brisbane: LGAQ.

LGAQ [Local Government Association of Queensland], 2006. *Size, Shape and Sustainability: Guidelines Kit*. Brisbane: LGAQ.

LGAT [Local Government Association of Tasmania], 2007. *Review of the Financial Sustainability of Local Government in Tasmania*. Hobart: LGAT.

LGFA [Local Government Finance Authority of South Australia], 2011. 'Annual Report 2011', URL: <http://www.lgfa.com.au/>. Consulted 15 June 2012.

LGFA [Local Government Finance Authority of South Australia], 2012. 'Services', URL: <http://www.lgfa.com.au/services/>. Consulted 15 June 2012.

Lin, W, and Raman, K, 1998. 'The Housing Value Relevance of Governmental Accounting Information', *Journal of Accounting and Public Policy* 17(2): 91–118.

Local Government Association of Queensland *see* LGAQ.

Local Government Association of Tasmania *see* LGAT.

Local Government Finance Authority of South Australia *see* LGFA.

Local Government Funding Agency, New Zealand *see* NZLGFA.

Local Government Rates Inquiry (New Zealand) *see* NZ Rates Inquiry.

Lopez, M, Dollery, BE and Byrnes, J, 2008. 'Financial Sustainability in Local Government: An Analysis of the *Roads to Recovery* Program in New South Wales Local Government', *Public Policy* 3(2): 141–58.

Lopez, M, Dollery, BE, and Byrnes, J, 2009. 'An Empirical Evaluation of the Relative Efficiency of the Roads to Recovery Expenditure in New South Wales Local Government', *Australasian Journal of Regional Studies* 15(3): 311–28.

Lyons Inquiry into Local Government, 2005. *Consultation Paper and Interim Report*. London: Stationery Office.

Lyons Inquiry into Local Government, 2007. *Place-shaping: A Shared Ambition for the Future of Local Government*. London: Stationery Office.

Macquarie Bank, 2007. 'MQ launches new product platform to access global investment ideas including water utilities', URL: <http://www.macquarie.com.au/au/au/aboutmacquarie/media_centre/20070226a.htm>. Consulted 28 August 2007.

Maddox, G, 2000. *Australian Democracy in Theory and Practice*, 4th ed. Sydney: Longman.

Marshall, NA, 2008. 'Local Government Reform in Australia', in *Local Government Reform: A Comparative Analysis of Advanced Anglo-American Countries*. Cheltenham: Edward Elgar. 16–45.

Martell, CR, and Guess, GM, 2006. 'Development of Local Government Debt Financing Markets: Application of a Market-Based Framework', *Public Budgeting and Finance* 26(1): 88–119.

Mathews, R, 1994. *Fiscal Equalisation: Political, Social and Economic: Linchpin of Federation*. Canberra: Federalism Research Centre, Australian National University.

Mathews, RL, and Grewal, B, 1997. *The Public Sector in Jeopardy: Australian Fiscal Federalism from Whitlam to Keating*. Melbourne: South Pacific Publishing.

Mathews, RL, and Jay, WC, 1972. *Federal Finance: Intergovernmental Relations in Australia Since Federation*. Melbourne: Nelson.

Matthews, R, 1983. 'The Commonwealth–State Financial Contract' in *A Fractured Federation*, eds J Aldred and J Wilkes. Sydney: Allen and Unwin.

MAV [Municipal Association of Victoria], 2005. *Trends in Local Government Finance*. Melbourne: MAV.

Maxwell, DG, 2006. *Corporate Overheads of Local Governments*, Final Report, Vol 2. Sydney: NSW Local Government and Shires Association.

McNeill, J, 1997. 'Local Government in the Australian Federal System', in *Australian Local Government: Reform and Renewal*, eds BE Dollery and NA Marshall. Melbourne: Macmillan Education. 17–39.

Megarrity, L, 2012. 'Regional Dreams: Local Government and its Relationship with the Commonwealth, 1943-75', in *Public Policy* 7(1), Special Edition: 'Local Government and Regional Governance', eds B Grant, B Dollery and M Kortt. 7–22.

MFABC [Municipal Financial Authority of British Columbia], 2011. '2011 Annual Report', URL: <http://mfa.bc.ca/sites/default/files/mfa_2011_annual_report_final.pdf>. Consulted 20 June 2012.

MFABC [Municipal Financial Authority of British Columbia], 2012a. 'History', URL: <http://mfa.bc.ca/about-us/history>. Consulted 19 June 2012.

MFABC [Municipal Financial Authority of British Columbia], 2012b. 'Governance', URL: <http://mfa.bc.ca/about-us/governance>. Consulted 20 June 2012.

MFS Group, 2007. 'MFS Water Fund – The Fund at a Glance', URL: <http://www.mfsgroup.com.au/mfsim/water.html>. Consulted 28 August 2007.

Morrissey, M, 2006. 'The Australian State and Indigenous People, 1990-2006', *Journal of Sociology* 42(4): 347–54.

Mueller, DC, 2003. *Public Choice III*. Cambridge: Cambridge University Press.

Municipal Association of Victoria *see* MAV.

Municipal Financial Authority of British Columbia *see* MFABC

Murray, D, and Dollery, BE, 2005. 'Local Council Performance Monitoring in New South Wales: Are "At Risk" Councils Really at Risk?', *Economic Papers* 24(4): 332–45.

Murray, DR, and Dollery, BE, 2006. 'An Evaluation of Performance Measurement and the Identification of "At Risk" Municipal Councils in NSW Local Government', *Public Administration Today* 6: 46–61.

Musgrave, RA, 1959. *The Theory of Public Finance*. New York: McGraw-Hill.

New Zealand Government, 2011. *Local Government Borrowing Act 2011*, URL: <http://www.lgfa.co.nz/~/media/LGFA/Files/LGFA_Local%20Government%20Borrowing%20Act%202011.ashx>. Consulted 15 June 2012.

New Zealand Local Government Funding Agency *see* NZLGFA.

NSW Local Government Inquiry *see* Allan Report.

NZ Rates Inquiry [Report of the Local Government Rates Inquiry (New Zealand)], 2007. *Funding Local Government*. Wellington: Department of Internal Affairs.

NZLGFA [New Zealand Local Government Funding Agency], 2011. 'Home', URL: <http://www.lgfa.co.nz/>. Consulted 18 June 2012.

NZLGFA [New Zealand Local Government Funding Agency], 2011/12. 'Statement of Intent', URL: <http://www.lgfa.co.nz/~/media/LGFA/Files/LGFA%20SOI%202011-12.ashx>. Consulted 18 June 2012.

NZLGFA [New Zealand Local Government Funding Agency], 2012. 'LGFA Bonds', available at 'Tender Data History', URL: <http://www.lgfa.co.nz/en/Investors/Tenders/Tender%20History%20Data.aspx>. Consulted 18 June 2012.

O'Dowd, MC, 1978. 'The Problem of Government Failure in Mixed Economies', *South African Journal of Economics* 46(3): 360–70.

Oates, WE, 1972. *Fiscal Federalism*. New York: Harcourt Brace Jovanovich.

Oates, WE, 1999. 'An Essay on Fiscal Federalism', *Journal of Economic Literature* 37(3): 1120–49.

Onyx, J, and Bullen, P, 2000. 'Sources of Social Capital', in *Social Capital and Public Policy in Australia*, ed I Winter. Melbourne: Australian Institute of Family Studies. 105–35.

Pagano, M, and Moore, RJ, 1985. *Cities and Fiscal Choices*. Durham, NC: Duke University Press.

Pape, B, 2005. 'The Use and Abuse of Commonwealth Power', paper presented at The Samuel Griffith Society Seventeenth Annual Griffith Conference, Coolangatta, 8-10 April, 2005, URL: <http://www.une.edu.au/law/publications/B.Pape%20-%20Commonwealth%20Finance%20Power.pdf>. Consulted 18 September 2009.

Parker, RS, 1980. 'Responsible Government in Australia' in *Responsible Government in Australia*, eds P Weller and D Jaensch. Richmond: Drummond.

PC [Productivity Commission], 2008. *Assessing Local Government Revenue Raising Capacity*. Productivity Commission Research Report, April 2008. Canberra: Australian Government Printing Services.

Peacock AT, 1977. 'The Political Economy of Devolution: The British Case, in *The Political Economy of Fiscal Federalism*, ed. WE Oates (ed.), Lexington: Lexington Books.

Peng, J and Brucato, PF, 2003. 'Another Look at the Effect of Method of Sale on the Interest Cost in the Municipal Bond Market: A Certification Model', *Public Budgeting and Finance*, 23(1): 73-95.

Petchey, JD, 2011. 'Fiscal Capacity Equalisation of the Australian States', *Australian Economic Review*, 44(2): 207-214.

Peterson, GE, 2002. *Banks or Bonds? Building a Municipal Credit Market*. Washington: Urban Institute.

PriceWaterhouseCoopers *see* PWC Report.

Productivity Commission *see* PC.

Putnam, R, 1993. *Making Democracy Work: Civic Traditions in Modern Italy*. Princeton: Princeton University Press.

Putnam, R, 2000. *Bowling Alone: The Collapse and Revival of American Community*. New York: Simon and Schuster.

PWC Report [PriceWaterhouseCoopers], 2006. *National Financial Sustainability Study of Local Government*. Sydney: PriceWaterhouseCoopers.

QLGRC [Queensland Local Government Reform Commission], 2007. *Report of the Local Government Reform Commission, Final Repor,*. Brisbane: QLGRC.

QTC [Queensland Treasury Corporation], 2008. *Financial Sustainability in Queensland Local Government*. Brisbane: QTC.

Queensland Local Government Reform Commission *see* QLGRC.

Queensland Treasury Corporation *see* QTC.

Quibria, MG, 2003. 'The Puzzle of Social Capital', *Asian Development Review* 20(2): 19–39.

RBA [Reserve Bank of Australia], 2007. 'Capital Market Yields – Government Bonds – Monthly Bulletin Statistics Table F2'. Sydney: RBA.

Reid, M, 2008. 'Local Government Reform in New Zealand', in *Local Government Reform: A Comparative Analysis of Advanced Anglo-American Countries*. Cheltenham: Edward Elgar: 46–74.

Reserve Bank of Australia *see* RBA.

Robbins, MD, and Kim, D, 2003. 'Do State Bond Banks Have Cost Advantages for Municipal Bond Issuance?' *Public Budgeting and Finance* 23(3): 92–108.

Romero-Lankao, P, 2000. 'Sustainability and Public Management Reform. Two Challenges for Mexican Environmental Policy', *American Review of Public Administration* 30(4): 389–99.

Roorda, J, and Associates, 2006. *The Present Condition and Management of Infrastructure in NSW Local Government*, Report Commissioned by the Independent Inquiry into the Financial Sustainability of NSW Local Government. Sydney: Independent Inquiry into the Financial Sustainability of NSW Local Government.

Sachs, W, 1995. *The Political Anatomy of 'Sustainable Development'*. Wuppertal: Wuppertal Papers.

Shah, A, 2005. *Fiscal Decentralization and Fiscal Performance,* Policy Research Working Paper Series 3786. Washington: World Bank.

Shah, A, ed, 2006. *Local Governance in Industrial Countries.* Washington: World Bank.

Simonsen, B, Robins, M, and Helgerson, L, 2001. 'The Influence of Jurisdiction Size and Sale Type on Municipal Bond Interest Rates: An Empirical Analysis', *Public Administration Review* 61(6): 709–17.

Sobels, J, Curtis, A, and Lockie, S, 2001. 'The Role of Landcare Networks in Australia: Exploring the Contribution of Social Capital', *Journal of Rural Studies* 17(3): 265–76.

Sokolow, AD, and Honadle, BW, 1984. 'How Rural Governments Budget: The Alternatives to Executive Preparation', *Public Administration Review* 44(5): 373–83.

Solano, PL, 2005. 'An Appraisal of the Interest Cost Savings of State Bond Banks', *Municipal Finance Journal* 25(4): 13–48.

South Australian Financial Sustainability Review Board *see* FSRB.

South Australian Government *see* Government of South Australia.

Stewart, J, 1997. 'The Governance of Difference', in *A Fresh Start for Local Government*, eds M Chisholm, R Hale and D Thomas. London: Public Finance Foundation. 65–78.

Steyvers, K, Reynaert, H, De Cuerninck, C, and Valckew, T, 2006. 'Mayors in Governance: Heading for Efficiency and Democracy', *Local Government Studies* 32(4): 429–46.

Stoker, G, 1998. 'Governance as Theory: Five Propositions', *International Social Science Journal* 50: 17–28.

Tiebout, CM, 1956. 'A Pure Theory of Local Expenditures', *Journal of Political Economy* 64(5): 416–24.

Tresch, CH, 2002. *Public Finance: A Normative Theory,* 2nd ed. San Diego: Academic Press.

Tucker, D, 1997. 'From Administration to Management' in *Australian Local Government: Reform and Renewal*, eds BE Dollery and NA Marshall, Melbourne: Macmillan. 69–88.

WALGA [Western Australian Local Government Association], 2006. *Systemic Sustainability Study: In Your Hands.* Perth: WALGA.

Walker, R, and Jones, S, 2006, 'An Alternative Approach to Identifying Councils "At Risk"', *Economic Papers* 25(4): 347–57.

Wallis, JL, and Dollery, BE, 1999, *Market Failure, Government Failure, Leadership and Public Policy,* London: Macmillan.

Wallis, JL, Dollery, BE, and McLoughlin, L, 2007. *Reform and Leadership in the Public Sector: A Political Economy Approach*. Cheltenham: Edward Elgar.

Warren, N, 2008. 'Reform of the Commonwealth Grants Commission: It's all in the Detail', *UNSW Law Journal* 31(3): 530–52.

Watson, A, 2007. *The Flawed History of Irrigation in Australia: Faltering Attempts at Reform*, Paper prepared for the Symposium 'Water Matters' organised by the ANU Emeritus Faculty, the ANU Water Initiative and the ANU College of Science as part of the Australian Science Festival, August 24-25 2007, Canberra.

Weisbrod, BA, 1978. 'Problems of Enhancing the Public Interest: Toward a Model of Government Failures', in *Public Interest Law*, eds BA Weisbrod, JF Handler and NK Komesar. Washington: University of California Press. 30–41.

Western Australian Local Government Association *see* WALGA.

Williams, R, 2005a. 'Federal-State Financial Relations in Australia: The Role of the Commonwealth Grants Commission', *Australian Economic Review* 38(1): 108–18.

Williams, R, 2005b. 'Fiscal Federalism: Aims, Instruments and Outcomes', *Australian Economic Review* 38(4): 351–69.

Wintrobe, R, 1997. 'Modern Bureaucratic Theory', in *Perspectives on Public Choice*, ed DC Mueller. Cambridge: Cambridge University Press. 429–54.

Witherby, A, Dollery, BE, Marshall, NA, and Auster, M, 1999. 'Local Government: One Industry, Many Perspectives'. Sydney: Australian Institute of Urban Studies (NSW).

Wolf, C, 1989. *Markets or Governments*. New York: MIT Press.

Woodbury, K, Dollery, BE, and Rao, P, 2003., 'Is Local Government Efficiency Measurement in Australia Adequate?', *Public Productivity and Management Review* 27(2): 77-91.

Woodhouse, A, 2006. 'Social Capital and Economic Development in Regional Australia: Case Study', *Journal of Rural Studies* 22(1): 83–94.

World Commission on Environment and Development *see* Brundtland Commission.

Worthington, AC, and Dollery, BE, 1998. 'The Political Determination of Intergovernmental Grants in Australia', *Public Choice* 94(3/4): 299–315.

Worthington, A, and Dollery, BE, 2000a. 'Can Australian Local Government Play a Meaningful Role in the Development of Social Capital in Disadvantaged Rural Communities?' *Australian Journal of Social Issues* 35(4): 349–61.

Worthington, A, and Dollery, BE, 2000b. 'The Debate on Australian Federalism: Local Government Financial Interrelationships with State and Commonwealth Governments', *Australian Journal of Public Administration* 59(4): 25–35.

Yusuf, JE, and Liu, G, 2008. 'State Infrastructure Banks and Intergovernmental Subsidies for Local Transportation Investment', *Public Budgeting and Finance* 28(4): 71–89.

Index